one small bite

one small bite

Anti-Diet Stories that Help You Build
a Positive Relationship with Food

David R. Orozco MS, RDN

Copyright © 2022 David R. Orozco

All rights reserved. No part of this publication may be reproduced, distributed, or transmitted in any form or by any means, including photocopying, recording, or other electronic or mechanical methods, without the prior written permission of the publisher, except in the case of brief quotations embodied in reviews and certain other noncommercial uses permitted by copyright law.

SEL027000   SELF-HELP / Personal Growth / Success
SEL014000   SELF-HELP / Eating Disorders & Body Image
HEA048000   HEALTH & FITNESS / Diet & Nutrition / General
HEA017000   HEALTH & FITNESS / Diet & Nutrition / Nutrition

orozconutrition.com

Contents

1: Commencement ... 1

2: Curiosity ... 7
    David (Yours Truly)—His Awareness Journey ... 12
    Angela—Open Mind: Curiosity Comes in Waves ... 24
    Ericka—Experimentation: Moving Past Repetition ... 43
    Meredith—Enjoyment: Finding Her Hum ... 61
    Catalina—Experimentation Is the Way Out ... 75
    Curiosity—What Did We Learn? ... 91

3: Compassion ... 93
    Jeff—Discovering Self-Compassion ... 95
    Interlude—Self-Prioritization, Self-Kindness,
        Self-Awareness ... 104
    Nathaniel—Fear ... 107
    Isabel—Self-Compassion Came as a Surprise ... 125
    All—Self-Prioritization, Self-Kindness, Self-Awareness ... 134

4: Commitment ... 137
    Isabel—Unwavering Commitment ... 139
    Tiffany—Control Is an Illusion ... 143
    Claire—Remember, The Tortoise Won the Race ... 152
    Summary—Commitment ... 156

5: Consistency ... 157
    Anita—The Tortoise Keeps Winning ... 159

Contents

    Interlude—Consistency 170
    Joel—Heading toward Scary Foods 173
    Marcie—Our Fine-Tuned Biological Machine 189
    Interlude—Consistency 197
    Steve—Stuck on Autopilot 199

6: Conclusion 208

Complementary Section 213

Appendix A:
    Bariatric Surgery 218

Appendix B:
    Fat Burning = Oil Rig Comparison 223

Notes 230

About the Author 234

1

Commencement

Dinner with the Family

One of my favorite moments of the day is dinnertime with the family. It's not because I'm looking forward to working more and cooking over a hot stove after a long day at work. Well, actually, let me clarify that just a bit. I do enjoy cooking. It's a creative outlet for me and somewhat cathartic because it's not the same as working or consulting with people. To me, dinnertime is wonderful because it is the one simple things, we do almost every single day as a family. We gather around the dinner table, share our day, and enjoy our time together; therefore, creating a meal and sitting at the table together helps us strengthen our family bonds. As I say this, however, I'm keenly aware that for various reasons not everyone has the privilege of being in a thin and able body or has the financial ability to enjoying dinner with a family each night. Many people might not have the time or even a home to enjoy dinner together. They may be working two jobs, or have to take care of an elderly parent, or be a single parent with one or a few children. Numerous marginalized individuals are living in poverty or deal with multiple challenges such as financial, language, or transportation barriers, and just don't have access or availability to food. I have been extremely privileged to grow up in modest middle-class immigrant family, and although my parents struggled, fought, and clawed their way into some resemblance of a social class, dinner as a family was always a must. For my family, dinner was definitely one small thing we were able to do together. In retrospect, one could consider this the poor person's chance at group therapy and support.

Now with a family of my own, I knew it was important, but what I came to realize was how it would affect us in such a profound way. I mean, it wasn't like something miraculous and magical happened because we had dinner together as a family. Or was it?

Yes. We noticed subtle and incremental changes that really started to unfold.

I remember when my daughter, Helena, was just learning to eat and trying new foods. Like most kids, as she started to get a little older, somewhere around age two or three, she began to have second thoughts about certain foods. Particularly those green ones. Sound familiar? We took a simple but very impactful approach to get her to eat a greater variety of food, enjoy her food, and make dinner a little less stressful for all of us, especially after a long day of work. We would tell her, "Just take *one small bite*." This one statement has rocked our world, but not in the sense that a lightning bolt crashed out of the sky and enlightened us. It was more its simplistic nature, a simple little behavior that we embarked on together that over time has really changed us. Take note of what I just said—*simple little behavior* and *over time*. These are the two critical components.

This concept of trying the food and self-autonomy wasn't always easy for us to do because it wasn't how my wife and I learned to eat. We were always forced to clean our plates and not complain about the food. Our parents didn't realize they were inadvertently putting food police voices in our heads on how we should eat, despite our own experiences, tastes, and hunger or fullness cues. We didn't want to take that same approach with our daughter, but what we didn't know was how impactful those dinner meals would turn out to be, and how powerful that one simple statement would be. We wanted to instill in our daughter a secure relationship with food, helpful eating habits, and the ability to recognize her own physiological as well as emotional signals. That is, we were subtly teaching her about autonomy.

This subtle yet impactful change has made our dinners as a family less stressful because it is just one small change. Helena gets to try new foods, and over time, the exposure to a less stressful experience of eating reduces the likelihood that she creates strong negative feelings or false stories about food in her head. While this isn't always easy, we are committed and consistent. We don't yell at her, there isn't fighting at the table (at least not always), but what we try to do is find a compassionate approach that builds on curiosity and find kind ways of communicating.

That's what I mean with that one single statement, *one small bite!* It has changed not just me and my family's lives but that of so many of my clients. So many people have come to realize how important it is to allow curiosity to guide decisions, to instill compassion, to be committed to one small incremental change over time, and to be consistent. It has also changed my counseling style with clients. More importantly, these four components—curiosity, compassion, commitment, and consistency—are what *one small bite* is grounded on, and it changed the life of so many people I work with.

What *one small bite* does is speak to various aspects of human nature and how we can enhance our health through small changes over time. Health is cumulative! With *one small bite*, we learn so much over time, build experiences, and develop an ability to practice small moments of learning that will drive change. It is the type of change we can accept long-term: manageable and incremental. Easy on the body and the mind. The sense of accomplishment will drive further desire to accomplish more, to work harder, to further enhance health through small steps and changes—and you'll see that motivation take off!

Let's take walking as a simple example. No one is born walking out of their mother's womb, yet people don't give it a moment's thought. Walking seems so natural and instinctual. Actually, it takes time to learn, one step at a time. It takes most of us about twelve to eighteen months to figure the whole balancing and walking thing out, and then another two to three years to walk without tripping. So, while walking may seem like second nature, it certainly did not come overnight.

This is true for anything new you embark on in life. Take martial arts, for example. You don't just learn overnight how to block, parry, jab-jab-uppercut, throw the attacker to the ground, and then pin them to submission. Heck, most times you start by taking a punch, and only after a long period of small, incremental improvements (and lots of bruises and black eyes) will you give as good as you get. Accomplished martial artists might make it look easy, but their grace and agility come from years of small steps forward.

One Small Bite is about taking what you love or value most in your life and developing those abilities consistently over time. We all have a special superpower—some of us are amazing at helping others, some of us have incredible organization skills, and some of us are natural leaders. *One Small Bite* is about helping you realize and reconnect with that superpower, and slowly but surely exercise it little by little so that you build momentum and get really good at it.

What you won't get in this book is any fancy-schmancy diet or false hopes that will "do the trick." Nope, that's not what this book is for. There are no hidden agendas or bait-and-switch tricks that will get you to lose weight. I'm not here to make you think that if you work on intuitive eating principles, mindful eating approaches, or get in tune with your value system that your blood sugar or cholesterol issues will magically improve. Sorry, there is no quick healthy meal plan, special fat-burning foods, or the next miracle juicing detox program in this book.

Instead, you will get a wonderful opportunity to hear about the journey of some of my clients. The real-life stories of Sheroes and Heroes. People just like you that made small changes—and how that one small, fundamental change transformed their lives. You will learn how they focused on one small eating pattern and built compassionate internal voices that helped them pay attention to their body. How they became interoceptively aware of what their bodies needed *and* wanted.

1: Commencement

You'll learn how they were motivated to change and inspired to act differently. They created a new mindset and view on life, not focused on their weight or physical appearance. You will read how some people had drastic changes that were predicated on the small steps they took to get there. In some of the stories in this book, you'll see how major traumatic events in some people's lives were catalysts for small changes, which led to major improvements and paradigm shifts. Or vice versa. Some people started with just one small approach to enjoy food or movement again, which in turned led to huge changes and opportunities in life.

In this book, I will guide you through people's experiences and evolutions, particularly focusing on how they incorporated *one small bite* in hopes that you'll be inspired to create small new habits that will help you build greater awareness of your own physiological and emotional signals.

This book is divided into the four main pillars of the one small bite approach. These four sections take you through each person's journey and transformation.

- **Curiosity**—You will discover how curiosity leads to greater awareness, how awareness enhances your ability to see pain points, challenges, and patterns that can therefore be changed. You will develop a greater sense of awareness and open-mindedness and learn to experiment and explore a variety of new foods and discover your body and joyful movement.
- **Compassion**—By developing compassion, you will open your mind's vastness and depth and endless positive strength to work on that one small change. You will see that you are not the totality of what you think or feel, and you will become the mind's observer to see what really matters in life (spoiler alert—it is not about being thin).
- **Commitment**—You will find that one small change and commit to it. It will be the driving force to continue even when some of these new changes will be hard or slow, but the sense of accomplishment will be right in line with your values.

- **Consistent**—You will not use catchy diet approaches, fancy tricks, or techniques that go against your body's physiology. You will learn how to be persistent and patient, and continue to practice, determined to make that small change on a regular and frequent basis, because it's sustainable, it satisfies you, and it gives you that sense of wholeness.

With these four pillars, you will learn how one small consistent and committed change in your eating patterns, sleep, activity, or mood has a domino effect on other areas of your life, just like the Sheroes and Heroes in this book. I will point out the various social determinants of health and privileges, such as being in a thin and able body, white or other privileged groups, financial security, food security, higher education, and safe living environments, that can offer the same opportunities to marginalize BIPOC and other communities of color, disability, or sexual orientation.

I am so inspired by the Sheroes and Heroes in this book—but know that I've altered the actual stories and names of these people to protect their privacy and identities. However, all these stories are true experiences with the goal of resonating or inspiring you as well. I look forward to having you join me on this journey, to help you discover and transform your life, so that you can thrive and live fully.

OK, now let's get started on your transformational journey!

2

Curiosity

"I have no special talent. I'm only passionately curious."

—Albert Einstein

What often happens in many of my nutrition counseling sessions is that clients have moments of curiosity. They talk about certain habits or behaviors and then have that *hmm* expression on their faces. It's like talk therapy—a moment of finally listening to themselves aloud. I find these breakthrough moments extremely pivotal in the progression of the person's journey. Curiosity is one of those essential human traits that allow us to slow down and start observing ourselves in a different light. Curiosity doesn't require any special abilities, and most importantly, it's available to all of us. Yet, I believe it is one of the key methods of human adaptation, and thus human survival. I've been at this counseling game for close to twenty years, and I have discovered that five components of curiosity are essential to helping people transform their lives. When that client gets their curiosity going, I passionately swoop in and seize the moment with them to initiate that journey. Just like any Shero or Hero, their character runs into this moment that catapults them into their journey.

Curiosity is that catalyst. To me, it is one of the most interesting human traits I have observed during sessions because people who are genuinely curious tend to be happier, driven, and more positive, optimistic, or hopeful. Curious people tend to be more open to discovering a secure relationship with food and their body. In my experience, there are six main components of curiosity that most people demonstrate. They include the following:

1. **Awareness**—paying attention to themselves, their body, patterns, and nuances in life
2. **Open-Mindedness**—being open to possibilities, to body signals, to the simple things
3. **Experimentation**—doing as the famous Nike tagline says—"Just Do It!"—and seeing what happens
4. **Doing**—actually embarking on what they are curious about
5. **Learning**—learning from past experiences, ongoing self-discovery, and mistakes—it's a teaching moment
6. **Changing**—growing from their experimentation and learning

Curiosity is an interesting yet basic human trait. It serves as an intrinsic motivator for our desire to play, experiment, seek information, learn, and grow. Curiosity is brilliance. Einstein said it best: "Imagination is more important than knowledge."[1] A very simple, yet powerful statement. Being curious allows our imagination to open up, to see the vast opportunities and possibilities, to expand our young minds. And at the same time, it perpetuates our innocence, our vulnerabilities, which in turn make us brave and courageous. By being curious, we can cultivate relationships, learn to trust one another, and establish deeper connections with others, and more importantly, with ourselves.

Of the five major components of curiosity, awareness is the one I initially focus on and advocate the most for people. Living with a greater sense of awareness is not something many of us do in our own lives, yet it plays a critical role in helping us recognize how to begin taking small steps toward bigger goals and dreams.

Awareness happens in three different ways:

1. When major or dramatic events occur throughout our lives, such as a career change; moving to a new town, city, or school; a

car accident; a major illness; or some type of physical or mental abuse such as a very emotional breakup with a partner.
2. Through incremental moments over time within our daily habits or behaviors. For example, it could happen while playing hide-and-seek with your children, getting a paper cut on your index finger, while in the middle of a nice warm hug from your partner, or while taking a break from the computer and going for a walk and noticing how much better you breathe or feel.
3. When we least expect it—possibly in combination of major events and during incremental moments. But more than likely it is when we slow down, become mindful, and can see our thoughts and feelings and know they are not the totality of who we are.

To observe our minds and be ready to receive our natural thoughts is critical, but we have to learn to consciously and consistently catch them. Numerous experts have talked about the importance of being mindful and building awareness. Dr. Russ Harris, physician, psychotherapist, and author of *The Happiness Trap: How to Stop Struggling and Start Living*, says that we need to be our minds' observer: "The observing self is fundamentally different from the thinking self. The observing self is aware, but does not think; it is the part of you that is responsible for focus, attention, and awareness. While it can observe or pay attention to your thoughts, it can't produce them. Whereas the thinking self thinks about your experience, the observing self registers your experience directly."[2] This ability to be observant or mindful of our thoughts, feelings, images, memories, or beliefs is profoundly helpful to assist us in climbing out of our lived perceptions. Kristin Neff, author and psychologist, writes in her book *Self-Compassion: The Proven Power of Being Kind to Yourself*: "Mindfulness brings us back to the present moment and provides the type of balanced awareness that forms the foundation of self-compassion. Like a clear, still pool without ripples, mindfulness perfectly mirrors what's occurring without distortion. Rather than become lost in our own personal soap opera, mindfulness allows us to view our situation with greater perspective and helps to ensure that we don't suffer unnecessarily."[3] And I love how she continues to say that mindfulness is awareness of awareness: "When we notice our pain without exaggerating it, this is a moment of mindfulness. Mindfulness entails observing what is going on in our field of awareness just as it is—right here, right now."[4] And it is just like best-selling author and spiritual teacher Eckhart Tolle describes in his book *The Power of Now*, "So when you listen to a thought, you are aware not only of the thought but also of yourself as the witness of the thought."[5]

This section is about curiosity. What is curiosity? Why is it essential for transformation? What does it help you with? How does curiosity help people make that one small nutritional change that is sustainable and in line with the body's needs and wants? More importantly, how is awareness intricately linked with curiosity?

Ivan Pavlov, Nobel Prize winning physiologist, developed the concept of the conditioned reflex. He conducted the famous experiment of the dogs trained to salivate at the sound of the buzzer. Pavlov wrote that the spontaneous orientation of dogs was a "What-is-it?" reflex to explain their form of curiosity.[6] As humans we carry this very same primal trait, one that is part of our reptilian brain. Harry Harlow, the famous rhesus monkey psychologist and behaviorist, also explained curiosity as a basic driving force, a "manipulative motive" that engages the puzzle-solving behavior.[7] How else would we have been able to build a space station, get to the moon, create the internet, or develop smartphones, apps, electric cars, and quantum computing? We now have augmented reality software, autonomous self-driving vehicles, drones, and AI (artificial intelligence). We are living in the future! We dreamed it, we imagined it, and all because we were curious! We took action!

Just as I was writing this, I watched the launch of the SpaceX Crew Dragon rocket from the famous Kennedy Space Center, and I was reminded of the speech President John F. Kennedy gave at Rice University back in 1962:

"We choose to go to the moon in this decade and do the other things, not because they are easy, but because they are hard, because that goal will serve to organize and measure the best of our energies and skills, because that challenge is one that we are willing to accept, one we are unwilling to postpone, and one which we intend to win, and the others, too. We have to be open minded and trust curiosity."[8]

It is these five key curiosity components that light a fire in people's hearts. The key elements that successfully transform their health. In the following chapters, you will learn about a variety of Sheroes and Heroes and their journeys so that you can learn, be inspired, and discover how to maneuver through these five components to transform your health one small bite at a time!

One small thing you can do right now is visit my website to download my free guide to enhancing your curiosity at www.orozconutrition.com/curiosity-guide. You can get started right away to enhance and develop that curiosity voice.

David
(Yours Truly)
His Awareness Journey

The curiosity journey for me began about twenty-five years ago. At the time, I thought I was on top of the world. I was running my family's travel business, and it was at the peak of financial success. We had two offices and six employees, and we were grossing about five million dollars in sales, with about twenty percent in profits. I was also reaping all the benefits of travel—going off on these *familiarization trips,* or *fam trips* for short, which were all expense-paid trips by vacation companies, airlines, hotels, and resorts as a way to incentivize travel agents to sell their vacation packages. The travel business was rocking it!

However, I hesitantly have to say that I was also on quite an ego trip! To start, I was emotionally disconnected to myself and so many people in my life, and I was clueless to that disconnection. I dated often and would try hard to impress women with those elaborate fam trips or set up romantic weekend getaways hoping to fill some emotional hole that was missing in my life. I bought my first home, a condominium, and it was such a bachelor's pad. I decorated it with the latest furniture and technology. It was right out of one of those modern home décor magazines, but it was more to impress others than for my own comfort. I also bought a brand-new sleek and fast Acura sedan, and just thought I was living it up. I never once considered the expense and how others in my family even thought about it. At the same time, I also reached third-degree black belt in Aikido and thought I was such a badass. On a positive note, I will say that the Aikido training and classes were very cathartic and therapeutic, though unfortunately not enough. At the time I thought I was just on top of the world. With all that said, there's nothing wrong with having nice things and enjoying life. Unfortunately, the more I had, the more emotionally empty I felt. Like something was missing or wrong with me. I was definitely a perpetual bachelor, pretty cocky, and blinded by all the material things filling some internal void. These fam trips, material possessions, and shallow romantic relationships just did not fill me. Something deep inside of me just didn't feel right, like there was something more in life that was missing.

Let me back up a little and give some family history for context here. I am the youngest of nine siblings but grew up with my three immediate older sisters. I was fortunate to get to college but really did not have much guidance on what college life was like, what to do, or what to expect. My parents worked so hard and most of my siblings already had families. It took me a little over five years to graduate with a bachelor's degree in biology. At the time, I contemplated becoming a researcher or physician, but I didn't have much direction and was just living in the moment. I did not attend a traditional university. I lived at home, commuted to school, and worked through most of my education. Being the youngest of nine, I was left to fend for myself and figure out the whole life thing.

When I finally graduated, I worked as an assistant manager at The Gap with no real direction in my life. I didn't get into research or become a physician after all. Instead, my mother asked me to run the family business. It was an easy fit. I worked in the travel agency throughout college, so I knew the business really well. I felt compelled to jump right in when she asked. The family travel business had a lot of perks, and it was easy. The business was a family-based endeavor. I grew up in a very interdependent Colombian American family that helped each other as much as possible, which at times left little privacy or independence. I also realized the years of challenges and hardships my parents faced migrating to the United States. All throughout my childhood my mother worked in the garment industry of New York City, and my father as a night shift security guard at a warehouse to help make ends meet for a family of six. They were all in with the American dream,

2: Curiosity

and even tried running various businesses like a restaurant, a software company, a bridal gown boutique, and a few other business endeavors until they finally landed on the travel agency. I often remember how my parents were not always around, and most of my life I either just did my own thing or worked with siblings. It was a rough life for my parents, and they did what they could to survive. Therefore, when my mother asked me to run the business, I felt obligated and proud to be a part of it. To me, it was like giving back for the sacrifices everyone else made for me in order to get my college degree. You'll hear more about that guilt feeling from the various stories in this book.

At the time, my best stress relief was an intense regimen of physical activity: Aikido three nights a week, weight training four days a week, and then three-to-five-mile runs on weekends. My diet consisted of eating out, fast food, and drinking soda, and the only green or colorful food consisted of bags of M&Ms and sweets near my desk. Not that there is anything wrong with eating out, sodas, or candy—the problem was that I wasn't aware how much I was eating unconsciously. I was eating anything to help deal with the career I did not want to be in. I was pretty oblivious to how I was eating for quite some time. Working out and Aikido was my way of escaping that emptiness, and it went on for another eight to ten years. I really didn't make the connection between my lifestyle and my emotional state. I just worked hard, kept my head down, and did my thing.

Then my life started to unravel. A few unfortunate events happened one after the other. First, I went through a couple of tough breakups that shattered my heart. A few years later, my mother was diagnosed with diabetes and then colon cancer. As if that wasn't devastating enough, shortly after my mother's devastating news, my father was diagnosed with prostate cancer and cardiovascular disease. Lots of medical issues all at once! At the same time, the travel business was starting to crumble right underneath me. Several employees were stealing, booking fraudulent trips, and running the business to the ground. Together with my exuberant lifestyle, the business and my life were just not looking great. It was further complicated by the fact that, like my family, I had these conspiracy theories and beliefs that pharmaceutical and medical industries were out to get us. I even suggested that my mother try an extremely strict raw-food diet and take supplements because I believed that drug companies were out to kill her. I was convinced that these pseudo-sciences and snake oil type treatments were a much better option than conventional medicine.

Life had finally knocked me down. The combinations of jabs, hooks, uppercuts, and blows were devastating. Life for me was just falling apart. Up to this point, I was blind to the deeper, more profound understanding of myself, and more importantly, to my curiosity that was practically nonexistent prior to my mother dying. Yet, life has an amazing way of tapping one on the shoulder and offer opportunities to climb out of the misery and stagnation. Unfortunately, I had to go through these difficult life circumstances. At some point, we all go through difficult moments in our lives. While they are not pleasant moments, they help us to grow. Getting through these challenging moments in our lives strengthens our minds, just like exercise strengthens our muscles.

When we stop being curious, we stop growing. Think of a child and how often they question life. Why is the grass green? Why is the sky blue? How do fish breathe underwater? Why, why, why? And open-ended questions for everything! This just demonstrates their innocence, their kindness, their desire to learn—their curiosity reveals a desire to grow. Give that child some guidance and love, and sprinkle in a little hard work, and that child will thrive. It's the same for all of us. Curiosity is at the core of what drives behavior change, and this is what we will learn from this journey.

The Awakening to One Small Bite

My eyes were finally opened. Life was forcing me to pause, getting me to slow down and open and expand my mind. With that awareness, curiosity started to fill my mind and my heart. I finally saw what was

2: Curiosity

hidden in plain sight. I was finally listening to what I like to refer to as The Force (sorry, big *Star Wars* fan here). It was telling me to listen to my heart and my mind and be open and aware of my emotions and needs. But complete clarity was not quite there yet. I would get hit with even more challenges and difficulties before finally deciding to change.

The first small bite was simple, but it had the most profound effect on me and for the rest of my life. It was simply a mindset change. I was now more curious. I started asking what I wanted out of life, one small question at a time.

I started with "What is my purpose?" Of course, I didn't know the answer right away, although this time I stayed curious and willing to think it through. And that was enough to get me started on a path toward real change. One of my first decisions was to take an oath of celibacy for a couple of years and completely stopped dating. I realized how shallow my relationships were and how they may have reflected the lack of self-compassion, love, and kindness for myself as well as others in my life. This gave me time to find myself, to better understand my emotions, and better see myself a little more profoundly. I was curious of what it meant to be a better man. This "time off" was one small way of slowing down and allowing me to see other small bites I was blinded to.

The curiosity bug continued. I became more curious about my health and started reading several self-help and diet books. Keep in mind, these were diet books, and I wasn't completely *woke* at that point. Those books contained food rules and judgment about what I was eating, or better yet, how I should be eating. I wanted to enhance my health and avoid the same illnesses my parents developed. Little by little, I started to become more interested in cooking and didn't eat out as much. All these small curiosities led to action, which led to changes that gave me a newfound purpose in life. I was inspired and motivated, and it was all from that simple mindset change.

I began to see the power of curiosity. This mindset change was the antidote to inactivity or stagnation. When we are curious, we feel a desire to try something new, often something small at first. There's an itch to be scratched, so we gotta scratch it! This creates inertia, momentum. It leads us to a sense of true awareness and realization, a place of learning and adaptation. Darwin stated that the likelihood of a species' survival depended not on its strength, speed, agility, or even its intellect, but on its ability to adapt! Awareness could lead to action, which can lead to clarity. Clarity is a form of being open-minded, which can allow us to be creative and explore. That exploration can provide us with further experimentation, so that we can enjoy our lives. Curiosity leads to further action. Curiosity is therefore at the core of behavior change because it allows us to become aware of our past mistakes from a factual, nonjudgmental, and level-headed view. I was becoming curious, and my mind opened to other possibilities, which led to more small actions. By slowing down, I started responding to my body's needs instead of reacting to them like I had in the past with anger, rash decisions, and poor habits. I adapted! I began to transform my health, my life. Survival of the fittest, right?

Little by little I started adding other changes over time. For example, I wondered what would happen if I stopped drinking coffee. Actually, giving up coffee was easy partly because I never really liked it, and partly because it made me so jittery. Again, it was about listening to my body. Well, I gave it a try, and then I realized how my appetite started opening up again. I went back to having breakfast most mornings, and because I was cooking again, I started being creative with my breakfasts. It wasn't very foreign to me since I had always enjoyed breakfast as a kid anyway. Just this one change was enough that I felt amazing. I had more energy throughout the day and slept better at night, which helped me be sharper the next day and make better decisions. It was amazing how one small deed led to another—inertia, momentum—the falling dominos effect.

There were some setbacks, though. I was doing well, so I experimented with a variety of diets, but then I slowly realized that diets just were not sustainable, and in fact they ended up doing more harm than good. I actually developed orthorexia and tried eating perfectly, and, boy, did that backfire on me. Fortunately, I learned about Intuitive Eating from a colleague and then let curiosity guide me. Needless to say, I learned the hard way from those experiences. However, there was no failing, just a lot of self-discovery. Actually, it was just having that time to enjoy a delicious breakfast in the morning, to give myself that time to start the day and at least enjoy more time for myself in the morning. Soon after, I started realizing I had more time in the morning, so I started packing my own lunches from time to time and therefore avoided eating out a little more. I like being creative with meals, so I dabbled with new recipes quite often, and even though I burned a few meals at first, I discovered a new passion, a new way to relax, and a new way to be creative. A pleasant surprise was how much money I saved by not eating out—I would spend about $250–$300 a week on just lunches and dinners sometimes. At one point, I remember calculating that over six months I saved just over $1650! WOW!!!

Another pleasant surprise was how I began to observe my own thoughts and feelings more often. I started asking and talking to myself more, asking questions like *What do I need or want now? What would happen if I changed this one thing?* I started to become aware—that something so small like eating at home more often just simply made me feel better—and the extra cash was just a bonus! So now, what else could I do? If it were this simple (of course not easy), what other amazing things in life could happen?

I wondered what would happen if I went to the gym in the morning instead of at night. It was challenging at first to wake up earlier, but I realized that going to bed earlier meant having more time in the morning. The benefits really started to add up. And it started with curiosity. It opened me up to other changes and what life was offering me. But it still took work, but this time the work was listening to my body. That was it! Curiosity was my body's communication conduit.

And here's what I learned. Again, I had to go through these explosive and difficult moments in my life. I had to transform my eating and learn to balance my life. It was both painful and enlightening, and curiosity was my beacon. I was slowly, bit by bit, becoming the man I wanted to be, the man I needed to become. This transformational point turned a new leaf on my life—to be a better man—and that new way of thinking is what continues to drive me today. It is a mind shift. A light that shines within me, and it serves as the foundation of motivation and inspiration in my life. I now work with others to pay attention to the circumstances that lead to my mother's and father's health challenges. That light helps me to become aware and curious that old beliefs can change. To help people avoid getting sucked into propaganda and misleading diets and fitness routines that promise to cure them, or somehow miraculously they will "lose 30 pounds in 30 days!" But more important, I have realized that change happens in small doses. Small, incremental changes over time. Interestingly, these small changes and challenges seem to happen either like one major explosion in life, or small challenges that build over time, and this is how the transformation happens as well. It can occur in a few months or over the course of six or seven years. For me, it continues still today.

After the Awareness

Let curiosity drive you. Don't force it. Let yourself be curious to change things you suspect need to be changed. For me, food and nutrition became the guiding light—the Force—and I love nutrition and food but not more than I love myself. I'm not willing to sacrifice other vital elements of my life, like enjoying time with family and friends if they choose to eat fast food. Nor do I sacrifice my hunger because the only thing that is fast to eat is drive-thru. Nowadays, if I'm hungry and fast food is all that is available, then that's what I'm having. I am just more curious as to how food will make me feel, instead of getting sucked into the collective believe that I should feel guilty or shame for eating junk food. I now approach eating and nutrition with a sense of curiosity and experimentation. A sense of playfulness and wonder. I pay attention to what my body is telling me.

Often in our crazy busy lives, our bodies are repeatedly telling us to slow down, but instead we are swept away by diet culture ideals and beliefs that suppress our ability to listen and trust ourselves. Yeah, I too drank from that same water cooler, and at one point thought I could perfect my eating. I ended up dabbling with "clean" eating, in addition to a diet or two. I was a big believer in this 40-30-30 diet (not going to give those diets any more publicity), if you can remember that one. I was partial to it because it was written by a biochemist, so the scientist in me thought he understood food and nutrition. Spoiler alert—he didn't! Yet, I fell for it, and not only tried to eat that way, I made sure to eat the "healthiest" food available (whatever that meant)—organic-only fruits and veggies, lean proteins and fish (no red meat), fats like olive oil, grapeseed oil, or the latest and greatest phytonutrient food out there—kale, chia seeds, and quercetin from apples and red onions. You know, anything with a fancy Latin chemical name that sounded important. Then I started realizing that eating "perfect" was a farce, a ruse intended to make me think I needed to fit into these narrow expectations of what it means to be a man. Being open-minded and listening more to my body gave me a sense of freedom and peace that was amazing, powerful, compassionate, and scary. Experimenting with diets and developing a disordered eating approach forced me to pay attention to the fact that I was living a lie. I was trying to become something that wasn't authentically me. I realized that my way of living was also an "in-your-face" and an "I-am-better-than-them" approach. Yup, that didn't fly.

On the contrary, what started to happen when I was on that orthorexia kick was watching my friendships disappear. Ignoring people telling me that I was too difficult to have around food, and a food snob. There were times I was feeling isolated and lonely because I didn't get invited out with friends. I later discovered that they didn't invite me because they didn't want to hear me complain about the food. That was tough, but I was blinded by my desire to be "healthy." Little by little, the

"I'm-gonna-show-them" attitude was actually backfiring on me. Over the years of becoming this "nutrition expert," getting my fancy-dancy master's nutrition degree, and a dietitian, I thought I could cure people of their diseases (like my mother). I tried to get people to eat "healthy" (I'll talk more about what I mean about that later), and what started to happen was that I was isolating myself even further. Now don't get me wrong, I'm extremely proud of my nutrition degree and career, and I totally geek out on the science, but there was a part of me that was doing it to "fix" myself. Cure my mother's cancer and my father's heart. Hell, to be honest there was a part of me wanting to somehow fix my own transgressions. Bear with me here a little, if you're a *Star Wars* fan, you might understand this—I had an Anakin Skywalker moment. What I feared the most was actually coming to fruition, and the worst part was that I was unaware of pushing people away and hurting inside.

After four to five years of practicing like a food police, I was introduced to Intuitive Eating and Health at Every Size. This was the anti-diet and weight inclusive approach I so needed. Again, I was opening my mind, and it felt amazing! I started with one small step and listening to my body, my eating habits, and now I spend time with many people I work with on just homing in on their body's communication. Sometimes it's hard, other times it's not.

What are your eating habits telling you? Are you having heartburn? Are you dealing with bloating? Slow down and listen fully. Give your body a break and be curious about what it needs. What is it telling you? Help yourself live life to your fullest.

Use more questions: How would you feel if you changed just a small part of your eating pattern, but not diet? Would having a regular breakfast help you? What would you feel like if you drank more water in the morning, or have tea instead of coffee a few days a week?

There is a not-so-famous quote from Dr. Martin Luther King, Jr., that talks about the importance of our interconnectedness and shared humanity regarding food, and coincidentally, it's about breakfast.

2: Curiosity

"And before you finish eating breakfast in the morning, you've depended on more than half the world. This is the way our universe is structured. It is its interrelated quality. We aren't going to have peace on earth until we recognize this basic fact of the interrelated structure of all reality."[9]

Dr. King has always been an inspiration and idol of mine, as for many people, but when I found this quote early on in my career, I was truly moved. I instantly thought of my parents and how much they had to sacrifice in a new country and with a new language to get food on the table each day for the six of us. I now realize how much we need others and I routinely think of all the people it takes to bring just one small bite of food every day. We can easily forget how intricately connected we all are with each other. Food is so vital to our existence, yet it is also that connection we feed off as well. We take these unseen actions and hard work for granted. It's the very first moment in the day when we are receiving sustenance from a dependence on so many others—the farmer or workers that pick or grow the food, the clerk at the grocery checkout counter, the corporate employee coordinating the marketing and distribution, and the truck drivers hauling the food to the stores. We are all so interconnected that eating is partly a moral imperative as much as a spiritual connection to our fellow person. It is part of the "common human experience," as Kristin Neff states—one of the three principles to reach self-compassion.[10] We are also social beings. Eating is a way to connect and belong to our group, our family. To me, having breakfast was a way to connect to my past, my emotional state. To fuel me, to start and appreciate yet another beautiful day that I get to spend on this amazing planet.

Next Steps

A few times throughout the day, stop. Slow down. Get away from the computer or put away your smartphone. Get ahead of challenges like frustration, anger, irritability, sadness, and anxiety. Pay attention to what your body is asking or telling you. That morning coffee is only going to get you so far before you need another cup. Be curious and listen to what will endure instead. Look for the changes that are small but permanent—not fleeting, not temporary, but long lasting. Experiment a little and see what happens. Be curious and open to what your body is telling you. And if you don't get it at first, keep at it.

Remember, one small thing you can do right now to get started is to visit my website to download my free guide to enhancing your curiosity: www.orozconutrition.com/curiosity-guide. You can get started right away to enhance and develop that curiosity voice.

Next, you'll learn how Angela was curious. Her changes didn't happen overnight. This is what I call "Act 2" or the "messy middle." This is where we learn how to climb up the mountain, when the process of change comes in waves.

Angela

Open Mind: Curiosity Comes in Waves

> "Curiosity is an act of vulnerability and courage. . . . But curiosity is uncomfortable because it involves uncertainty and vulnerability."[11]
>
> —Brené Brown

Angela was focused on making peace with her body, but how she got there came in waves. It wasn't a straight line. The peace came after years of diets and fitness programs that were just maddening, and she really wanted to enjoy food again. Angela felt like there had to be a different way. After multiple attempts to lose weight, "eat clean" (which is a co-opted term for dieting), Angela discovered that there was more to life than the hamster wheel of chronic weight cycling, more commonly known as yo-yo dieting.

Approximately ten years prior to working on a more compassionate approach, Angela returned from a not-so-positive routine yearly physical visit at her doctor. Let's just say the visit left a pretty traumatic scar in her mind. Her mortality was thrown in her face. "You're prediabetic." "You have high blood pressure." "You're going to die if you don't lose weight." Just WOW! Words like that can make a deep negative and emotional impression in even the strongest of minds.

Unfortunately, while it may seem helpful to warn someone of the fate of chronic illnesses or the risks of death, I have never seen negative approaches become enduring motivators or even an efficient tool at keeping people healthier. Those types of comments are more like a militant approach to healthcare, like knocking someone over the head with a blunt instrument to get them to change their behaviors. Initially, these negative approaches may spark some people into action, but what often happens is the person develops a slew of negative self-narratives that become more like "I'm less of a human, I'm not normal, I'm not healthy, I have a disease, why can't I do this, I'm such a—" You fill in the blank. But to many health professionals, it's the only approach they know or were ever trained to use.

Like many people, after that visit, Angela started on a low-carb diet and a strict workout routine. At first things looked good (or what would seem to be classified as good by diet-culture standards). She started losing weight, improved lab values and health indicators, and initially felt like she was in a better place. But after about a couple of months, life happened. There were various events that slowly started to take her off track—she went on a cruise with her family, then injured her hip during one of her workout routines, and the stress at work was quite overwhelming. And all of this was pre-COVID pandemic. She started slowly gaining a little weight again. She tried to go back to her fitness routine, but it was inconsistent. Some weeks she could go, but the hip pain would set her back. She tried cutting out the carbs again, but she had a new position at work, and the pressure and the demands were tough. And then a common negative narrative started to develop. Angela started believing she just didn't have the discipline. *Discipline* can be such a triggering word, but so many people use it to try to control a natural physiological change. It was never about discipline; it was about diet culture dictating her fate.

At first it seems like an easy solution. Put the fear of God in someone's mind and it gets them moving, right? Angela loses weight, and *voilà* the illnesses are gone, right? But that's just not the case. It isn't so black or white! The short-term gains (fleeting feelings of being lighter, healthier, and having more energy) don't last and are impossible to maintain. Many people that have tried losing weight multiple times, or tried keeping it off, know oh so well that it is by far a mind game. And

2: Curiosity

yet, Angela kept at it. Diet culture is ubiquitous and unescapable, like a drug addiction that forces people to continue despite knowing otherwise they have to stop. Do you know what happens when you try to lose twenty to fifty pounds in a few months? It's torture. Cravings are amplified, obsessive behaviors are created, and mental stress is intensified. The body is in a perpetual state of chronic starvation, which the primal brain is designed to keep you alive and avoid hunger. It's innate animal instincts—metabolism slows, and organs and muscles start releasing stored energy that is actually needed for the day-to-day physiological functions. Yet Angela tried fighting it. Her thoughts were constantly filled with the need to be disciplined: "No cheating," or "I can't enjoy food, or else." Angela was left feeling like a failure because why couldn't she do "it"? Is that really a way to live? Angela was constantly worrying about gaining weight. The worst part is that the chronic conditions may not go away just from losing weight. Then what? What happens when, not if, the weight comes back? After all, the single biggest predictor of weight gain is weight loss!

One of the most powerful types of research is what is known as a review or meta-analysis of multiple studies. This is where experts in a specific area of science sift through, pick, and analyze similar studies to help demonstrate what the body of research is indicating or telling us over time. I mention review and meta-analysis type studies to help drive the point about how diets and weight loss attempts lead to weight gain, and only exacerbated Angela's fears. Another proof of how weight loss predicts weight gain is from research with Dr. Michael R. Lowe, professor of the Department of Psychology at Drexel University in Philadelphia. Dr. Lowe and colleagues investigated over twenty-five different studies that contained dieting, restrained eating, and predictors of weight gain. They found that every study showed that dieting and restrained eating approaches displayed weight gain from as little as five months to as far out as nine years after the initial weight loss.[12]

(Trigger warning—I'm about to give examples of calorie levels and talk about starvation, so for those of you that would be triggered by this please just skip the next few parts.)

What this study also confirms is what we know from the famous body of research derived from the Minnesota Starvation Experiment. Back in 1944, Ancel Keys and researchers at the University of Minnesota took a group of thirty-six college men and put them on a semi-starvation diet for six months that consisted of a range of 1,200 to 1,700 calorie restriction based on each of the participants age, height, body size, and base calorie requirement. In today's diet-culture mentality, those calorie levels may not even be constituted as a low-calorie diet. Heck, you're probably thinking those are the amounts of calories your nutrition and fitness app tell you to consume—guess again. These men lost on average 25 percent of their body weight and had significant psychosocial challenges during the six-month study. They dreamed about food, chewed large quantities of gum daily, licked their bowls and plates dry, and added large amounts of salt and pepper to the food to enhance the flavor. They avoided any and all activity to decrease their appetite and became extremely antisocial. They had extremely low interest in sex, which was confirmed by hormone samples taken on a regular basis. The men were then placed on a re-feeding program for the next three months, and most gained the majority of their body weight back, but most was fat weight. In at fifty-seven-year follow-up investigation of the Minnesota Starvation Experiment, Dr. Eckert and colleagues, found that nineteen of the men took several years to regain their muscle mass back to pre-study levels, but had abnormal eating habits before they returned to pre-study levels.[13] Moreover, when we look at the vast majority of individual weight loss studies, without the help of a meta-analysis or review study, we can see various patterns—few studies go beyond a few months, and fewer still could look at diets and weight loss beyond two years. Most weight loss studies follow the same problems—participants don't last, there is a slew of exclusion criteria, and the ability to track and manage the exact amounts of food is quite challenging.

2: Curiosity

Of course, Angela was feeling like a failure because she was walking into a failed system. Diets and starvation might help someone drop a few pounds, but evidence shows that diets, food rules, and rigid fitness plans don't last. Using the Minnesota Starvation Experiment above as an example, imagine trying to feed an elite athlete 1500 calories while training for the Olympics . . . good luck with that one!

Look—let's be real. If you want a successful career, a family, a home, or just be social, it's near impossible for people older than thirty to sustain diet after diet, and weight loss attempts after weight loss attempts. And as for the tiny number of people in their twenties that might be able to maintain diets or weight loss, few would be able to sustain that weight loss for five years or longer, and by that time they're getting close to their thirties anyway.

Yes, of course there was an initial improvement in Angela's health—blood pressure improved, blood sugars decreased slightly, and her sleep improved somewhat. The problem is that whatever measures she took to lose the weight, especially dieting and increased physical activity, just weren't sustainable (especially with a busy lifestyle). It's not realistic, nor is the human body designed to continue running in a twenty-year-old's body at forty or fifty. Life throws so many more responsibilities and physiological changes as we all age. Angela, and anyone in life, just can't expect to work out two to three hours a day and follow rigid diets and food rules, when her work consisted of traveling two to four days out of the week, raising children, and caring for an older parent or family member. Angela had a great career and a great marriage, yet dieting and excess exercise were getting in the way. Life changes and what got her there wasn't going to keep her there. And this happens to people in their twenties as well—the body just can't keep up with the energy demands without a daily balance of food and enjoyment. Our bodies, and our minds, need to be filled not just with food or sustenance, but with deep human connections. Diets, food rules, and militant fitness programs are attempting to fill an abyss.

However, the damage was done. The belief that people with higher weight are doomed has now become ingrained in our collective narrative, and that the best way to manage, eliminate, or cure ourselves of these chronic diseases is to lose weight. Yet, weight gain is vastly complex, and certainly not strictly unhealthy. Various people I know, work with, and love are in a heavy body, and they are healthier than many people in thin bodies. There are copious variables to the development of chronic illnesses; large-body people are not a disease and large bodies aren't singularly responsible for the development of co-morbidities—despite the fact that the American Medical Association has classified obesity as such. I'll talk more about the Body Mass Index and the misguided and misused affects it has in our society more in detail later. A more psychologically damaging belief exists in our culture today: the diet mentality and the belief that thinness is "next to Godliness." The desire and push to live up to this belief also increase the production of stress hormones and negative chemical effects in the body. All this has certainly blinded many, including healthcare professionals, with the idea that excess weight is bad. It's a bit of a cop-out, a call-out culture.

Several years later, Angela felt like she had no choice because she had gained more weight than when she started. Regardless, she was determined to "beat this," as she put it. She decided to start vegetarianism and a very high fat diet both at the same time. And as was expected, after a few months of dieting and more activity, her doctor seemed pleased with her lab values—her blood pressure improved, and her A1c (which is the measure of the average blood sugar levels over the last three months) was now 5.1 percent (below the pre-diabetes classification). Things were looking good, right? But then her doctor dropped a bomb on here (again): "This is great, *but* you should try to lose some more weight."

That was it! Just that one little, yet devastating piece of unnecessary, unsolicited advice: "*But* you should try to lose some more weight." I mean, come on! Focusing on the negative is not going to endure—telling people they need to do more or else only causes people to regress.

2: Curiosity

This is what I meant by the collective narrative. Healthcare professionals get caught up in the idea that weight is the cause of a patient's illnesses and problems, and it's just not the whole picture. Unfortunately, this belief system and lack of understanding and training in the complexities of higher weight and chronic illness blinded Angela's doctor to see all the progress she had made. Angela had made several changes, and she improved her health significantly (albeit not in a sustainable way). Instead of building on the positive, her doctor set her back with just one little word: "but."

Again, we cannot singularly blame all physicians. Many mean well, and of course want to help us. Part of the problem is that this is our healthcare system at play. Many physicians and health professionals are stretched thin, overwhelmed, and stuck in a healthcare system that is inherently flawed. You see, Angela really wanted her physician to be pleased with her changes. Angela wanted her doctor to be proud of the strides she took and all the hard work for the last few months. That one tiny comment, *"But* you need to lose some more weight," was like a punch in the gut. But that narrative wasn't just from her physician; it was also the self-criticism in Angela's own mind that blinded her. She'd been here before, and her mind thought there was a pattern . . . a pattern of failure.

One of the functions of the body when it's in a starvation-like mode is to open the floodgates to a slew of energy-releasing hormones like glucagon, epinephrine, norepinephrine, and cortisol to allow glucose and other energy compounds to enter the blood and provide the body with rapid energy. Therefore, when the body senses a perceived threat like starvation, we then get this short burst of adrenaline, or energy from the natural stress cycle. Add some caffeine and you get this false sense of energy—a jolt of "I feel great!" So, when someone diets or cuts out food (all a form of starvation to the body), it blinds the person to what will happen eventually.

Remember my story about my early mid-life crisis and striving for that perfect body? I was burning a good amount of short-term and short bursts of adrenaline and liver- and muscle-stored glucose, but not an enduring source of energy. The body just cannot sustain a constant burn of stored fuel, despite this notion of gluconeogenesis that you will hear from diet culture. Allow me to digress just a little bit about gluconeogenesis. People believe that because the body can regenerate and produce glucose from triglycerides (fat molecules), protein, and byproducts of energy metabolism, that there's a belief that humans don't need to eat carbohydrates. That the body has an endless supply of glucose. Uh, not so, but, boy, wouldn't that be convenient? Actually, the body needs that fuel for other emergencies or just natural bodily functions—maintaining adequate body temperature, acid-base balance, heart pumping blood, diaphragmatic movement to keep the lungs functioning and us breathing. Who knew? The body does! The brain alone consumes about 20–25 percent of the body's entire resting energy, and when there's stress it drives heart rates, sweat rates, and use of stored energy even faster.

Vegetarianism, high-fat food choices, or any type of restrictions of carbs all seemed like good ideas, but Angela just couldn't sustain them. Her cravings and hunger would come roaring back. Again, diet culture is like a rolling a boulder up a mountain—it's a failed system!

However, Angela wanted to do it differently this time. She knew and felt something else was out there. She was curious and wondered whether she could get more guidance instead of doing it alone. She didn't want to go back to crash dieting again. When Angela came to me, she was ready for a different approach. We started with small steps, like going to bed early and having a balanced breakfast. I also suggested that she start reading *Intuitive Eating: A Revolutionary Anti-Diet Approach* by fellow dietitians Evelyn Tribole and Elyse Resch. This book was and continues to be fundamental to *One Small Bite* because it helps lay a strong foundation of anti-dieting and establishes how we should build a positive and secure relationship with food and our body. The ten principles (such as Reject the Diet Mentality, Make Peace with Food, and Cope with Your Emotions with Kindness) are tools to help rebuild a person's relationship with eating and health.[14] This anti-diet approach really resonated with

2: Curiosity

Angela. She felt this sense of liberation and finally discovering peace and enjoyment with food and eating. I didn't try to push the agenda of a non-diet or weight-inclusive approach. I told Angela I didn't want to get in her way if she wanted to lose weight or continue dieting, but I wasn't going to help her in that way. We were going to start listening to her body's cues, to her life circumstances, to her energy levels, and to what her eating patterns were telling her about herself. We were going to start a journey of body trust and self-compassion.

At first, intuitive eating was not very intuitive for her. Angela struggled honoring and understanding her hunger. She struggled because, up to this point, it was the years of rigid food rules and restrictions from numerous diets that blinded her to developing the ability of listening and understanding her own body. The fear and guilt derived from vast amounts of misinformation; from years of low or high you-name-it diets; from society telling her that carbs will make her fat; the fear and guilt was singed into her psyche. It created a form of traumatic experiences that seemed to be relived over and over again. One of Angela's greatest challenges, believe it or not, wasn't overeating or snacking on treats or sweets, but in actuality it was dealing with an overwhelmed and busy life, both at home and at work. The sweets and snacking at night were her body's method of communicating to fuel herself, to feel better, to relax. She needed to slow down to hear those subtle but available signs and signals from her body. Angela was learning to allow her curiosity to guide her.

Over time Angela made great strides in learning to honor her hunger and understand that overeating at one time, regardless of whether it was carbs or candy, would not cause weight gain or poor health. She started to build that curiosity to become interoceptively aware of her body and its physiological needs. Angela began to understand how to eat more mindfully and in a way that was appropriate for her lifestyle. Over time Angela really started to understand her hunger and fullness cues much better, and she started to trust herself. She realized that if she continued skipping meals and not prioritizing eating or fueling her body when she needed it, she would be exhausted and starving by the end of the day. This would lead to her body compensating by snacking into the evening most nights.

The Awakening— What Did Angela Learn?

Angela finally found a way to accept her weight, move past the war of weight loss, and make peace with her body. Those waves of curiosity in Angela's case came in some interesting fashions. The key was not whether food decisions were bad or good, but what she learned from them. She learned to be present with her desire for sweets at night, and this wave was like the weight of an elephant being lifted off her shoulders. Snacking and overeating at night were not very interesting to her anymore, but the pull was still there. After listening to her own body, to her own wants and needs, Angela moved forward and found ways of living that were in line with her values and what she enjoyed. Slowing down and being present with herself at night helped her go to bed earlier, which helped her wake up more refreshed. In turn she had time to make a little something to eat before she left for work. Now, this breakfast wasn't a stack of pancakes, eggs, and sausages like a mid-Sunday brunch; that wouldn't have worked for her. And let's be real, who the heck has time for that, anyway? But she started with a sensible breakfast of tea, a granola bar, a hard-boiled egg, and a fruit cup she'd take to work.

Over time Angela started to sleep better and felt her clothes fitting looser, and she felt lighter. She had more energy, and more importantly, she was less irritable. Her husband even mentioned that she beamed and shined when she walked into a room. She felt amazing. Angela really learned to pay attention to herself. She realized that the belief about carbohydrates making her fat was so common around the office. She noticed that those types of beliefs were the key elements of how diets prey on the psyche of all people. Over time, Angela also realized her cravings for those snacks at night would intensify if she continued having food rules or follow diets. For instance, when she went on a low-carb diet in the past, she would eat more compulsively and snacked mindlessly at night, but this time she was onto it. She remembered how important it was to listen to her body's signals. She was curious, and this time she paid attention.

Curiosity was opening her mind to her behaviors, to her patterns. Angela started becoming aware that the years of dieting had only brought more false hopes and further eroded her self-trust. Like most of us, she had learned the hard way: the vicious cycle of weight gain, weight loss, and then gaining it back. Most of these nonsensical diets will cause physiological changes that can become practically irreversible. Angela realized that being interoceptively aware of her body, listening to her physiological and emotional signals, was so much more beneficial to her health. She trusted her intuition and let her curiosity guide her instead of following strict diet rules that went against her natural physiological needs. Angela learned to listen to her body—her intrinsic goals—instead of something extrinsic.

Trust is a major component in seeing the change come to fruition, but this is not an easy or simple process. In *Daring Greatly: How the Courage to Be Vulnerable Transforms the Way We Live, Love, Parent, and Lead*, Brené Brown so eloquently explains that "the bad news is that it's a chicken-or-the-egg issue: We need to feel trust to be vulnerable and we need to be vulnerable in order to trust,"[15] and that's just the key to seeing change in ourselves. We need to rumble with vulnerability, which means we need to experiment and ride the figurative waves of curiosity in our own lives. We hop on, we hop off, and in many cases, we land flat on our faces, much like Angela did after riding many waves of diets and the weight-loss mentality. She then became vulnerable, and it wasn't easy. She knew she needed to do food differently, because those diet and weight-loss waves were just not going to satisfy her. Brené Brown further describes learning to trust in her latest book, *Dare to Lead—Brave Work. Touch Conversations. Whole Hearts*—that trust is built on small changes, and it means we need to fall flat on our faces to get there. She talks about the importance of setting self-boundaries, of reliability, of counting on yourself, having accountability in your own actions, respecting yourself, having integrity, being nonjudgmental, and being generous.

> "While trust is inherently relational and most pronounced in practice with other people, the foundation of trust with others is really based on our ability to trust ourselves. Unfortunately, self-trust is one the first casualties when we fail or experience disappointment or setbacks. Whether it's conscious or not, when we're wondering how we ended up facedown in the arena, we often reach for the blanket statement 'I don't trust myself anymore.' We assume that we must have made a bad decision and therefore it is a fallacy to count on ourselves to deliver."[16]

What helped Angela become more aware and trust her curiosity? She started with one simple technique: she kept a journal. But this time she didn't just write what she ate, the calories or grams of anything, or how much she was eating—she journaled what she was feeling and experiencing when eating. For her, it became one of the best methods to slow down and reconnect with herself. It was part of her "me-time." She analyzed, reviewed, studied it, so the journal opened herself up to curiosity. It wasn't just an accountability log she had to present to me; it reflected her state of mind. A data of behaviors and emotions around eating. She was more vulnerable and became accountable and nonjudgmental to *herself*, not me, through her food journal. She looked for patterns in her habits and signals from her body, noting what led to the return of her heartburn, or how to deal with the constipation or other issues around eating. Conversely, I've witnessed other people work and work all day long, ignoring and barreling right through any physical signs from their body. Grind-culture limits people's ability to slow down and pay attention to those subtle signals from the body that something is awry—heartburn, bloating, constipation, headaches, exhaustion, fatigue, irritability, lack of concentration or focus, missed periods, low sex drive—all signs our body gives us to pay attention. Ironically, many

2: Curiosity

of us were never taught to pay attention or understand them, but that's why I am telling you about this Shero!

Not Angela. Angela was more receptive and expanded her mind. She slowed down and paid a little more attention. Her journal was an amazingly simple but extremely effective tool. By journaling, Angela noted that while skipping breakfast might have been convenient and easy most mornings, the longer she maintained this habit, the more she was also dependent on a stimulant throughout the day, like a diet soda, coffee, or iced tea, or she craved chips or sugary foods. This was a subtle but important signal that would have otherwise been ignored. If there's no food from a wholesome variety of food groups, our body steals energy from our liver, muscles, and other areas before starting to break down fat. But like many of us while on diets, Angela was so determined to lose the weight that she ignored those subtle physiological signals. She ignored the low energy, poor mood, irritability, lack of focus or concentration, and therefore her cravings for snacks and sweets increased. Her heartburn would happen more often because she was scarfing down food while in front of her computer or on a conference call. She would have difficulty sleeping the longer she did a vegetarian and high-fat diet (not giving any of these diets the spotlight so avoiding the actual names). Consequently, by lunchtime, Angela would be starving when she followed these food rules.

Using her journal, she slowed down and paid much greater attention to how her energy levels were decreasing. She noticed those cravings at night sneaking back in. She thought, *No, this isn't what I want nor what I need.* Sometimes curiosity is subtle, while other times it just smacks us in the face. She decided to focus on breakfast because she remembered how it helped with her energy levels, her mood, and her overall feeling. Because of the regular journaling and review, she tried experimenting more often with breakfast most days of the week. It was the next small step for her—just one small bite to focus on at a time.

Please understand, I'm not trying to push another food rule or diet approach; breakfast isn't a panacea. It's not a sneaky method or backdoor approach to losing weight or improve your health. Why was breakfast so important for Angela? Because for her, she realized that a balanced breakfast would break the typical overnight eight- to twelve-hour fast! Her body was starving and needed to replenish nutrients like carbohydrates, which was her body's primary source of fuel. And that worked for her to feel better and build more a secure emotional relationship with eating late at night. She was learning to trust her body again. Our liver supplies a steady amount of blood sugar, or glucose, overnight in order to supply the extremely active physiological functions while we sleep (though we're obviously not as physically active at night in the same way we are during the day, but our bodies are busy and need fuel). This is the time when a whole host of nighttime hormones and neurotransmitters start the healing, repairing, and replenishing process. We utilize a significant amount of nutrients such as glucose, fat, and amino acids from protein for a whole host of physiological functions. What the body wants or needs is to replenish these stored fuel sources from various carbohydrate sources like whole grain cereals, starchy vegetables like potatoes, and yes, even bread and pasta, but also from fruit and some from dairy. We need a variety of these carbohydrate sources to fuel all the physiological functions; fruits and veggies alone won't sustain our energy needs throughout the day.

We also need amino acids, which come from animal (beef, pork, poultry, and fish and sea animals) and plant-based protein sources (beans, nuts, and high-protein grains like quinoa, fonio, and farro). These amino acids are the building blocks for every single cell in our body—blood cells, nerve cells, and organ and tissue cells (like the heart, liver, lungs, and muscles), and our immune cells, which, of course, are vital to keep us healthy and fight infection. These amino acids from protein are the building blocks of our entire body.

I mentioned the importance of carbohydrates and protein, but fat is the third major macronutrient, and it is equally as important as the other two. Fat provides the building blocks for myriad biological functions, such as creating cellular membranes for every single cell in our body. It insulates our body and cells, and it serves as a great conductor for chemicals and electrical signals from our nervous system, enteric system, lymphatic system, and our circulatory system. We get fat from animal sources like dairy such as butter, cheese, and creams, as well as from plant sources like nuts, olives, olive oil, peanut oil, and even coconut and avocado oil. And this is just the tip of the iceberg among the vast biological and metabolic processes of the human body.

We also need to replenish a slew of vitamins and minerals each day, and *no*, not from synthetic man-made supplements. From food! Supplements can be helpful, but our body does not process them as well. Synthetic vitamins and minerals are not as biologically available because they are not naturally combined within their precursor phytonutrients that are found in food. Another example of a nutrient that is vital for our survival is fiber. Yes, fiber is necessary to help get rid of the waste but to also fuel our gut microbes, which in turn help us digest food, get rid of cholesterol, enhance our mood—oh, and by the way, provide us with a bit more energy. One of the best descriptions for the relationship with our gut and our mood is described in an article published by the HEALTHbeat from Harvard Health Publishing, Harvard Medical School.

> "The gut has been called a 'second brain' because it produces many of the same neurotransmitters as the brain does, like serotonin, dopamine, and gamma-aminobutyric acid, all of which play a key role in regulating mood. In fact, it is estimated that 90% of serotonin is made in the digestive tract."[17]

And there are now copious amounts of research that are linking the synergistic relationship with the enteric communication system and our nervous system. Think about it: fiber is critical for good feelings. Don't you feel good after a good bowel movement?

We also can't live without water. About 60 percent of our body consists of water, and not just from what we drink alone, but water from food. Just like vitamins and minerals are readily available in food, water is better absorbed by the body when it comes from food—somewhere between 20 and 30 percent more than from the water we drink. Water is the medium through which all the body's physiology happens.

Angela realized that when she paid attention to her body, having a balanced breakfast most days a week would sustain her energy throughout the morning and until lunch. Again, she just felt better and was kinder to herself, less irritable, and more productive. One could argue that fasting in the morning or only having a protein breakfast provides the same sharpness or alertness, but not indefinitely. Meaning, the body will sacrifice a little stored fuel, but it hates using up stored energy to make up the deficit, regardless of whether that supplemental energy is coming from stored glycogen in the liver or muscle or from triglyceride chains in fat cells.

Interestingly, what started happening is that Angela started to wonder what food combinations would sustain her. Again, she let her curiosity guide her, and she experimented with different options for breakfast. I love the word *experimentation* because it is at the heart of curiosity. It helps inform us through the action driven by curiosity. That's a fundamental method of learning—we learn from our experiences. Angela learned that just a hard-boiled egg or oatmeal alone wouldn't hold her very long. She experimented with adding a mini bagel with a little cream cheese to the egg, which really didn't take up that much more time, and that combination seemed to hold her till lunch. Yes, there were still fears of carbohydrates, but I reminded her that it's the amount of food that causes the body not to feel well, not the food itself. Again, a form of interoceptive awareness that she started gaining by journaling, slowing down, and paying attention to what her body needed. She had to make time a few nights a week to prepare meals, which led her to think, *Well, what if I turn off the TV and go to bed thirty minutes earlier?* It was one small deed after the other. A domino effect! Angela started getting up a little earlier, which offered her more time to prepare lunch too. And then out of the blue, she thought, *Why not get a morning yoga session in as well?* Out of nowhere, she added a quick morning yoga and cardio routine of ten to fifteen minutes a couple days a week. Yet again, one small change led to another. The more she was curious, the more she would experiment. This was on top of feeling better, being in a good mood, having more energy, and improving her digestion. She started having regular bowel movements again, and more important, her cholesterol improved as well.

What Can You Learn and Do from Shero Angela?

Some people say they do better in life juggling many balls, and that just focusing on one small thing takes too long. There are so many other things to get done in the day. This argument is extremely valid. Angela, too, had a ton of other responsibilities in life. She didn't focus on dismantling her life or stopping everything in her daily routine to change her eating or improve her health. What she did is just focus on one small skill and ability she (and you) always had—listening to the body! I would argue that on the contrary, dismantling your life is exactly what diet culture is great at doing. Stopping everything! Changing every food and eating pattern you do in order to follow "the plan." Whatever that means. Well then, how well has that worked for most people? Heck, we've been at this whole diet craze for over sixty years now. In fact, diet culture and thin ideals have been around for centuries. If you don't believe me, just read *Fearing the Black Body: The Racial Origins of Fat Phobia* by Sabrina Strings. We've had one diet after another going on forever, and still people hopelessly waiting for the "next best thing." If diets worked, we would have only needed one. We can't continue trying to fool our bodies because when it comes to hunger and weight, our bodies can't be fooled.

What can you do? First pay attention to what your body is telling you. Stop for a couple of minutes each day and pay attention to your body. What do you feel? Do you have energy? If not, why? What will make you feel better? What new habit or behavior do you think will make you feel better? Be open and curious. Let yourself ride the wave of curiosity and then try it.

Pick one new habit. Try it several times. Learn from it and adapt as you go. You might not get it right the first time, and you'll often fail more than you'll succeed. But if you're doing what you know needs to change, then stick with it. It's like Master Yoda says, "The greatest teacher, failure is."

How does one learn to surf, fly a kite, build a sandcastle, or become a Jedi Knight? By doing, and doing, and doing. But you first must trust your curiosity. It's the antidote to inaction, inactivity, and stagnation. Curiosity leads directly to action, and together they are the foundation for lasting change. It's like learning how to surf. You must get past your fear of the ocean and the surfboard itself. If you've ever gone to the beach, your mind is full of curiosity. You might look out to the vastness of the ocean and wonder, "What would it be like to be one with the ocean?" Why not learn how to surf? When you start learning to surf, you learn to read the motion, timing, and patterns of the waves to catch just the right one or the right wind patterns. There isn't a perfect way of surfing that works for everyone, just like there isn't a way of eating that every human has to follow to live fully. And just like in life, if we pay attention to our body's needs and our emotional wants, we have the opportunity to enhance our relationship with food and therefore improve our health and wellness. We nourish our brains. We allow our logical left brain to communicate adequately with the creative right brain and do something new. We get creative and trust ourselves to jump on the metaphorical surfboard and ride the wave to shore. In many cases, it's a leap into faith.

Trust is a major component to seeing the change we need. Angela trusted her body's own signals. She became aware of hunger and fullness cues again. Angela still faces doubts about being more intuitive and mindful about her food choices, but she's much more aware and present with what she both needs and what she wants. Curiosity is her driving force going forward. Key to her transformation was paying attention to and practicing how to ride the waves of life that guided her to her interoceptive awareness. Like Angela, what you can do is to start practicing trusting your body and mind to become harmonious and make peace with food and eating.

By the way, Angela found a new physician, one who listened to her, paid attention to her experiences, and she felt fantastic. Her labs improved, her blood sugar levels were better, she had no signs of high blood pressure, she was off her blood pressure medication, and she was pleased. Her new physician even asked her to provide a testimonial.

What one small bite will it be for you? It only takes one. Practice, persist, be present, and be patient. Life will give you *gifts*. That's why we call today the *present*!

It is not, nor should it be, done alone though. We need to be like the astronauts that put their trust in NASA scientists. Changing the way we eat is no different. We need to trust curiosity. Only fear holds us back. Despite the fear of drowning or the fear of the rocket blowing up, we still find the challenge necessary. Otherwise, how would we enjoy life? How do we learn and grow? We learn more the more we do, and thereby we become better at spotting the right wave. Simply put, curiosity allows us to become aware and present with our body and therefore connect with our physiological and emotional needs. Curiosity is about self-trust, building the self-awareness necessary to change our behaviors in order to enhance our health, and reaching for the stars or riding that gnarly wave, just like Angela did.

Remember, one small thing you can do right now to get started is to visit my website to download my free guide to enhancing your curiosity: www.orozconutrition.com/curiosity-guide. You can get started right away to enhance and develop that curiosity voice.

Ericka

Experimentation: Moving Past Repetition

> "Trust is the stacking and layering of small moments and reciprocal vulnerability over time."[18]
>
> —Brené Brown

Ericka was a twenty-eight-year-old speech therapist who lived alone and worked at a local hospital. She would put in long twelve-hour shifts, three days a week. Some weeks she added an extra day for overtime to help pay off her student loans. She would see between fifteen and twenty patients a day and had little time for breaks or meals. You would think that by the end of the day she'd be exhausted. No way, not Ericka! Extreme activity was her jam!

Erika loved parkour—an obstacle course–type extreme sport that is typically done outdoors in urban settings (at local parks), but a few fitness centers have recently popped up catering specifically for parkour indoors. They are known as parkourers or traceurs (or traceuses for women), and essentially what they do is run, jump, flip, and climb structures as if they have Spider-Man abilities. Looks amazing if you ever get to check it out, and quite honestly if I were in my twenties, I'd be all over this sport as well. Think *America Ninja Warrior* (ANW) but street style, and in fact a lot of ANWs have done or are parkourers themselves. Ericka would train with a parkour group three days a week, often for two hours per session. Aside from parkour, Ericka also loved Jiu-jitsu and trained a couple of times a week, would then hit up a hot yoga class for a ninety-minute session once or twice a week, would take a sixty-minute body sculpting and strength training class on her days off work, and would go on a mile-long walk with her two dogs daily. At work, it was just as intense. She would often take on more work than she could handle, partly because she loved working and helping people, but also because it helped her escape her mind and stressful life. We calculated about two and a half hours of activity, and that didn't count the amount of activity (walking, taking stairs, and standing) she did at work. Like I said, high intensity!

From a nutrition standpoint, Ericka was equally intense. She had strong rules about what she'd put in her body. She heavily restricted certain types of food and maintained a rigid approach to eating. She had intense body image issues and insecurities that were adding to the already high level of stress at work. She had high anxiety, fear of certain foods, and a perfectionist personality; she often felt like she needed to control everything she ate. She would follow the exact same eating pattern most days, which mirrored her strict and extreme physical activity level. A typical workday included running out of the house with a twenty-four-ounce tumbler filled with coffee along with a few slices of toast that she ate dry on her way to work while sipping on her coffee. At work she would often avoid food except for energy drinks, protein bars, and the occasional bag of chips, and despite the very low amount of food she would typically still work out, get home most nights between 10:00 and 11:00 p.m., and then eat anything starchy while on her tablet or phone glued to YouTube or social media. Or on weekends and nights that she knew she would be off the next day, she might meet up with some friends after her workouts for drinks at a local bar, and sometimes not get home until 3:00 or 4:00 a.m. On her days off, Ericka would sleep in until 11:00 a.m. or later. Her eating was minimal. She would often have a protein shake smoothie and again live off protein bars, with occasional almond butter and rice crackers. She would go to hot yoga and body sculpting classes but wait to eat afterward and often binge in front of the TV with chips, salsa, and guacamole—(her go-to snack when she thought she couldn't control her hunger). Her eating was very sporadic, just as sporadic as her weekly schedule; it was either a go-go-go schedule or just couch out on her days off, except for her workouts. But she was extremely repetitive and restrictive with her patterns, mostly due to her intense fear of gaining weight.

Ericka started seeing an orthopedist for severe leg pains. Her doctor suggested she take a couple of weeks off from parkour and Jiu Jitsu to allow her body to heal, but that was hard because her activities were also a huge part of her social life. All her friends and people she hung out with were there, but it was also about the fear of gaining weight. However, Ericka had a good conversation with her close cousin; she was like a sister to her. She would often talk to her about almost anything, and she suggested she see a nutritionist because she thought some of her leg pains had to do with how little she was eating for her level of activity. She was significantly underweight and looked possibly anorexic. Her cousin suspected that she might have an eating disorder.

The Awakening— What Did Ericka Learn?

We all know that keeping busy helps us get things done. The better we get at a task, the easier it becomes, and we can be repetitive with our habits to make us efficient and effective. But there comes a point when repetition can cause more harm than good. Repetitive patterns can blind us to how our habits may be contributing to poor health or avoid listening to subtle but necessary signals from our body. The challenge is that we often can't see it for ourselves. Things are going too fast, and we are incapable of being properly aware. The consequences of daily repetitive patterns and habits is described in a great piece by neurobiologists Zachariah Reahg and Michael Yasa from the University of California, Irvine, on the effects of repetitive memory. They theorize that repetitive memory, like memorizing facts for an exam, may actually interfere with our ability to see important nuances and specific details that affect our lives in the long run.[19] The irony, however, is that repetitive behavior allows us to be fast and efficient; we get things done almost automatically.

But we might be missing some nuance as well. Yes, blinded repetition helps regurgitate answers on an exam or efficiently get us to complete our daily tasks, but it also makes it difficult to introspect, to take inventory of ourselves, or to be present. We lose ourselves in the repetition and busyness of life. We begin to ignore our deepest fears and what we most dislike about ourselves, and oftentimes these dislikes live in our subconscious. We may not even be aware of this if we are unable to slow down and pay attention. This is similar to Generalized Anxiety Disorder, where we tend to have constant and chronic worrying, nervousness, and tension of the things we fear—it's a disorder that involves our primal stress response of fight-flight-freeze. However, when we stop and listen, pause, and pay attention to the signs, signals, or patterns in our lives, we can become curious. This is the major benefit of slowing down.

Ericka was locked in a loop of extremes: restricting, over-exercising, overworking, and then crashing, either due to the leg pains (the body's way of signaling), or through binges, difficulties sleeping, or emotional challenges (the mind's way of signaling). The repetition in her life was blinding her ability to see what to change. This is a typical situation in a starved mind. The body will try to compensate by slowing down its metabolism to preserve energy, shut down nonessential body functions like sex motivation or bone or soft-tissue repair, all in order to maintain glucose to the brain and heart. A comparison I regularly tell people about a starved mind or body is similar to a doe in heat foraging for food. Although she is in heat and ready to take on a mate, her drive to survive and find food keeps her fitness at top priority because that strong handsome eight-point buck is no longer a perfect mate, but a threat to any food she is trying to find—bad luck, buck!

Ericka also grew up with messages that she wasn't good enough, that she needed to prove herself. Unfortunately, her self-worth was tied into the need to control—control what others thought about her. And

2: Curiosity

those fears and insecurities were intensified by a family history of diabetes, hypertension, cancer, and obesity. The story in her head was a determination not to fall into the same fate as other family members. She had a perfectionistic mentality, living in this chronic nervousness and tension of not measuring up. This was the consistent and nagging self-narrative in her head. She truly wanted to do better all the time, but it was exhausting. The repetitive self-identification was blinding her to what would help her move forward and enhance her health. Well, for Ericka, her purpose was to barrel through the day, at whatever cost to her body. That's like so many of us, right? We push it! Busy is the new status symbol. Slowing down in our society is synonymous with weakness, laziness, and being unsuccessful.

But is slowing down really a manifestation of weakness, laziness, or a lack of success? I argue to the contrary. The saying "slow down and smell the roses" means we ought to slow down and enjoy life. Enjoying life means to be curious, thus being open to life's opportunities and possibilities we would otherwise miss if we blindly continued the same routines, habits, and patterns every day. On the other hand, when we don't slow down, life is going to continue passing by, hammering or harming us both physically and emotionally.

In Ericka's case, she couldn't connect her behaviors to her challenges. She was stuck in a routine of extreme control, perfectionism, and anxiety, so the only outlet was the other extreme—over-exercise, restriction, overwork, and then in contrast, the waves of laziness or numbing in front of her smartphone endlessly streaming media at night.

Moving Forward

Ericka *did* start to slow down and pay attention. After a few visits, she started to realize that her schedule and routine was getting too intense, and she knew something was off. Her curiosity piqued mainly because she was forced to slow down. Her body was communicating; in fact, it was actually screaming—leg problems, nighttime binges, lack of focus at work. She was forced to listen to her body! And sometimes, that's what it takes to pique our curiosity, or simply a no-duh mentality such as, "*Stop* this craziness or you're going to end up in the hospital!" Unfortunately, for some people it takes hitting rock-bottom before they are aware of what's going on.

While challenging, Ericka reluctantly started working on making small changes, because she realized she just couldn't continue with her current extreme behaviors. At first, she tried making big sweeping changes, like eating three balanced meals every day, but she quickly realized that something like that was just too much. It set her back. That's a common problem with many of us. We think more is better, which is steeped in our societal collective narrative, our social beliefs to "go big, or go home" or "aim for the high-hanging fruit." Her perfectionist and critical negative self-narrative quickly disappointed her yet again. It's a vicious cycle. When we are in our own head, it's like being inside a bottle: we can't read the label from the inside. Progress is not a straight line.

I frequently draw a simple x–y axis graph on two sticky notes. One has a perfectly straight line sloping upward. On the second sticky note inside the x–y axis I draw a squiggly, looping, circling line that looks like a three-year-old doodling on paper, but the line also ends at the same point as the upward straight line. I tell clients that progress is not a straight line. So, the only option Ericka had was to focus on the one small change, and it actually didn't turn out to be a behavior at first; it was being aware of her mindset. She began observing her behaviors as a method to provide data and facts instead of emotional judgments or criticism. She had to figuratively step outside her bottle in order to read her own label; therefore, she first learned how to become her mind's observer.

We started with a simple awareness exercise. She had to overcome one of her most difficult challenges, which was her rigid daily routine. Consequently, this rigidity and repetition was offering her an alternative path to healing her starved body. At first it was a simple exercise of

2: Curiosity

pausing for thirty seconds to a minute sometime in the day to just check-in. Learning to pay attention to the body is not easy, partly because like many of us, Ericka was so use to the grind that she forgot how to tap into her body's wisdom. This was further complicated by an unusual work schedule—some days twelve-hour shifts, and then random days off. She didn't have a typical nine-to-five, Monday-through-Friday schedule. Ironically, her days off were a perfect opportunity to pause and pay attention to her body. At first even pausing on her days off was challenging because even though she wasn't working, her mind was somewhere else. Yet, she found the thirty seconds a couple of times a day, and it helped her pay attention. We were sitting in one of our sessions and we had a great discovery conversation about what she observed. She mentioned her thoughts about her diet and activity level: "You know, it seems like I have this really bad habit of going to bed late." Then she proceeded to say, "Well, it's just that I'm a night owl. I've been a night owl most of my life. I feel like I can get so much work done at night, and I enjoy staying up late watching TV or streaming on social media. It's my time to unwind."

I pressed it a bit and asked her, "What does it mean to be a night owl and unwind?"

She thought about it some more, and then said that unwinding meant she could relax and do the things she enjoyed. Get away from the hustle culture and everyone watching her. She gets her energy at that time, which ironically coincided when she ate the most. Her eyes opened wide. She paused right then and there and said, "Hmm, I never realized it was like that. All this time I was beating myself up for eating, when what I'm now seeing is that I was hungry." There was a long silence. "You know, that's what my mother did at night; I just grew up that way. No one in my family would go to bed early, there was always someone eating at night. My mom would regularly let out this sigh of relief after snacking." Ericka started seeing some patterns. Her relationship with food was built on a model of how others coped with their emotions through food; they, too, never learned to pay attention to their body's wisdom. How could she have trusted her body? She didn't learn how to cope or deal with her anxiety or fears, thus restricting or extreme activity blocked her ability to hear her body's signaling throughout her life.

Again, she paused and just sat with those realizations for a couple of minutes. I could see it sinking in. "Well, now that I hear myself, I think it's ironic. I mean, I see what you mean. It's like I don't want the day to end, but at the same time I need to escape, yet I get those strong urges to eat." It was a need to fuel her starved body. She started realizing how she would avoid her emotions or ignore her body's signals all day because her fear of developing a disease, gaining weight, not being perfect was such a powerful force that it blocked her awareness. Fortunately, her starved brain, her animal instincts could not be tricked. She started to discover about herself. "Hearing myself say that I'm a night owl out loud sounds so definitive. I go to bed late partly because I can't shut my brain off, partly because of my leg pain, and partly because I'm just so used to it." Therefore, on her days off she would wake up late, drink a couple of cups of coffee instead of eating, grab protein bars, and then meet up with her parkour or Jiu Jitsu group, and avoid eating by exercising more. "I don't get home till late and I'm not really tired, so I start streaming media late into the evening, and then snack. OK, I get it, it's a domino effect. It's as if I do this because it's just what I've always done before. I don't ever stop to think about it, certainly not this way."

In other words, the first thing Ericka needed to do was to become aware of her own behaviors and self-narrative. In her mind, she was unaware of how she was identifying herself. She was saying that person she was in the past—*because it's just what I've always done before*—and that alone was subconscious. She also filled her mind with narratives about negative body images; fears of chronic illnesses that she didn't have; self-criticisms and judgments about her self-worth. Yet, these beliefs and narratives had been building up for a long time.

We then proceeded to analyze what going to bed late does to her. "Well," she said, "for one thing, I tend to snack or I am tempted to eat

2: Curiosity

something at that time. It looks like it's also causing me to get up later the next morning, and then I have less time to make a balanced breakfast or pack some meals for the day. I'm hitting the snooze button on my phone about five times before I get up, and then when I do get up it's a mad dash to get ready. I'm not making time for myself, even though I feel like I enjoy that nighttime routine. I guess it's just something I've done for so long I don't think about it." Again, there was the example of not paying attention.

The funny thing is that so many of us are just like Ericka. We are conditioned to live in the past, clinging to old habits without realizing how they affect us throughout the day. We are blinded by how one small habit affects various parts of our lives, like our sleep quality, energy levels, or health. Ericka had high anxiety challenges (she was also on medication for anxiety), and part of the excess anxiety was lack of sufficient rest. Staying up late caused a cascade of various events, one of which was forcing her to rush the next morning. This would then set the tone for the rest of the day. These types of small habits seem so integral to our own self-identification, so we believe they are an important, essential, or unchangeable part of our lives. This is just how it is, and so we can't move past the repetition.

If this was what she discovered just from slowing down, then what else could she discover? Her curiosity was piqued. Ericka took a second look at other sticking points in her life.

"It's interesting," she said. "I really don't slow down at all, do I? I'm always in a rush going from my apartment to work, consult to consult, then off to parkour, out with my friends, and I'm also on my computer at work or on my phone all day. By the time I get home, I find myself scrolling through my social media or Netflix shows, and the next thing I know, it's 2:00 a.m."

She continued, "*Wow*, this is starting to make sense. Hearing myself say this is both revealing and exhausting."

As we were reviewing her patterns, Ericka said something pretty amazing next:

"OK, so what I'm realizing here is that because I think I'm a night owl, I'm actually creating this self-fulfilling prophecy; I'm setting myself up for greater challenges and I'm oblivious to them, right? If I stay up late, which is when all my demons start swirling [her expression for her extreme anxiety, negative self-talk, and deprecating self-criticism] and my eating behaviors kick in. Most nights I'm having the hardest time falling asleep or sleeping soundly. The next morning is a mad dash—I've hit that snooze bar a few times, which leaves me zero time for a decent breakfast. So, I just grab coffee, maybe toast or granola bars, and then the entire day I'm rushing around from client to client; I really don't take a break. I rely on snacks from the vending machine, which I know are not healthy for me, so I avoid or punish myself at that point by not eating. But by then my energy level just tanks most days, yet I keep using caffeine or snacks. Wow, this is a vicious cycle, isn't it? Just saying this out loud sounds crazy. Who can sustain this? No wonder I'm super stressed and anxious, which is the main reason that on my days off, I just wanna crash. Huh, I wonder if that why I hit a wall doing my Parkour and Jiu Jitsu techniques. I've been off for a while now, which is how I hurt my leg. My body just isn't getting what it needs."

I love it when the hero in the movie is self-discovering! They are beginning to see the light. "Yes, precisely!" I said to her.

Ericka had a light bulb moment and when clients have these moments, they are, well—to use a word—enlightened.

Ericka also started to discover how many unsustainable food rules she developed. For instance, she saw a documentary once about meat production, and then gave up red meat. This food rule was validated by the fact that many of her friends did the same. In another instance, she read somewhere that fruit gets converted into sugar in the digestive process—of course it does, fruit naturally contains fruit sugar. Yet, Ericka bought into that diet mentality, the one about how sugar is evil, it will make you fat or cause diabetes. And just like that, another food group gone! She decided to abstain from most fruit and instead supplement with protein bars, which she wouldn't have needed had

2: Curiosity

she not given up meat—*Trigger warning: I'm going to talk about grams of carbs*—At that point, I compared the amount of carbohydrates in a small orange with the amount in her protein bar. Her eyes open wide when she saw that the bar had eighteen more grams of carbohydrates than the orange, some of which came from fruit purees. Now, I wasn't trying to indicate that one food is better or worse than the other; it was a simple fact to help her see how food rules get created by fear of weight gain, or this thin ideal in a diet culture. Fundamentally, these food rules and diet beliefs set in our collective narrative, and it only perpetuates hunger, which creates a constant struggle with food and our bodies. Therefore, our bodies fight back and know how to compensate for not eating, regardless of our advanced executive brain abilities. I explained to Ericka that our limbic brain, our reptilian brain, can't be fooled. She may think sugar is the devil incarnate one day, and then another she's bingeing on cookies at a party because they look delicious, and her brain and body are starved.

Over time, Ericka started to slowly secure her relationship with food and make peace with her body. Fruit was fine and so was red meat, and it probably would have been cheaper than buying protein bars in the long run anyway. She discovered a few other food rules, and slowly started feeling less tension, but she struggled with trusting her body.

The problem with these types of rules we create in our heads is that they contain gaps of information. Facts like how various fruits naturally contain sugar, water, and fiber to help fuel the body, hydrate more efficiently, and support the digestive track; facts like how fruit provides essential vitamins and minerals—these facts are simply missed when food is demonized because of one nutrient like sugar. These food rules typically come from someone we know, trust, and maybe even love, so it's easy to incorporate those rules into are our personal belief system. It's a form of belonging and validates our identities—skewed as it may be. In other words, Ericka was restricting, avoiding, and controlling her eating, despite her body's energy needs. She didn't have a complete understanding or awareness of how those rules would affect her over time. What develops in the long run are gaps of information about our body that are then filled by our emotional experiences, not facts. Our executive brain then creates a fear narrative that blinds us to those long-term problems of what I call Starvation Brain. This form of stress is exacerbated by the fear of food, lack of body trust, and rules that become extremely strong belief systems that are almost impossible to break. As humans, we are designed to eat meat, just as much as we are designed to eat plant foods, and it's OK to choose one type more than the other. Starvation Brain, however, prevented Ericka from being aware of those types of comparisons. It never crossed her mind. She was in disbelief.

Ericka was not aware of the gaps in her mind. Those gaps were blinded by her daily routines. Those routines helped reinforce common behaviors that were so familiar to her, they became a thoughtless process. And it's not just her; most of us are not aware of the nuanced information all around us. Many of our habits or behaviors today might have started from an adverse childhood experience, like a traumatic event, which in turn our minds then create a story filled with missing information. The problem is that those stories then later become an ongoing self-narrative of how to act if or when we feel a similar threat. Like Ericka, we block body signals to avoid a similar feeling, but we may not realize that we're starved.

The Starvation Brain is all about conserving energy so we can focus. We try to numb ourselves, escape the feeling, fight it—it's our natural stress response. An alternative to conserving energy is finding it. Some people use food to help avoid feeling that perceived threat, which again is only created by our minds. Others avoid food all together because the starved brain focuses on something else. One example is eating ice cream to feel better. Not that ice cream is bad, but it's being eaten to help numb the pain we actually need to confront. The Starvation Brain is looking for a coping mechanism. Others, like Ericka, avoid eating throughout the day because the perceived threat of developing diabetes or weight gain was the narrative, but then at night emotions get more intense so food or extreme exercise or streaming becomes a coping mechanism, and lead to habituation. These new habits are then a way to avoid eating during the day because it is tied to the very feeling we are trying to avoid—some form of pain, fear, anxiety, or anger. But that starved brain is only going to further intensify emotions, leading down a vicious cycle. Other people might use alcohol, drugs, or gambling to soothe or cope. The challenge again is that we are just not aware of how eating habits or behaviors during the day affect us at night, which was happening with Ericka.

Throughout the day, our minds block out noncritical information in order to get work done or go on about our daily routines, this in turn helps us avoid feeling the pain or sadness. Essentially, we focus on the task at hand while our minds diligently filter out nonthreatening stimuli. For instance, we may be going through a tough relationship or a traumatic event in life, so we are oblivious to low energy levels from skipping meals. However, because eating is necessary, it also becomes intricately and emotionally connected to those traumatic moments. In other words, we might not be aware that an eating experience in our life—the tastes, smells, mouth feel—is an emotional situation simultaneously linked with the feelings of those foods. In the future, we might have a reaction to that food because of our current emotional state, and then suddenly that food is "bad" for us. Unbeknown to us, we create a story like how the treatment of cows is our fault; it pulls at our heart strings, and all of a sudden, we give up meat. We then find ways to try to justify the need to control eating and avoid that food. The stress can also increase our reaction to that food, like with certain carbohydrates; we might perceive bloating or heartburn, when in reality the digestive upset is due to a complex interplay with the gut microbes and the stress—the starved brain. However, this becomes a method to control our emotions. We don't want to feel the pain—unaware that the pain is caused by our minds. Our minds then fill in the information gaps, which is a form of counterfactual thinking.

Counterfactual thinking is a human tendency to create possible alternatives, "what ifs," to something that has already happened. We think, "If I could have changed that situation in my life back when it happened, then all I have to do is control what I do or eat now, and today will be better." The problem is that those situations and life experiences already happened.

For Ericka, the narrative was the pain of losing one of her parents to diabetes, which was tied to weight and eating too many carbohydrates or sugar. Connecting fruit to too much sugar was a counterfactual way of thinking, so she was going to avoid fruit—a form of control that was blinding her. One emotion was tied with the other, and because she, like so many of us, was so busy, her mind looked for the easy fixes, the counterfactuals. It filled in the details or missing information, and so then she didn't eat fruit. Then the repetition sets in, and it reinforces our beliefs, and so a belief is then automatic. Ericka was developing disordered eating habits. The "ah-ha" moment she had earlier was so important, but it was only the beginning.

Many more complex situations weave themselves into the fabric of our nourishment. By the way, this isn't just isolated to people like Ericka, or people with an eating disorder like anorexia, bulimia, or binge eating disorder. This happens to various people—wealthy or poor, thin or large bodied, people with chronic illnesses or not—all the time. Ericka was starting to see how one small habit was leading to a cascade of other habits, one after the other.

You might be asking, "OK, David, this sounds great. Thanks for the info, but how do I get out of this vicious cycle?" The truth is that there is no magic bullet! There is no electric shock treatment or hypnotherapy (nothing against hypnotherapy—good stuff). There is no magic pill a psychiatrist can prescribe. There is no supplement out there that can miraculously get rid of repetition, counterfactual thinking, habits, beliefs, or eating disorders. It really takes a concerted effort to change. Nonetheless, just as food rules and negative narratives about food develop through small experience slowly over time, so too is the

2: Curiosity

solution—small changes over time, committed and consistent effort, will help transform your health.

Curiosity allowed the establishment of a greater sense of awareness with Ericka, the problems started becoming more obvious. Her nighttime routine as well as her belief system was driving a huge wedge into her health and well-being. Consequently, we began collecting facts and paying attention to the data, looking at patterns in her typical eating habits: what she had to eat the day prior, and then what would happen on her days off. The obvious solution seemed so simple, which I'm sure you thought of as well. Ericka needed to go to bed earlier; yet again, another example of the need to slow down. But it's not always obvious to the person dealing with the problem. As I mentioned before, "You can't read the label from inside the bottle." So how can you see what's really going on in your own life from deep within your habits and challenges? After exploring what would be required to go to bed earlier, Ericka started to understand that simple doesn't mean easy. She quickly realized it would mean having to give up something like going out with her friends, her nighttime social media binge, or maybe one of her fitness classes. Still, baby steps, right?

A simple but powerful technique is to first ask yourself, "What does easy looks like? What's the simplest thing you can do each day to fix the problem?"

For Ericka, she said, "Well, the easiest thing I can do is just be aware. Really, David? Come on! This is just too simple, and it's not really doing anything." Subsequently, I asked her to tell me how she's able to jump from structure to structure, sprint up a wall, do a flip and twist backward, and then jump onto a tree branch and swing into a dismount, landing like a Marvel superhero. "Well, that doesn't come . . . ," and then she stopped. "Oh, okay, okay," she said, "I get it! I see what you mean. I have to practice slowing down. I have to become aware of what gets in my way. I have to visualize what I have to do, so I'm not doomed to repeat old habits." She became curious because she finally slowed down and paid attention. For her, "easy" was turning the screen off at night.

Ericka created ripple effects, transformed her life, and made a difference. She went from an "oh, why bother" type of attitude to "hmm, that sounds interesting." She stopped, looked at her evening routine, and thought, "OK, put my phone down, head to the kitchen, get a few things ready for tomorrow, and you can get back to whatever you're doing." She said that being aware of what was happening at night was enough to remind her to just get up and do it. Yup, this is probably why the Nike tagline is such an iconic marketing brand. It's what everyone needs to do. Stop, slow down, and assess yourself, and then get up and just make your life happen. Just do it!

Ericka started journaling, but she made it fun. Instead of just a calorie counting app on her phone, she used the good old-fashioned paper and pen journal. But it wasn't just any pen and paper—she bought an assortment of different color pens, markers, stickers, and even tiny fabric pieces. It looked more like scrapbooking than journaling. She made journaling an art project, and she was quite creative. She remembered discussions about balanced eating, various food groups, and sticking to a schedule, so she would color her entries to help her capture patterns. The she would make drawings of her emotions and use fabrics to create alternative textures to an emotion. It was artistic, and she enjoyed it. Colorful and creative journaling made it easier to tie positive emotions to eating breakfast more often, packing her snacks, remembering to stop and eat, and reconnecting to the joy of meals with friends and family.

Over time, Ericka also started reading more about yoga, and she found information about finding balance in life. Curiosity was flowing, and she wondered if hot yoga was really that helpful. She started going to a new body-positive yoga studio. Journaling (or should we say her creative outlet) was helping to open her mind to herself. Yes, slowing down and just paying attention to her body was empowering. Instead of fighting against her night-owl tendencies, she meshed with it. One night while sitting on the sofa scrolling through the feed on her phone, she stopped and just took a deep breath. It was enough to open her mind and listen to her body—*you need rest, girl!* She gave up hot yoga in exchange for better sleep.

There were definitely still bumps, hurdles, and some hills to overcome. Yes, she still struggled a bit at work, trying to get time to eat. She loved her work and helping people. Over time, however, she slowly started to change her schedule as well. It wasn't easy, but she chipped away at it. She remembered a conversation with a friend who was trying to get a new position at work, and she said, "My father would tell me that you have to ask. The worst that can happen is that they say no, but it's not about you." Listening to herself give that advice was empowering her, not just her friend. She knew she needed a little more flexibility at work, so she asked her boss to give her a few more flexible hours. Instead of working three days a week, she added one more day but reduced her daily hours from twelve to eight. She varied her starting times and worked a couple of Saturdays a month to allow her to have a day off during the week. This gave her more time to prepare meals, get more rest, and enjoy her friends and activities.

Finally, Ericka focused squarely on one major change: stopping, slowing down, and checking in with herself. It was the singular focus that led to more changes. "It's like one good deed leads to the others," she commented. Yes, it's a domino effect, and that's the whole point of curiosity. Allowing your curiosity to explore one small bite leads to significant and long-lasting positive changes over time.

Interestingly, I've had people tell me that focusing on one thing just isn't helpful for them. They tend to be more productive and creative when they have a few balls in the air. Yet, when I explore that argument, each time I come up with the same answer. When they focus on multiple things, something breaks pretty fast. I ask them how they were so successful in life, and they often give me a similar answer: they focus. They are committed to what's important despite everything else that's going in their life. Same difference! Obviously, I'm not trying to tell people to stop everything in life to focus on only one thing. That's no different than dieting—give up carbohydrates; give up fat; give up meat, blah, blah, blah. We know how that turns out. No, that isn't what *one small bite* is about. It's about slowing down and focusing on what's going to help you thrive.

Look, regardless of who you are, if you don't eat, sleep, move, go to the bathroom, or connect with people, you'll pretty much burn out. One Small Bite is about paying attention to your body so that you can get really good at something, and people seek out your expertise for it. It was scary for Ericka to slow down; it certainly wasn't easy, but she learned how to do it over time, and the cascade of improvements in life were astounding.

You too can slow down and pay attention to your body. It takes practice, but the key is to allow yourself to be curious. Please feel free to visit my website at www.orozconutrition.com and set up a fifteen to twenty minute discovery call with one of my clinicians, and we can help you get things started.

Meredith

Enjoyment: Finding Her Hum

Has this ever happened to you? You arrive home after a long and busy day with an hour-long commute. You pick up the kids at their respective after-school activities and then immediately start cooking dinner for the family. Alright, maybe not the cooking part, but work with me. Meanwhile, you have to feed the pet, wrangle everyone for dinner, but then no one eats at the dinner table. You might have a quick minute to get a bite yourself, but you have to check that they did their homework. At this point you're beyond exhausted, but you have to hop on the computer to finish some work. At the same time, you're trying to get the kids to bed, and you're arguing with your spouse about financial problems and whose parenting method is the best.

It's like we just don't get a break, a moment to relax, or a chance to take time for ourselves. We're pulled in a million directions, and we're overwhelmed. This was no different for Meredith.

Meredith is a mother of three with a full-time director position at a large technology company. She was living the dream. She had three kids and a top-notch job with a great salary, and they were starting to build their dream lake house. She was revered at work because she was a go-getter, fast and efficient, organized, excelled at her job, and her employees loved her; she led through inspiration and compassion. She definitely put in her time, traveled often for work and pleasure, and was fortunate to visit numerous cities across the US and around the world. Growing up, she was the youngest of four and the only one in her family to graduate with honors with a business degree and then complete her MBA. She was killing it! A true Shero!

The picture-perfect life, right? On paper everything looked fantastic, but in reality, not so much. Over the years the stress, late hours, inconsistent eating, and on/off dieting and fitness really started to set in. She started to dislike her body, and at her last physical she was diagnosed with prediabetes. Meredith was so overwhelmed. Her marriage was on the brink of collapse, partly due to her husband's infidelity. But they were still trying to make it work. She was up at 5:00 a.m. most days, getting everyone ready and fed (except herself), and then out the door. Most days she would drop her youngest at elementary school, one at middle school, and the oldest at high school. Talk about child taxi service! Mornings were once her favorite, but over the years her husband did less, and the demands were greater that all she wanted was to get to work. At home, Meredith was left doing all the work, yet she somehow made it in the office by 8:00 or 8:30 most mornings. She also traveled quite a bit for work, which would often mess her eating and fitness schedule. It seemed like she just never caught a break, so it was obvious that she didn't have the energy to cook. She was on antidepressants and sleep aids as well, but sleep was constantly challenging, to the point that it would interfere with her workout schedule. She just didn't have the motivation to keep all of it up. Even her weekends were packed with the kids' activities, sports, competitions, and recitals. Meredith's picture-perfect life was creating havoc on her eating patterns.

A typical eating pattern began with two cups of coffee with just half-and-half first thing in the morning. Interestingly, this was the only time of the day where she really had a moment for herself; it was her "me-time" where she had twenty to thirty minutes of peace and calm in her day. Breakfast used to be her jam, and she knew she needed something to eat, but she had to wait to get to work, which would usually consist of either a packet of instant oatmeal or a protein shake. It all depended on time.

Her lunch was often at odd hours, or she'd skip it altogether because of meetings, calls, or one deadline or another. At times she would be on the road or catching a last-minute flight and scarfing down half a taco. She would often eat leftovers from home, but lately it had been quick taps on the Uber Eats or DoorDash apps to deliver to her office. She would even order ahead of a meeting with a client so they would deliver to the parking lot of a client's worksite, and then she'd scarf it down right before the meeting. Often her company would cater food for meetings, so she'd grab anything available, frequently tacos, sandwiches, pastries, and a large diet soda. She would often find herself mindlessly snacking in the afternoon, not once but at least three or four times. Most times it would be nuts, but from time to time it would be another protein bar, a diet soda, and some fruit. Again, it really depended on what was available and what she might have in her bag. Of course, that's if she'd remembered or had the time to grab something before leaving the house. But we all know how challenging that can be. She would have about a forty-five-minute commute to pick up one of her kids from an after-school program or practice. Meredith had all the right intentions to cook dinner, but she just didn't have the energy or the motivation, and her husband was often no help. That was another point of contention in her marriage, among so many others. Therefore, it was just too easy to get something quick and convenient at a drive-thru and not have to mess with making dinner.

Ironically, Meredith also tried various diets—low nutrient this, high nutrient that, fasting something or other—you name it, she tried it (sorry, not giving any of those diets any free ad space here). Each one gave her false hopes, like *the next one will do it*, yet it was one failure after the other; self-criticism filled her mind. She thought something was wrong with her body. She'd get tests done thinking something was wrong, and discovered she had a low thyroid function, which is often a sign of a slowing metabolism. Eventually, all those diets created a sense of starvation, an energy deficit in the body. Unfortunately, the body responds by lowering its metabolism since there is less energy coming in. The funny thing is that she wouldn't eat much at dinner either, or it would turn out to be a free-for-all at night anyway. Everyone in her household would just do their own thing. The kids would plate their own meals, head to their own rooms, and eat while on their screens or doing homework. Things were quite a mess, and the family rarely had dinner together. So often Meredith would get back on her computer and work from around 8:00 p.m. until midnight most nights. Another habit she had was constantly snacking most nights. She didn't eat much dinner, but chips, ice cream, soda, or whatever was available in the refrigerator was fair game.

The Awakening— What Did Meredith Learn?

Clearly, Meredith was completely overwhelmed, facing incredible challenges and being peppered from all directions by life's punches. However, she was determined to make changes, and obviously, she's a hell of a go-getter! She didn't want to end up in the same situation as her mother and older sister—both with diabetes. Meredith remembered how her mother would often neglect her health. She would rarely take her medication and hardly ever checked her blood sugars. I truly connected with Meredith at this point. Very much like myself and my own mother as I mentioned in chapter one, Meredith's mother believed her diabetes was a conspiracy theory, and she felt fine. It was the medical and pharmaceutical industries out to make money on her illness. Distorted beliefs of how the medications and the side effects of conventional treatment would make her sicker, and Meredith's mother believed it was all a hoax to make her spend time and money in a system that would just kill her. Unfortunately, this belief system prevented Meredith's mother from getting treatment, taking medication, and adequately managing her diabetes. For me, it was as if I was living my mother's illness in Meredith's pain as well. Meredith's mother died of complications from diabetes and heart disease at an incredibly young age of sixty-three. I had mentioned to Meredith about the similarity of my experience with my mother, and it really strengthened our relationship. Meredith's older sister was also dealing with diabetes and breast cancer, and had similar beliefs as their

2: Curiosity

mother, so Meredith just didn't want to end up in the same boat, and she wanted to enjoy her life and family.

Repeatedly, clients tell me that they just don't have the time to eat healthy or to even work out. I get it! I mean, look at Meredith's life. It was just a whirlwind of crazy days for her, one after the other. What's worse, just like Meredith, we too often don't see what's going on day in and day out or pay witness to our own reality.

Remember how Ericka was blinded by counterfactual thinking and anxiety about the food for the same reasons? It is what I call autopilot syndrome: day after day. It's so easy, so familiar, and convenient to stop in the drive-thru or order takeout, and not even realize it sometimes. Heck, we all have days like Meredith, where all we want to do is just plop down on the sofa and get lost in streaming Netflix, TikTok, YouTube, or social media. Moreover, this escapism is so often tied with food, and after a while this becomes habitual. This is how one may relate to food or their eating style—used as a coping mechanism (which by the way, is not a judgment). That was how both Meredith and Ericka learned to cope.

You don't even notice it happening yourself—mindlessly eating while reading this. That's OK! Coping with food is an emotional act. There are few things we put in our bodies so frequently like food that elicits a physically emotional response. Food is emotional just as much as it is physiological, so for someone to tell me they are an emotional eater, I often respond that "yes, we all are." Accordingly, there's no judgment if choosing to eat to feel better was Meredith's coping mechanism . . . it probably helped her when she did. Conversely, what is more important is to become our own observers. Pay attention to our emotions and reactions to them so that we may better respond in the future.

For Meredith it was the early morning "me-time" that started it all. She began to pay attention to what she needed and wanted. Realizing she needed help was challenging because asking for it was not in her DNA . . . a common trait for many of us. She wanted to *do it right* this time, which is why she wanted professional help from a dietitian. Yes, she wanted to lose weight, but she came to realize that her weight wasn't as important as wanting some enjoyment back in her life. Doing it right meant having time to go the gym. She loved Zumba and indoor cycle classes because of the great music and connections she makes. Doing it right meant finding time to enjoy food with her family a few nights a week. She discovered that it wasn't so much about losing weight; she wanted to feel good, and that meant slowing down, having more energy, getting more sleep, enjoying life, and, yes, looking good too. We started with that *me-time*. She knew it would prove to be the catalyst for her transformation. Consequently, it wasn't about cutting out that early morning me-time with her coffee to be replaced with a balanced breakfast or going to the gym. No! Just spend those twenty to thirty minutes to pay attention to herself. Give her time to plan her day with a little more *me-time* sprinkled in for herself as many days as she could. This autonomy to choose instead of being told what to do was liberating to her.

Meredith discovered that the diets and years of battling with her weight was about a misperception of health and a lack of trust in herself. She'd rely on diets and experts to tell her what to do, but this time, she was the one in charge of her own body. Autonomy through self-reflection allowed her to start listening to her body's subtle signals. That was all she did at first! She started to realize that the best way to relax was to learn when to say no, or better yet, when to say yes. It's the difference between that subtle but oh so important "hmm" voice. You know, that little voice of curiosity we all get from time to time? Not that dreadful and disregarding voice "ugh . . . not now," which then avoids the confrontation. More importantly, she discovered that she needed to stop and pay attention to the voices regardless of what they were; to pay attention to that tiny little expression on her face or the mood she was in. Life would be so much easier if she spent the time to slow down and listen. Meaningful change would occur. Consequently, this is what therapists, coaches, or gurus mean by being in present. Pausing and paying attention is a form of self-observation that is a critical step to transformation.

2: Curiosity

Another big ah-ha moment that manifested in her me-times was the need for a sounding board: someone to talk to, to support her. She often came home and went straight to work and tried to get more done; she was in a whirlwind of automatic actions day after day with no one to help and listen.

I mentioned to Meredith about the amazing TED Talk that the TV titan Shonda Rhimes presented a few years ago. Shonda Rhimes is the bestselling author of the book and memoir *Year of Yes: How to Dance It Out, Stand in the Sun, and Be Your Own Person*—THE Shonda Rhimes, famous creative genius behind *Grey's Anatomy*, *Scandal*, and *How to Get Away with Murder*. In her TED Talk, she talks about the premise of her book, how she lost her *hum*. Her true, deep, and meaningful hum. Below is a small excerpt transcription from her 2012 TED Talk.

"For one year, I would say 'yes' to all the things that scared me. Anything that made me nervous or took me out of my comfort zone, I'd say 'yes.' Public speaking? Yes. Acting? Yes. A crazy thing happened—the very act of doing the thing that scared me undid the fear. It's amazing the power of one word. 'Yes' changed my life. 'Yes' changed me. Saying 'yes' to playing with my children likely saved my career.

"Three shows in production at a time, sometimes four. Each show creates hundreds of jobs that didn't exist before. The budget for one episode of network television can be anywhere from three to six million dollars. Let's just say five. A new episode made every nine days times four shows, so every nine days that's 20 million dollars worth of television, four television programs, 70 hours of TV, three shows in production at a time, sometimes four, 16 episodes going on at all times: 24 episodes of *Grey's*, 21 episodes of *Scandal*, 15 episodes of *How To Get Away With Murder*, 10 episodes of *The Catch*, that's 70 hours of TV, that's 350 million dollars for a season. . . . Four television programs, 70 hours of TV, three shows in production at a time, sometimes four, 350 million dollars, campfires burning all over the world. You know who else is doing that? Nobody. So like I said, I'm a titan. Dream job.

"But I understand a *dream job* is not about dreaming—it's all job, all work, all reality, all blood, all sweat, no tears. I'm not complaining. I work a lot. Too much—much too much. And I love it! When I am hard at work, when I am deep in it, there is no other feeling. It's a hum, it's my hum. The hum sounds like an open road and I could drive it forever. The hum is a drug, the hum is music, the hum is God's whisper right in my ear. The more balls in the air, the more eyes on me, the more history stares, the more expectations there are, the more I work to be successful, the more I need to work. Am I anything besides the hum? But my hum was broken; all I heard was silence. . . .

". . . And then the hum stopped. Overworked, overused, overdone, burned out. The hum stopped.

"And then my Southern waitress toddler asks me a question. I'm on my way out the door, I'm late, and she says, 'Momma, wanna play?'

"And I'm just about to say no, when I realize two things. One, I'm supposed to say yes to everything, and two, my Southern waitress didn't call me 'honey.' She's not calling everyone 'honey' anymore. When did that happen? I'm missing it, being a titan and mourning my hum, and here she is changing right before my eyes. And so she says, 'Momma, wanna play?' And I say, 'Yes.' There's nothing special about it. We play, and we're joined by her sisters, and there's a lot of laughing, and I give a dramatic reading from the book *Everybody Poops*. Nothing out of the ordinary.

"It's all peace and simplicity. The air is so rare in this place for me that I can barely breathe. I can barely believe I'm breathing. Play is the opposite of work. And I am happy. Something in me loosens. A door in my brain swings open, and a rush of energy comes. And it's not instantaneous, but it happens, it does happen. I feel it. A hum creeps back. Not at full volume, barely there, it's quiet, and I have to stay very still to hear it, but it is there. Not the hum, but a hum. And now I feel like I know a very magical secret. Well, let's not get carried away. It's just love. That's all it is. No magic. No secret. It's just love. It's just something we forgot. The hum, the work hum, the hum of the titan, that's just a replacement."[20]

This passage and Shonda Rhimes's entire TED Talk epitomizes exactly what Meredith was beginning to discover—that one subtle statement: saying yes to what really matters in life is profoundly transformative while at the same time pretty hard to do. It's an awkward sensation to many of us, foreign and difficult to self-advocate. Yet, love is fascinating because it truly recharges our batteries. Love is belonging and connection. It gives us the ability to stand firm and know that we don't need to binge on chocolates or work endlessly to fill a deep void in our lives, or to control and restrict every gram of food we try to put in our bodies to find the true hum.

We have to slow down and listen. Meredith started to notice something. Like many successful clients, one key element started to happen. Meredith started noticing her hum voice. This voice was starting to become a predominant voice in her head. It's that curiosity voice instead of that give-up, throw-in-the-towel, or I-don't-care-right-now voice. It is what Anna Gatmon, author of *Living a Spiritual Life in a Material World*, describes as Expansiveness—the first of the Four Keys to Fulfillment and Balance. An experience of presence, being, or putting yourself in a place to receive curiosity and opportunity. It's like being at the beach and watching the sunset, but instead it's happening because we choose to stop.[21] Like Shonda Rhimes, we choose to say yes to ourselves, and begin to live. That image of the sunset or surfboarder riding those waves, we're hit with the enormity of that beauty for only a few seconds, but it fills our heart. The soft white sand, the beautiful orange-red-pink-blue hues of the sun touching the horizon, and you look out in awe and realize the importance of life. Meredith could have been swept away by the currents of her life, and like surfing, it's not easy. We wipe out, over and over, but we get back up. At first, Meredith was riding her curiosity like a surfer rides the waves of the ocean, crashing and causing chaos all around.

It's as Anna Gatmon describes as her second key element to finding and reaching that fulfillment and balance in life: Active Listening. It is about paying attention to what the universe, God, the Force, or the energy source is telling us. The third key element is Inspired Action. The power of knowledge is great but it's not knowing something; it is taking Inspired Action with that knowledge. Similar to the nerves of fear of jumping *on* the surfboard and riding those waves, curiosity may lead us down a scary path, but we know the journey will be wonderful. Once in that expansive or conscious mind, we are allowing ourselves to ride the unfortunate diagnosis yet choosing to pay attention, learn, and move toward change because the alternative is just more of the same. It's experiential learning at its best, not just watching the YouTube video and then suddenly doing it. It's allowing that information to become available, really listening, being aware of the larger interdependent opportunities and factors, and coming from a place of intuitive knowing. In the book *Intuitive Eating*, authors Evelyn Tribole and Elyse Resch focus on expanding our minds in order to reject diets, honor hunger, challenge the food police voices, make peace with food, and learn to develop our interoceptive awareness. *Intuitive Eating* is a method of engaging with our bodies so that we can build a positive and secure relationship with food. Therefore, when Meredith took Inspired Action by paying attention to her needs during her early morning me-time, it was one small bite that started her transform. She was therefore engaged in the action and manifesting her dreams, goals, and purpose, albeit little by little. But hey, Rome wasn't built in a day either.

2: Curiosity

Forward Momentum

Along her journey of self-enlightenment, Meredith confronted numerous moments of frustration and thoughts of failure. Ironically, that very same me-time gave her the opportunity to observe how failure was only a destination of many along her journey. Failures served as teaching moments and growth. Therefore, we did a simple exercise. I asked her to name what eating behaviors or positive changes had made her feel good and that she could sustain for the rest of her life. "Oh, David," she began saying, "it's interesting that you want me to do this exercise because it's very simple things like the following:

- Cutting back to one or two sodas a week
- Enjoying a simple breakfast most mornings
- Going out for quick walks after work
- Having dinner together as a family
- Getting organized
- And finding love in my marriage again."

I asked next, "OK, now which one is the lowest hanging fruit?" (Sorry, can't help the food puns.) "Which one will have ripple effects in your day?" In other words, I asked her to pick the easiest behavior that could be applied with little effort, the one that required little thinking or wouldn't get in the way of her daily routine or cause the least disturbance. Hearing this piqued her curiosity, but she wasn't quite sure which one to choose. I gave her an example of a client that wanted to work out. I told her that I suggested he put his sneakers next to the coffee machine because that was the first repetitive thing he did every morning—I call this little trick the *Captain Interrupter Technique*. It's simply a way to break the mindlessness or automatic motions of our moments. I told Meredith that he thought Captain Interrupter was a bit loony, but he figured it wouldn't hurt. Well, as it turned out, that simple little cue of just seeing the sneakers next to the coffee machine was enough to subconsciously, and consciously, distract his automaticity. He would have to move his sneakers out of the way to make his coffee. Well, that was enough to make him slow down and think to put them on and just go for a walk. Over time he started laying out his workout clothes and sneakers because he figured, "Well, why not? It's here and I can just go on a quick walk." That then turned into a couple of short easy runs a week, then having breakfast, then making a couple of delicious lunches to take to work, avoiding social media first thing in the morning, which then helped him connect more with his kids. Meredith was intrigued.

The next words out of Meredith's mouth were like magic: "Huh, that's interesting." It was a moment of self-discovery. To play along though, I asked her what she meant by that comment.

"At first, I was thinking, OK, let me start journaling because that really helped me in the past to slow down and pay attention to what I was eating, and it would make me accountable. But, boy, I hated journaling in the past. It felt like it was such a chore and ineffective."

I said, "OK, tell me more. What else went through your mind?"

"I remember in high school, I used to love my Trapper Keeper. I had a plastic transparent bag where I kept all my colored markers, and I remember how organized I was. How much I loved coloring certain days of the week, keeping my calendar, and doodling images on the bottom and corners of my calendar. Now it [journaling] became fun! I'm going to journal Trapper-Keeper style!"

She continued describing more ah-ha moments.

She then said, "Well, I liked the Captain Interrupter technique with the sneakers. I thought I could put my workout clothes together for the next day right at the entrance when I get home from work. I really like to make it thoughtless and break my routine to help motivate me to get to the gym. I really miss it you know." And then she continued: "Yeah, I like that simple little trick. I think I'll do the same. I'll put my sneakers and workout gear right where I place my keys when I get home. I just know I'll have to move the clothes out of the way."

At her next appointment, we checked in on her new *interrupter* technique. She explained that she did put her gear on top of the bowl, and the very first night after work she went for a ten-minute walk. She

2: Curiosity

felt a whole lot better the first night, and although she didn't always go for a walk each night, she had to move her gear out of the bowl. It was simply interrupting her automatic habits. This actually pleased her because it felt simple. She was excited because it wasn't a fitness program or a restrictive diet approach. Again, she would make the choice on her own, and she felt more in control, the more control she would give up. Meredith was amazed how often she slowed down and became more mindful. One simple act made her shift her thinking. After a few weeks, Meredith was walking regularly, but what was more important was that she started making other changes. Again, the domino effect. One action was leading to another.

At her next visit, Meredith had a smile on her face. She said that because she was walking more, she slept a little better those nights, which in turned helped her have more energy the next morning. The walks helped motivate her youngest to go on walks with her a couple of days as well. Those mornings, she would have the energy to make a couple of meals for her family and lunch for work. She started a whiteboard organizer for the family to divide some of the tasks, a way of asking for help. This way, the kids felt like they had the freedom to choose, which in turn helped them all feel better as well. Meredith got to a place where she could make her own decisions. There was no diet, no food rules, no fitness programs that would complicate her life. All she did was let one small curiosity bug bite her to start the transformation. She didn't give up sodas or eat dinner with her family every night, but she paid attention more to her body. She realized on her own that the sodas were a way to keep her awake, and they substituted her hunger.

Most importantly, Meredith learned that she didn't have to make major changes. Her life was still complicated, work was super busy, and not every day was easy. But, to this day, she continues to put her workout gear on her bowl and now she's learned to slow down and pay attention to what she needs and wants. She's learned to listen to her body and create boundaries at work and home. Finding her me-time was her superpower. It was one small bite that helped her start journaling and paying attention to her needs.

We have a great journaling tool you can also use to help you to slow down and pay attention to your body. For a free copy, visit www.orozconutrition.com/awarenessjournal so that you can get started on your journey of self-enlightenment.

Catalina

Experimentation Is the Way Out

Meet Catalina; she is a forty-three-year-old single mother of a teenage son with some skills on the soccer field. Catalina works as a human resources manager for a manufacturing company, and like Meredith, she works long hours at the office with long commutes to and from work. However, she has had the opportunity to work from home one to two days a week, which allowed her to be a little more available for her son as he was growing up. Catalina really enjoys her current position helping people in her company, yet the stress from work and life circumstances have been taking a toll. She has been unhappy with her weight and blames herself for letting herself go, but she recently read *Intuitive Eating* and wants to work on building a secure and positive relationship with food and her body. She wants to be more active and spend more quality time with her son, but she's had three herniated discs in her back and a trochanteric bursitis on her left hip that have led to less activity over the last several years. With all that said, we can stop here and just say that she's a true Shero! But let me tell you a little more.

Catalina had dreams of getting a degree in psychology, but life happened. She got pregnant and dropped out of college to focus on raising her son. Eventually, she went to night school and finished her undergraduate degree in human resource management, which has helped her advance her career. Things haven't been easy as a single parent, and she longs to have her own therapy practice. Like many people that come for nutrition services, she was looking for a nutrition expert to "make her right, once and for all," as she put it, but this time she was amazed with *Intuitive Eating* and thought she really needed someone to help her. In the past, she wanted to control her weight and had tried various diets: she thought at one time that a high-fat diet, which had been all the rage with many of her friends and colleagues, would finally do the trick. This time, she really wanted to end the roller-coaster ride of unsustainable dietary requirements and ridiculous food rules.

Catalina faced strongly held beliefs of excess weight and what she thought that would mean to her health. Diets were part of her identity because she was on one or another for most of her life. They gave her hope that she would finally be the person she was in her twenties and look acceptable and healthy. At the same time, she was fearful that she would develop a chronic illness or not be accepted by her peers or family. Diet culture feeds off this negative emotional false hope roller coaster. Catalina suffered from an unfortunate negative association of her self-worth and lack of self-acceptance. She was blind to the fact that she was already a beautiful, strong, and successful woman. Furthermore, this warped belief system and low self-esteem were also intrinsically connected with her body image.

When we finally met, I let her know that I held no judgment about her wishes to lose weight, and we spent some time giving those feelings space and agency because embarking on Intuitive Eating and a weight-inclusive approach to her health and body was going to be radically different than anything she'd ever done before.

She had worked with a dietitian in the past and was pleased with her services, while at the same time, ashamed that she didn't lose as much weight. There was a lot of judgment and self-criticism, and a lot going on in her life. She often felt that she just couldn't maintain the diet requirements and restrictions in calories, which led to a flood of negative feelings about herself. Of course, with those responsibilities, who could? Our encounter, however, was quite different than what she expected. No one had ever explored her desire to lose weight, what it meant, nor how she felt. We discussed what her goals were: have more energy to enjoy life and her son, sleep better, and—she was honest with me—she wanted to look better. She was considering dating again and thought she wouldn't be able to find a partner. We took some time to explore how these beliefs were tied (or not) to her weight, and that eating in line with her values is completely valid and important. We discussed how diets may have at first seemed to help her in the past, but they didn't last. She discovered how difficult they were to sustain, how much work they took, and the challenges she'd come across. How each time she was excited by the possible results, but how she was disappointed with the outcomes. She noticed how emotionally connected she was to losing weight, and for the first time she paid attention to the intense stress and anxiety of what would really happen.

Catalina was intrigued with the ten Intuitive Eating principles and wanted to try a more mindful approach to building her trust around all foods. She was eager to move away from diet culture and curious about feeling better, but there was a lot of fear. Without judgment, we explored her experiences with diets and weight-loss programs from the past. What did they mean, and what did she experience? Just a couple of years prior, she had experimented with a high-fat diet and discovered that while she lost some weight, she couldn't deal with the regular and intense levels of constipation and increased cholesterol levels. Frustration was another common challenge because that diet required ridiculous amounts of preparation of meals with butter, coconut oil, bacon, nuts, seeds, avocados, and various types of oils. Shopping for those foods alone was both challenging and super expensive. More importantly, she discovered how extremely socially isolating the diet was, alienating her from friends and family. For example, she was active in her church and would attend various social functions a few nights a month, which usually involved food and eating. As a result, she would either deviate from her diet or choose not to go to these events because the temptations and social pressures were too problematic. These social and emotional pressures are often overlooked or not even known to most people, regardless of the diet. But these social constructs create deep divisions between our values, and diets are not worth the sacrifice. Health is so much more than just what you eat; it's about the deep-seated values and connections in life, like sharing food experiences with people we love and care for.

Catalina hired a personal trainer and started going to the gym early in the morning, which meant skipping breakfast. Ill-advisedly, the trainer suggested she fast the rest of the morning to help burn more fat. Allow me to explain the problem with this recommendation. A lot more happens metabolically and biologically than just burning fat when people exercise after a prolonged fast. For instance, the body uses up a considerable amount of lean tissue due to the ease at which glycogen can be broken down faster than fat stores. Yes, fat is broken down too, but at the expense of the fuel stored in muscle and lean tissue. Not just glycogen—amino acids are also taken from protein to be converted as energy too. In other words, it's all hands on deck for what the body perceives as starvation. Consequently, personal trainers are not aware that the body needs that stored energy for basic biological functions such as neurological, reproductive, endocrine, or lymphatic functions, just to name a few. So yes, she would technically be burning fat, but at the expense of the rest of her body.

Another unforeseen consequence of time-restrictive eating while strength training is there will be a natural increased demand of energy required by the process of tearing down muscle fibers to rebuild newer, stronger muscle fibers. The muscle needs to replenish glycogen stores and protein, especially after workouts. Therefore, the body (and mind) will respond by enhancing the desire to eat both more carbohydrates as well as more protein to replenish muscle loss. Actually, the body will crave whatever it can, and it might be something recent, something from a childhood eating experience, like candy. To put it another way, it's simply unsustainable and dangerous.

Catalina discovered that her mealtime window was only seven hours in the day—12:00 p.m. to 7:00 p.m. Additionally, the problem was that the more she increased her physical activity level, the greater her hunger level increased. She would complain of incredibly strong urges to snack at night and difficulty focusing during the day the longer the fasting plan continued. Another challenge to this feeding approach was dealing with temptations and desires to eat all the

2: Curiosity

delicious breakfast food that her company catered for their twice-weekly morning meetings.

Catalina also tried a gluten-free approach a few years ago on advice from a friend about how good she felt after just a week off gluten. Needless to say, this gluten-free thing didn't last very long either, and the fact that her friend was only on it for a week should have been a major red flag. When Catalina did try the whole gluten-free thing, she discovered that it took a lot of time to prepare her meals most nights, which meant giving up precious time she wanted to spend with her son. Grocery shopping was not any easier because her son wasn't eating the same way, and it was difficult to find gluten-free foods he would enjoy. Finding recipes was difficult because the instructions were intricate and detailed. They took Catalina hours, not to mention that trying to find the ingredients was frustrating. Again, Catalina realized these rigid rules were just unrealistic and simply unsustainable.

When she dipped her toes into a vegetarian diet (mostly pescatarian), she inadvertently caused considerable social challenges again. She would come up with interesting excuses to avoid certain foods with her colleagues at work. Many times, she would just work through lunch to avoid having to explain to everyone what she was doing. On various occasions, she would waste time online searching for acceptable food choices. However, when entertaining clients at work or at functions she was required to attend, she felt ashamed of herself for lacking the willpower to resist the forbidden foods. Some moments caused such intense emotional challenges that in the past would have meant giving up on diets. Shame is a poor motivator because it creates an emotional disconnection with the food that tastes good and belonging to a group, a tribe, or, in Catalina's case, her colleagues.

Despite Catalina's wonderful idea of getting more physically active and hiring a personal trainer, she faced other major challenges. Remember the two herniated discs and her hip bursitis? As it turned out, both problems got progressively worse and not better, which really disappointed her. She had hoped that being more active would help her tone and strengthen her body, and in turn help her back and hip. Catalina thought she hired an experienced trainer; unfortunately, that wasn't the case. Now, I certainly don't want to start getting any hate emails here, so let me just say that not all personal trainers are ill-trained fitness people out to make a quick buck. There are those out there. But more and more, I'm finding weight-inclusive, body positive fitness instructors, personal trainers, and yoga instructors that really bring a well-rounded, empathetic approach to training people. The trainer Catalina hired didn't take the time to pay attention to her back and joint needs, which wasn't what she expected from all the positive reviews about him. It seemed like he was more concerned about his reputation of high intensity workouts that attained the fastest results possible. He never adjusted the workouts to help improve her mobility or feel better, but instead aggravated her back and joint pain. Because she enjoyed working out, we discussed the concept of joyful movement, and finding a fitness expert that is more HAES (Health At Every Size) and weight-inclusive informed. Catalina was more curious about this anti-diet and Intuitive Eating approach, which helped her realize she needed to advocate for herself and let the personal trainer go. In the past, she might have continued paying for classes out of embarrassment that she wasn't fit enough, or even needed to punish herself. Not this time.

Despite all her great new discoveries of a weight-inclusive and body positive approach, Catalina continued to hear how much more weight someone else lost, how much better other people felt, or how easy their new diet and lifestyle was. "Easy and feeling better" was not how she remembered the dieting process, and it certainly wasn't a mindful approach. Needless to say, she struggled with her new approach. It was hard to shake the allure of diets and images of fit people; her social media feeds were replete with images of ideal body types and weight-loss successes stories. Or at least that's how it seemed. A person's social media feed is one place I often recommend people start paying attention to more often. Who do they follow? Are new people constantly posting new images of weight-loss or are they seeing years of success by the same people? What happens to those people that posted all their supposed huge weight-loss successes after a few months? They tend to disappear and stop posting success stories after a few months or years. Is that something that's ever questioned? In reality, many people like Catalina struggle with diets, body image, and keeping weight off for more than two years, and certainly even fewer people are able to sustain the same loss longer than five years. These false expectations lead toward false hopes, and diet culture feeds off people's fear and anxieties because it's a business—a $72 billion industry (at last count) that relies on shaming people into thinking they are not worthy, don't belong to the thin ideal, and bank on restarting the process every five years since diet fads have about a five-year cycle. A new one will swoop in and deliver all those false hopes and dreams yet again.

Catalina really drank the Kool-Aid this time around, mentioning how this new diet is different from the rest because this celebrity, that doctor on TV, or that fitness guru on social media looks great and said it was. Don't be fooled! Fad diets are all the same. All fad diets tend to follow the same recipe (yup, more food puns). Here are my seven ingredients that prove diets don't work.

- **Unsustainable**—Simply put, diets are not sustainable! They usually have specific rules about when, what, or how to eat. Diets tend to tell you what foods to eat or avoid, or specific nutrients to eliminate. They typically have two to five phases or levels, like the two-week fat burn phase, the power-up phase, or the replenish phase. Don't phases mean that it is not sustainable? Some diets may require special food combinations or restrict specific types of foods, which you probably never ate to begin with. For example, some diets require a genetic test, an elaborate physical, a ten-page questionnaire, and then they provide an elaborate multi-page glossy results report that takes a PhD to read, and several pages of foods you should avoid, are OK to eat, or have the green light. Talk about unsustainable! People are just overwhelmed and confused. Diets may have restrictions on when to eat like the time restrictive eating that Catalina was trying, but the body will dictate what and when we need to eat, and it can't be tricked. People look for modifications because the diet doesn't fit their lifestyle, and to be successful, they have to modify the diet. When you don't stick to the diet's rules, that by definition is unsustainable!

- **Unscientific**—Most diets are not evidence-based. This means that most diets were started or invented by a personal trainer, a doctor, or a celebrity with no nutritional background or training. They decided one day, "Hey, why don't I take what I do and make it into a diet book?" and of course a publishing house eats it up (sorry, I couldn't resist), it becomes a bestseller, and we're sold. Look, the point is that most diets are certainly not well researched. The "it works for me, it should work for everyone" philosophy isn't evidence based. Only a handful of diets have significant volumes of research, like the Mediterranean diet, which has been shown to help cure almost everything, but no one invented it, and even experts can't agree to what exactly is eating Mediterranean. What's worse is that diets like these marginalize populations and perpetuate systemic racism by other people that don't eat this way. I was born in Colombia and grew up in New Jersey with a predominant Latinx population. Mediterranean food was certainly not on my plate growing up (unless you consider pizza and croissants). People in the island of Okinawa, Japan, have one the longest lifespans around the world, yet they're not eating a Mediterranean diet.
- **Unrealistic**—When a diet claims that you will lose an unrealistic amount of weight in a short period of time, like ten pounds in ten days, run! That's not only unrealistic, that's unsustainable and starvation. You know that saying, "If it's too good to be true, it probably is." Not to mention the negative emotional side effects that affect your metabolism and body. But the allure of these claims of weight loss, these false hopes of having a beautiful body or images of a thin woman or muscular

young man are intense. You see and hear only a few loud voices of people that were so successful on this or that diet, but you never hear the challenges and struggles from the millions of others for whom the diet never worked or they gained all the weight back. Even the mighty Arnold Schwarzenegger no longer has his Terminator or Conan the Barbarian body any longer. Again, it just ain't realistic.

- **No Exercise or Extreme Exercise**—When diets claim you don't have to move at all, or when they require some extreme level of exercise (simply unsustainable), this is a *huge* red flag. I mean, which is it—none or extreme? If it's not joyful movement, then it's just hard work. Technically, increased or high intensity physical activity or exercise, over the long term, is not helpful in persistent weight loss. In fact, most research shows that exercise only helps 20–30 percent in the initial weight loss, and that's typically mostly water weight from the breakdown of muscle. Physical activity or exercise is a necessity in life, for all of us, but it's not helpful in losing weight indefinitely. To maintain our health, we need to be physically active. In my experience, people in fat or large bodies get lured into these fitness programs that require high-intensity, "fat-burning" exercises, and nine out of ten times they injure themselves.
- **Supplements**—When diets require you to take supplements, that's just another *huge* red flag. Catalina told me that she had been on another diet where they required her to take a B12 shot weekly, a specially formulated set of "proprietary" supplements that would aid in rapid fat loss and energy enhancement. Yes, there are chemicals and herbals that do that. For example, caffeine helps stimulate the pituitary gland and increase adrenaline, but we all know you can't lose weight on caffeine alone. If that were the case, with all the coffee and energy drinks we consume, millions of people around the world would be a bunch of skinny-minnies. Then there are various caffeine-like

derivatives like guarana, l-carnitine, ginkgo biloba, ginseng, and others. These derivatives are typically found in energy drinks or added to supplements to stimulate your metabolism and supposedly aid in fat burn. Yeah, that doesn't happen, but a panic attack or crash is pretty likely.

- **Endorsements**—Watch out when diets need a celebrity, doctor, athlete, or fitness guru to sell the diet or program. Endorsements are not science; they are just an emotional hook that drives people to the site. By the way, the more subtle approach to endorsements are testimonials. They may not be celebrities or athletes, but people feel a stronger connection because "those are people just like me."
- **Increased Desires**—Any time we start eliminating a habit (a way of eating, for example), we find ourselves noticing its absence and craving more of it than ever before. This is specifically true with foods because our bodies require food to live. Many fad diets involve completely eliminating specific foods or food groups, or tell us when to eat, which invariably leads to more cravings, relapses, binges, and worse problems than the foods may have caused in the first place! Additionally, by trying to replace healthy foods and nutrients with supplements, stimulants, or other alternatives, we often deprive ourselves of what we really need and want, which further increases our desires for them. Or we continue to avoid those foods we eliminate, and we start eating greater quantities of other foods. It doesn't matter; it's still a sign the body knows something is wrong, so desires, temptations, cravings, and urges are exaggerated.

Catalina had been here before. Weight cycling, also known as yo-yo dieting, is quite common for most of us. We hope and believe something is out there that will finally do the trick. Get the weight off for good. But this is just not the case. Diets are inherently designed to fail us. Oh, don't get me wrong. Initially some diets work extremely well at depleting water stored in our bodies; however, they are directly responsible for causing our bodies to gain weight and regain more weight over time.

A good example of this is the Minnesota Starvation Experiment Study mentioned in the previous chapter. *Trigger warning—discussing calorie levels in the next few sentences.* This study was performed between 1944 and 1945 where thirty-six college men were placed on extremely low diets of about 1500 calories for six months. Ansel Keys and colleagues published their findings in 1950 in a 1300-page book and concluded that the prolonged starvation diet (ironically what we consider to be a standard low-calorie diet these days) led to significant increases in depression, hysteria, and hypochondriasis, and periods of severe emotional distress. Some men tried self-mutilation and one person amputated three fingers. The men in the experiment also exhibited a preoccupation with food, both during the starvation period and the rehabilitation phase. Some men had drastically reduced sexual drive and signs of social withdrawal and isolation, decline in concentration over time, and decreased comprehension and judgment capabilities.[22] Over several years, various researchers did follow-up studies on the experiment volunteers. One profound study was from Elke D. Eckert, MD, and colleagues, where they published a fifty-seven-year follow-up and review investigation on nineteen of the thirty-six volunteers. Their findings confirmed the severe challenges with diets. Many participants reported higher weight gain, difficulties losing weight, and various eating disorders and tendencies, including anorexia nervosa, which initially was more commonly seen in women than in men.[23]

I'm going to play devil's advocate a little here. Catalina initially reported that she had an increase in concentration, focus, and energy, even a sense of euphoria, as a result of the various diet approaches in the past. Again, this is commonly due to the body's ability to release glucose stored in glycogen bonds in the liver and muscle, along with other hormones (such as cortisol, epinephrine, and norepinephrine) that increase delivery of energy and chemicals to the brain, but it is at the cost of the stored energy necessary for other functions the body will need later.

Today, most of us don't experience starvation conditions such as those promoted during the Minnesota experiment. Many people have plenty of food, and access to food is everywhere in the United States. However, some people have low socio-economic levels or poor availability of fresh foods like fruits and vegetables, meats, and fish. In fact, many higher weight people in low-income populations don't eat large quantities of food. It is a struggle to find adequate food sources, yet they find themselves gaining weight. Dieting causes extreme physiological and chemical changes in the body, slows metabolism, and leads to more weight regain, not to mention all the social, emotional, and financial stressors faced by these people.

Catalina had to explore her own path, much like Luke Skywalker from *Star Wars*. Luke had to explore the dark side to find his path. It's like that iconic scene with Luke Skywalker training with Master Yoda in *The Empire Strikes Back*. (If you're not a *Star Wars* fan, then hang with me a minute.) This is the scene when Luke Skywalker (while on a journey to become a Jedi Knight hero and training with the great Jedi Master Yoda) is resting with Yoda near a dark cave in the swamp planet of Dagobah. Luke Skywalker is curious and heads toward the dark cave. Master Yoda knows to let him explore, because only he can face his own fears. Diets represent the same dark cave: a way to escape, to not face our fears. Just like Catalina heading toward the diets. In the cave, Luke confronts the image (spoiler alert—but man, if you haven't seen this movie, then what are you waiting for?—I digress) of his father, Darth Vader, with his lightsaber. Luke then strikes the head off what he thinks/sees is the image of Darth Vader with his lightsaber. As Darth Vader's helmet rolls to the ground next to Luke, the front of the mask explodes open and we see Luke's face instead of his father's. The significance of this scene was that the hero had to confront his demon. Likewise, Catalina had to confront her diet and weight demons. In order to transform, she had to continue with her diets to learn how they didn't work.

As mentioned previously, Catalina had turned the corner with diets and intense fitness programs. She started to realize that diets were rigid and actually dangerous: years of worsening cholesterol, very bad constipation, worsening energy, and just frustrations with herself; moments of self-deprecation because she failed at losing weight was all she could handle anymore. There had to be a better way. While emotionally stepping into an anti-diet and weight inclusive approach was difficult, she appreciated her experimentations with a new identity. She didn't feel judged, and she had support. Catalina was transforming, and it felt awkward and thrilling at the same time.

The Awakening— Curiosity Opens the Mind

Curiosity opens the possibility of experimentation. Through experimentation we can learn to let go of the rigid rules and counterfactual narratives and instead unearth the hidden gems of our abilities. Experimentation and awareness can help lead us to a place of change, one small bite at a time. Just like Catalina did. She began to see how one small deed led into another, whether positive or negative, and all she had to do was stop, pay attention to herself, and tune in to what she felt and needed. What Catalina did was to tap into a powerful ability we all share: the ability to listen to ourselves, to what the universe, God, or the Force has to offer. We just need to stop and listen and become our mind's observers. We have the capability to induce change—positive and helpful change that can transform our lives.

One book that helped Catalina really slow down and smell the roses was *Joyful: The Surprising Power of Ordinary Things to Create Extraordinary Happiness*. Author Ingrid Fetell Lee describes how the simple act of watching the petals of cherry blossom flowers fall can be a method of entering the vastness that is our universe.

> "The opening of the cherry blossoms, or sakura, is an occasion almost of madness in Japan. In the brief season of their bloom, a culture known for its quiet reserve opens up and becomes giddy. People throw themselves into the evanescent joy of the season,

taking time off from work to gather for hanami, the traditional blossom-watching picnics that date back to the eighth century. In Ueno Park, the site of more than a thousand cherry trees, men in suits and women in dresses lay sprawled out on blue and green plastic tarps, gazing up into the canopy. Friends gathered in clusters, laughing and talking, taking turns snapping photos of one another with their faces next to the blossoms. . . .

"Watching Japan plunge headlong into the delight of the sakura was reminder that while the fluctuations of joy in our lives can be unpredictable, our planet has rhythms of renewal that regularly bring joy back to us. As the earth traces its annual loop around the sun and pirouettes daily on its axis, we co-travelers are subject to a host of natural cycles. We can't feel the earth's movement directly, but we see it in the oscillations of light and color, temperature and texture, that sweep through our surroundings. The blossoming of the trees, the rising of the sun, the flow of the tides: these recurring events remind us of time's circular nature and create an underlying cadence of joy that we can rely on."[24]

It's a way of being expansive, like Anna Gatmon explains. Expansiveness is the first key element that allows us to be open to and aware of the messages life brings us. When we listen, we can manifest the changes we want in life because we move into position. If we take one small step toward our dreams, toward what we value, then life will deliver, sometimes when we least expect them.[25]

Catalina saw the changes she needed to take. Like Luke Skywalker, sometimes we must prepare ourselves for what is inevitable, facing our fears to solve them. Yes, Catalina lost some weight through her past dieting experiences, but like many diets, she noticed some weight come back, the constipation and cholesterol problems from a high fat diet, and the social isolation that prevented her from enjoying events at church or with family or friends. This just couldn't continue! Additionally, dieting and fitness programs also disrupted her metabolism and her hormone and energy levels, which destabilized her life in various ways. In time, she restabilized her energy by paying more attention and experimenting with her hunger and fullness cues, and she was able to enjoy food again. She was able to pay attention to how shame led to those emotional disconnections, and by being present with those feelings, she wouldn't get swept away by them.

Interestingly, what she really wanted most from diets was to feel better. Eating more balanced, adding more fresh fruits and vegetables, and finding foods that helped her feel better was part of identifying with a thinner younger self. Like many of us, she had challenges confronting her age. She missed out on her youth because she had to take care of her son. In a distorted sort of way diets and fitness filled that void. It was a futile endeavor because she would eventually gain the weight back and feel miserable in the long run. The little she lost was short lived by all the challenges and complications in her life.

Little by little she discovered that being a mother, getting her psychology degree, and becoming the new woman she needed to be was not tied to an image but to purpose. Self-actualization required her to let go of the Dark Side and step into her light. OK, I know, enough with the *Star Wars* metaphors, but they make so much sense. Just one more—it's like Rey Skywalker, she too had to confront her identity and it no longer belonged in the past. Those types of realizations are truly a Shero's journey! Not easy for sure, but how else would we expect a Shero to become such?

Forward Momentum

Now let's look at just how Catalina got back in business. You know it: she started with just one thing. For Catalina, it was all about planning. That was her strong suit. Catalina was a type-A personality and she liked organization. She had a checklist of to-do's each day that were tied into her weekly goal(s), and she kept a planner. She had to do this for her work because she managed various employee development programs and schedules. This was her expertise!

I asked her, "What is the low hanging fruit?" To reach her health goal, what does easy look like? (I learned from Pat Flynn, and if you don't know who that is, he's an amazing online entrepreneur with a podcast and company called Smart Passive Income. He talks a lot about starting an online business, and the challenges entrepreneurs face when starting out.) What was the easiest thing Catalina could do to make the change she wanted?

For Catalina, it was having at least one serving of fruit or vegetable with at least one meal every day, as long as she put it in her planner. To her it was liberating and helpful. She felt better in the process because it wasn't restrictive—it was self-guided. She only had to do it once, and she didn't have to be perfect at it, because as she learned from diets that failed her, perfection is the enemy of progress. She also experimented with various fruits or veggies. It may sound simple, but it was powerful because it was familiar. Her superpower was organization but this time with mindful awareness of keeping it simple. Focusing on one small goal every day and learning more about herself. She already knew that she liked how diets offered her the opportunity and the challenge to try new foods. This time it was about paying attention to what her body needed versus how many fruits and veggies she had to consume daily. Eating just one serving of fruit or veggie at only one meal a day was what easy looked like for her.

Catalina started with just one small bite. She felt better having more fruits and veggies, but like bad relationships after bad relationships, she was tired of being disappointed and frustrated by the illusion of the Knight in Shining Armor (diet) coming to save her. This one small act led to a greater sense of purpose. It wasn't the I-have-to-eat-fruit-and-veggies-diet, or a strict food rule; it was a sense of autonomy that she discovered herself. By doing such, it freed her mind to enjoy life with her son, take more time off work, and pursue her dreams of becoming a therapist. It was going to take time, for sure, but this time it felt right. One small change had a positive domino effect on her life. Did she continue to struggle with diets and her hip and back? Absolutely! But this time she paid attention to herself and only did what she could and wanted to do.

Curiosity
What Did We Learn?

By now, I hope we can see the various methods the Sheroes in this section reached their enlightenment. Catalina's took a while before she reconnected with her radical self-acceptance. Although the journey was messy, she focused on one small change, adding only one fruit or veggie to a meal, which in turn lead to discovering Intuitive Eating and a new path. Meredith discovered that slowing down and setting aside her workout clothes was a simple little change that also gave her superpower back. Ericka learned that journaling for her was the key to making that everlasting change. She journals now once or twice a month, but it's enough to help her tap into her creative side.

All the Sheroes in this section had to rumble with their vulnerabilities and fears in order to break free from the Dark Side and avoid the temptations of diets and that of the skewed realities of thin ideals. The allure of weight loss and a fake promise of a better life, a thinner life, to be more beautiful, is taken right out of the story of the Shero's journey. Think about the many Hollywood movies and classic novels where the main character is tempted by a better life, money, or power and comes out a better person after leaving all that behind. Catalina's story was the same. Her curiosity led her through challenges and toward sustainable one small bites.

We saw these five components of curiosity in each of the Sheroes and Heroes:

1. **Awareness**—The need to start paying attention to ourselves, patterns, nuances, etc.
2. **Open Minded**—Be open to possibilities you don't yet realize.

3. **Experimentation**—Just Do It!
4. **Enjoyment**—Enjoy what you explore.
5. **Exploration**—Learning is ongoing.

Each of these components inspired the Heroes and Sheroes, got them to move, and allowed them to each discover their path. Are you ready to do the same? Remember, visit my website www.orozconutrition.com/curiosity-guide so that you can download my free guide to enhancing your curiosity.

Now, let's look at how compassion keeps your newly discovered one small bite changes on track!

3

Compassion

> "When we give ourselves compassion, we are opening our hearts in a way that can transform our lives."
>
> —Kristin Neff

Over the years, I've seen self-compassion help recharge people's emotional and inspirational batteries. There are various common denominators in the personality and characteristic types of the people I've worked with. For instance, as we already saw in the last section, many of the Sheroes and Heroes were overwhelmed, selfless, and depressed, and often self-criticized themselves to ruin. A lot of people run on autopilot and lack of self-prioritization or self-kindness. These traits drain people from transforming their health. The extreme of these personality traits and characteristics keeps them from choosing one new eating habit or being consistent with movement that will help enhance their health. When people slow down and truly learn self-compassion and find empathy for themselves, when they learn to be nurturing to themselves and be open to curiosity, to learning and exploring new possibilities for themselves, this eternal energy source, this light shines the path to true transformation. This means being vulnerable to our fears, shames, insecurities, and limitations, and rumbling with those takes enormous amounts of courage. This is a Shero's and Hero's calling.

One Small Bite

What you will read in this section is how the following Heroes and Sheroes discovered self-compassion in various ways and transformed their lives. Visit my website at to download information on how I can help you discover your self-compassionate voice to begin your transformation.

Let's discover how these Heroes and Sheroes did it!

Jeff

Discovering Self-Compassion

It was March 2015 when I got a call from Jeff. He had my phone number for about seven months and finally decided to call me. It was serendipitous! I had just become credentialed with his insurance plan, and I answered the phone right when he called. We started talking and he mentioned that he was forty-eight years old, not married, five feet eleven inches tall, and weighed about 375 pounds. He was a man of very few words, and he only had two questions. He asked me if I'd ever worked with obese people, and whether I recommended weight loss surgery or not.

First, I told him I don't use the word *obese* to describe someone because it's a term that came from a value within the body mass index; otherwise, famously known as the BMI. While the American Medical Association defines obesity as a disease, it shouldn't define the person as diseased. I personally don't see a person in a heavy body or as fat as diseased, just as much as I don't see a person living with diabetes as a diabetic. These terms only alienate people and make them feel othered, when in reality they are human just like you and me.

Second, I gave it to him straight. I told him, "Look, Jeff, I take a personalized and individual approach specific to the client and work with them to find a way of eating that's more in line with their values. I don't provide diet plans, tell you what foods you can or cannot eat, or focus on helping you lose weight. My approach is to help you build a more positive and secure relationship with food, your body, and your mind. This work is messy, at times awkward and extremely difficult, and it takes time, but it can be done; however, you need to be committed, be patient, and understand that this work will truly be enduring."

There was this long silence on the other end and then he said, "When is your next available appointment?"

When Jeff came to the appointment, he was quiet. He'd filled out all his intake forms and the three-day food journal. He didn't say much, sat down, was to the point, and said to me, "I'm really interested in losing this weight. I've been this weight for over fourteen years and a heavy person most of my life. I've only tried a few diets, but I'm not very athletic, so I haven't had much success." I could see the energy drain from his face when he heard himself. He wasn't enthusiastic; he was pretty stoic and barely broke a smile in his initial session. I explained to him again that this journey is not about weight loss, but about securing his relationship with food and his health. He completely agreed and understood, but I was worried he might have gotten the impression, like many people do, that an anti-diet, weight-inclusive approach means there's a backdoor to weight loss. Thus, I explained again, and he was all in.

He continued coming to our sessions. He was committed to the change, but I could see the hesitation on his face. At first, we worked weekly for six or eight weeks, and then it was twice a month thereafter. Most sessions were simply reviewing and repeating recommendations from previous sessions, but again, he was committed. Sometimes the conversations were a little challenging because he was so reserved and only said what he needed to say. But he continued coming visit after visit. For the first ten months, he really started to feel better. We never talked about his weight, and I never weighed him. The focus was always on new behaviors and prioritizing himself to do things that made him feel internally better. We didn't discuss a number on a scale or the calories or grams of anything on an app. In each session, we discussed his behaviors and why he would choose to eat out and have seven alcoholic drinks in one night. Or in some sessions we would discuss why he decided to order from Uber Eats despite having food in the home. We discussed how having a salad for lunch felt made him feel both emotionally and physically better, but often he didn't want people to see him eat that. Although he enjoyed eating salads, somehow it represented he was less of a man, or he was trying to lose weight. There were skewed beliefs about his identity, just like with our previous Sheroes and Heroes. Sometimes our conversations during sessions were pretty short, and all we would do was review his journal and learn to pay closer attention and understanding to his how food made him feel, which I have to admit was foreign to him and many people.

It is particularly difficult for people that identify as binary male, since male roles and ideals don't typically explore emotions. It's not something Jeff was ever taught, but he knew he had strong feelings about food. Jeff knew he needed help maneuvering the complexity of emotions around eating. His stoic personality was one of his methods of disassociating himself from his reality. He knew what he needed to do, yet the fear of gaining more weight was too challenging. Often, our sessions were about having someone to lend an ear to his diet and food challenges. That alone was extremely helpful for him. He was in a safe space where we could talk about these things without judgment, save space for what he felt around his body and food, and listen. Sometimes it was just a matter of letting Jeff work it out and guiding him, and he would stop beating himself up.

The Awakening— Compassion Filled His Void

One day we were reviewing Jeff's food journal during one of our regular sessions. I asked Jeff why he didn't write what he had for dinner one day. He hesitated for a minute and then said, "OK, so I ended up going to my old pub hangout two nights ago and had six shots of Jägermeister, about half a dozen chicken wings, and then some pie for dessert. It was just automatic! I went in there because I just wanted to get away. It was what I used to do after a horrible day at work."

I asked him what happened.

He said, "I was ready to quit my job." And before I could ask him what he meant, he just broke down. It took him some time to compose himself, but I told him to take a few deep breaths and then we stood up. I told him to shake it off, and we waited some more.

He then began to tell me about his day. "I was so nervous about coming here today. I totally knew you were going to ask me about two nights ago. I was doing so good for the last few months, but I just broke down and went to the pub. It is my go-to when shit at work is just unbearable." Then I asked him what he meant by "doing so good." He said, "I had the worst day at work. My boss was such an ass, and he just insulted me and made me feel like a complete idiot at work. He yelled at me in front of several people. What was worse was that I didn't do or say a single word to defend myself or try to reason with him."

"All right, so what did you do next?" I asked him.

He then explained, "I took the rest of the day off; in fact, I took the remainder of the week as PTO, and that was the night I went to my old pub. I was there alone and just wanted to drink and eat. It was bizarre! It felt like riding a bicycle. I felt like I had this tractor beam, like this mental Jedi mind trick, this hypnotism where I had to go to the pub and do what I've always done to sooth my pain. It was bizarre because I could see myself do it, but I couldn't break out of it."

I then asked him how he was able to break out of the mental and emotional fog. "It was right after the last bite. I ordered twenty chicken wings, extra spicy, with a side of fries and blue cheese dressing for dipping, and then after about six wings I had enough. I'm not sure if it was the second shot of Jägermeister or what, but it hit me like a ton of bricks."

"What do you mean?" I prompted.

"I mean it was like I was having an out-of-body experience. I felt a hand cover my mouth and a little force just take over my stomach, and I stopped. I didn't want to throw up, I didn't feel sick, I just felt this need to stop."

I asked him why he thought that happened.

3: Compassion

"It was weird, David. I felt horrible for doing it, but at the same time I just didn't want to do it. The food didn't taste as good, and I just wasn't enjoying the feeling. In the past I would have just devoured and almost inhaled the food and alcohol without even skipping a beat—without even thinking." And then he stopped.

He looked at me, and I could see he realized something. Now, you have to understand that prior to this day he wasn't very talkative. He said more to me in this one session than he had in the past ten months. It's interesting because I never know when something is going to click for someone, and sometimes it takes that person having to go through a rough patch, a difficult experience in life, to discover it. Not always though. Some clients hit those epiphanies through very casual or simple moments in their lives. So what did Jeff realize? He realized that he *was not* his negative thoughts. He was able to observe himself for the first time. A bit of an out-of-body experience. This isn't the way that will help sooth him. He was not going to do the same thing over again just because he'd done it before. Jeff was being empathetic and kind to himself. He realized he didn't need to fall into the same trap, filling his body with more food and alcohol, which might help him not feel the emotional pain for a little while but wasn't going to work. He knew that the physical pain he would feel with heartburn, upset stomach, and then all the emotional guilt and shame from eating and drinking wasn't going to help him feel any better. Jeff observed for the first time that his mind was filled with the same negative thoughts—"I'm not worthy; I'm an idiot at work; I'm not handsome; people hate me"—and so on. Food and alcohol were not going to truly soothe him. That void instead needed to be filled with more self-compassion.

Jeff was finding that self-compassionate mindful voice as I described earlier from Kristen Neff's work, "Mindfulness brings us back to the present moment and provides the type of balanced awareness that forms the foundation of self-compassion. Like a clear, still pool without ripples, mindfulness perfectly mirrors what's occurring without distortion. Rather than become lost in our own personal soap opera, mindfulness allows us to view our situation with greater perspective and helps to ensure that we don't suffer unnecessarily."[26]

The work we had been doing included intuitive and mindful eating exercises, hunger and fullness awareness techniques, and balanced eating exercises but nothing related to calorie counting or classifying food as bad or good. The more intuitive and mindful approaches had really helped Jeff be more aware of what his body was telling him. Going to the pub was a way of using food to sooth, escape, or drown bad feelings. By far, all of this was extremely difficult for him to discover and to express when we first started working. He had never shared his feelings this way with others, and throughout his life he was masterful at burying his emotions. But he was now curious as well. That small amount of compassion that came from paying attention to what really mattered in life was starting to come through.

He then wondered what else he could do.

Forward Momentum

We explored the idea about enjoying a pub meal with friends, and the need to escape and cope a little more. He expressed how he didn't really feel that good after eating there; he would feel both physically and emotionally heavy. Each time he went there, he explained that he'd leave with heartburn, and he wouldn't be able to sleep. He'd have to take antacids or heartburn medication, which he hated buying, partly because it reminded him of how horrible he was for eating that way to begin with. Contemplating his actions further, he then realized what he was really enjoying was the ritual—the routine of going to the pub and coping with food. Yes, the food and alcohol numbed him, but he realized at that moment how sad it was. Going to the pub was like a trigger, a tractor beam that would draw him in and repeat the behavior over again, which would reinforce the depressive feelings, not to mention the uncomfortable digestive problems. He looked at me and then asked, "OK, so what should we do?"

3: Compassion

I gave him an exercise to help deconstruct his eating patterns.

This exercise comes from Intuitive Eating, and it's called the Deconstructing Eating Behavior exercise. The most important element of this exercise was to help him pay attention to his emotions. I asked him to try and put a name to the uncomfortable feeling the next time he wanted to eat to soothe himself. The exercise provides a list of emotion words like *frustrated, disappointed, angry, sad, lonely,* and others. I asked him to just record what he was feeling, circle the word(s), and just *be* with the ugly or uncomfortable feeling. Once he was aware of what he was feeling, the exercise then asked him to think about what he needs or wants instead of food to help with his emotion. For example, if he were feeling lonely, would he need to call a friend or go hang out with someone? I'm not going to kid you. Just because this exercise can be helpful, doesn't mean it will miraculously "cure" him, or anyone, of his behaviors. Jeff would often forget to practice the exercise, and he continued going to the pub a few more times for the same reasons (he was lonely and frustrated with work). Eventually, Jeff started to practice the deconstructive eating exercise more on his own. Once he started, he immediately began feeling better. Just the act of naming and confronting what he was feeling gave him energy and enhanced his mood. I told him to practice this exercise when he felt good as well. He said to me, "David, it was interesting. The more I named my emotions, food became less appealing. I was a little upset that I didn't enjoy the same foods anymore. What was better was that I really didn't think of going out to the pub very often."

This exercise gave him the muscle memory, the practice he needed to develop a level of awareness that comes from slowing down and paying attention to his body's needs. When Jeff started working with me, it was as if a new student was learning to play a guitar for the first time. It feels a little awkward. He knew he needed to practice. So he did—he really practiced, and practiced, and practiced, and over time, he built a level of expertise at recognizing his emotions, not just around food, but at the various triggers throughout his day. At first paying attention to what he was feeling and then naming it was awkward and he stated that it sounded weird, but over time he got better. Like the guitar, strumming the strings and holding notes felt weird and even gave him calluses, but (OK, get ready, another corny analogy) after a while he was able to play a whole musical composition.

Jeff was learning to confront his difficult situations and emotions. Going to the bar and eating twenty chicken wings, fries, and six shots of Jägermeister just wasn't what his body wanted, and it only made him feel worse later. I'm going to add that there is nothing wrong with chicken wings or alcohol; it's about slowing down and paying attention to what he needed and wanted. It was the practice that helped him develop new neural connections. He developed a positive relationship with food, and more important, he developed self-compassion. He became his mind's observer and understood that his actions were not a consequence of his thoughts. He was more than his thoughts and his experiences. He was transforming.

He then surprised me with an important question. "So why would I go back to the pub even after knowing that it didn't make me feel good after all?"

I said, "Because it happens." I know, I know. A pretty canned and incredibly lame answer, right? But no. I told him that in martial arts we have a saying: "The student gets hit a thousand times before they realize they need to duck, and even then, they are just beginning to learn." In other words, old habits die hard. In fact, they never really die at all because old habits are so familiar to us. We do what we've done in the past because it's familiar, which makes it automatic and easy to fall right back into them. Awareness and acceptance of that fact can be liberating. The difference is that now he is more aware of what going to a pub used to mean: old ways to cope.

Jeff discovered new ways of coping and understand how to deal with his emotions. It wasn't easy, and it took working on one small change—paying attention to what he was feeling and what he needed. What he discovered to do was to be more self-compassionate. He needed

3: Compassion

to understand that he is not defined by his past actions. Being the person he wanted to be meant that he needed to take one small bite at a time, build self-compassion, and be present with his feelings. This doesn't mean he is any less of a man; it just means he is rumbling with vulnerabilities that can open doors for him. Weight loss may have been the initial motivator, but what we both realized was that he needed to shed the weight of self-loathing and negative self-criticism first. He needed to learn to love himself!

Interlude

Self-Prioritization, Self-Kindness, Self-Awareness

> "The purpose of life is to know yourself and love yourself and trust yourself and be yourself."
>
> —unknown author

I'm not offering any new Hero's perspective or describing their journey here. You've already read how Meredith needed to slow down and pay attention to the things that really mattered in life. She began to prioritize her needs before others. She had to slow down to figure it out. Just like someone as busy as Shonda Rhimes, we all need to recharge and find our true hum, and *it* will fuel and nourish us. We learned about Angela and her back-and-forth with curiosity until she truly found her direction, her purpose. We learned how I discovered my inner voice. That voice was always there to guide me, but it was lost in a material and make-believe world, which couldn't fill me. That inner voice made me feel whole and inspired me to be a better person. Catalina was curious about finding a new way. The old diets and approaches of the past were not about her. They were about becoming something, someone that others had told her she should be.

When I talk to people about self-prioritization, it's not about being selfish, ignoring other people's problems, or only thinking about what we must do for ourselves. It's about pausing—taking small incremental moments in your life, every day, to pay attention to your body and understand your basic physiological needs, as well as your desires.

Self-prioritization sounds simple, but it's not easy. What makes it hard is that we are used to old familiar habits. We have learned numerous habits over the years to ignore our basic needs. I often tell clients we have five basic needs we must do every single day:

1. **Eat**—We can't survive if we don't eat. Our bodies need food, plain and simple.
2. **Move**—We were designed to move, and besides, we have to get from here to there.
3. **Sleep**—Our body has to rest, recover, repair, replenish, and rejuvenate.
4. **Digest**—We all pee, poop, brush our teeth, bathe, and brush our hair (well, most of us at least).
5. **Connect**—We need human interaction; we are social from the day we are born.

Prioritizing yourself means making sure you don't skip any of these steps. This way we will have more to give to others because we are healthy, because we are connected, and because we model what we wish in others as well!

Self-compassion means that we get to be playful and enjoy that the struggles we deal with regarding food, weight, bodies, and life in general *today* will provide us with happiness *tomorrow*. Play is such an important component of compassion. I talked about it in Curiosity—how you need to make things enjoyable. Kids play in the playground. They don't usually think about the rules until they have to. They learn as they go. Playing helps us be more compassionate because we are in a moment of joy. Stuart Brown, MD, puts it in the very title of his book *Play: How it Shapes the Brain, Opens the Imagination, and Invigorates the Soul*. This is what I mean by nourishing your soul. It is one of the three taglines in the opening to my podcast—"Chop the Diet Mentality, Fuel Your Body, and Nourish Your Soul!"

Finding self-compassion is messy. I love this depiction of how I help clients find their purpose, their true compassion, and enhance their eating, make peace with their body, and have a positive relationship with food.

| The Ideal Path to meaning and purpose | The Real Path to meaning and purpose |

In the following chapters you will learn about two extremely important Heroes. Their transformational journeys began with the realization that self-compassion was being squashed by an incredibly strong emotion—*fear*. You will learn how their food and life choices were dictated by a compulsive reaction to what frightened them. By frighten I'm not speaking about a snake, bear, or dog jumping out at them and biting them, but by a deep-rooted emotion that many of us are unaware is shaping our lives. Let's take a look!

Nathaniel
Fear

Fear is a four-letter word! At a person's core, this one emotional state is single-handedly the one thing that pushes everything back. Fear keeps so many of us from changing, from moving forward. In my mind, when we get stagnant in life, when things don't change, or when we're not growing and prospering in life, it's probably because of fear.

Take Nathaniel, for instance. He was referred to me by a therapist for nutritional help for a condition called orthorexia, which is an obsessive and compulsive behavior with eating super healthy. Orthorexia is not formally recognized by the DSM-5 Diagnostic and Statistical Manual of Mental Disorders as an eating disorder, but it was first coined in the late 1990s and has become well understood by mental health clinicians in the eating disorder world.

Orthorexia is by far one of the most common conditions I see with people who identify as male that come to my office. I know this condition like the back of my hand because it's the very condition I dealt with prior to becoming a dietitian. It is this crazy obsession about eating the best quality and healthiest food available. I read, analyzed, and scrutinized every nutrient on food labels. I would do the same for each ingredient, and I would obsess about the production and packaging of the food as well. Was it in a recyclable container? Was it made with only organic ingredients? Did it have five ingredients or less? Was the food grown in an environmentally sound farm? Was it fair-trade, and were workers treated well? Each of these components was extremely important. Because I believe we all had to be good stewards of the earth, I self-identified with being a "good steward," as if that was some secret society. It was the society of being perfect, controlling everything. But in reality, fear was driving my belief system. Fear was at the root of many of my problems, and not just the quality of food. Fear was making me obsessed. I counted calories, I tried several diets, and I, too, became a vegetarian for a while. In fact, when my mother was dealing with colon cancer, I was the one that suggested we *only* drink a specific type of water designed with a patented five H_2O molecules. As if that's actual science. I was obsessed with one specific and perfect way of eating. What was I scared of? What was going on with me, and why was I so rigid with my diet? My answers to these questions were very similar to what Nathaniel found.

Nathaniel had the very same obsession and compulsion, a way of living that was just completely unsustainable. An important point of clarity, it's not common for men to be diagnosed with an eating disorder. But as I mentioned earlier, it is common for me to see men obsess about the perfect "manly" body and their diet. In fact, many men would probably laugh at even the suggestion of an eating disorder. But orthorexia is a condition I see quite a bit in men like Nathaniel. I feel that because men don't often seek medical care, and possibly because of societal norms, men aren't aware they have a problem. Disordered eating and eating disorders in men present slightly differently than in women or non-binary people. Heck, many men don't even have a primary care physician, nor would many physicians even consider a disorder of eating in men. And therapy? What? Heaven forbid men seek mental health counseling or therapy; that would mean we are not men; that would mean we're crazy or weak or that something is wrong with us. Yeah, fellas, how's that working for us?

There is a common and relatively new term discussed in psychology called alexithymia, which helps us understand why some men try to control their bodies through strict dietary standards and extreme fitness regimens. Alexithymia is the inability to understand or notice subtle emotional conditions. People have difficulty identifying different feelings, challenges understanding what causes their feelings, difficulty expressing their feelings, limited or rigid imagination, and challenges managing their emotions around others. Research shows that alexithymia seems to occur in about 10 percent of the population,[27] is more common in men than in women, and is one of the challenges within the context of masculinity—the imprisonment of many men that can lead to intense social and emotional challenges. This type of imprisonment is described best by Ronald F. Levant, EdD, ABPP, and Shana Pryor, MA, and doctoral student of counseling psychology at the University of Akron.[28] This silent and often missed psychological condition was not very different from what Nathaniel was dealing with. He was trapped by a fear he couldn't explain or understand—one he wasn't even aware of. I find that disorders in eating tend to have strong roots within the complexities of masculinity, and the fear of not being masculine is deeply rooted within our social and emotional narrative.

Fear is at the root of being unable to be vulnerable and courageous, of being unable to sit with our emotions and becoming aware of our mental and physical health. Brené Brown puts it best:

> "When we spend our lives pushing away and protecting ourselves from feeling vulnerable or from being perceived as too emotional, we feel contempt when others are less capable or willing to mask feelings, suck it up, and soldier on. We've come to the point where, rather than respecting and appreciating the courage and daring behind vulnerability, we let our fear and discomfort become judgment and criticism. . . . Vulnerability is the core of all emotions and feelings. To feel is to be vulnerable. To believe vulnerability is weakness is to believe that feeling is weakness. To foreclose on our emotional life out of a fear that the costs will be too high is to walk away from the very thing that gives purpose and meaning to living."[29]

Many men have a strong perception that vulnerability is a sign of weakness. I was taught this same ideal growing up. It is steeped into the fabric of various cultures around the world. Many men are not taught to understand or relate to their emotions. Therefore, because of these cultural and stereotypical male expectations, an eating disorder like orthorexia goes undiagnosed, or not even noticed in a lot of men because that's what it would mean to be masculine. Nathaniel was taking control of his body, getting stronger and faster, and toning up at the expense of his emotional state. It's a thing! It's really a thing.

When I saw Nathaniel for the first time, you wouldn't believe he had a problem. Good-looking young man, in his late twenties, tall, slender, and just a stellar dude. When he walked in the room he had a bit of a swag, and sense of confidence that leaned a little toward cocky. A very successful biomedical device salesperson, and one of the top performers in his company. He traveled quite a bit for his job and also enjoyed traveling for recreation. He worked remotely from home and had no commute except for a few times a year for quarterly sales or staff meetings. All of this prior to the COVID pandemic as well. He worked out quite a bit and was a sharp dresser with the latest kicks. He had a great smile, and he was just wicked smart. He looked like one of those male models right out of a fitness magazine, which is the look he was obsessed about. Those magazine and images of what we think a man is supposed to look like is no different than the plethora of woman's magazines and social media ads that flame the weight-stigmatizing, fat-phobic, diet-culture mentality that marginalizes so many men and women. It's extremely insidious and pervasive in our society. In many cases we are oblivious to it. In fact, many of us are attracted to it, which is why it sells so much.

Yes, Nathaniel had a great life. He was a single, good looking (by, of course, those magazine standards), and intelligent individual. He enjoyed living with two roommates in a trendy up-and-coming neighborhood in a city apartment. After reviewing his intake forms and food journal prior to his first appointment, and after the first few minutes in our initial session, I started to understand a little more what was underneath the façade.

Allow me to also point out some generational differences between Nathaniel and me. Nathaniel was in his late twenties, and I, at the time, was in my late forties. I'm a Gen Xer and Nathaniel is a millennial. Now why is this important? Because, a bit earlier I mentioned that us guys rarely seek medical or mental care, right? Well, that's tending not to be the case for many millennial men. I find that millennials tend to be a little more health conscious than us older men, but health isn't about working out and eating "clean" (clean is just the new co-opted word for dieting these days). Yes, Nathaniel was willing to make an appointment with me, but dealing with his eating issues wasn't what he was coming for. It was still about the hypermasculinity and need to be more of a man. In our modern society, diet culture has infiltrated every aspect of gender identities and cultural norms that it confounds the tenants of what health really means. Health is not about a magazine image of a perfect body . . . whatever that means. I see many people in thin bodies that have various physical conditions like hypertension, arthritis, back and joint problems, or mental health challenges.

A great perspective of the importance of mental health comes from Daniel J. Siegel, MD, authored *Mindsight: The New Science of Personal Transformation*. He points out that health is an "Interpersonal Integration." This means it is a delicate balancing act between the independent body systems like the lymphatic system, the digestive system, the respiratory system, the circulatory system, or our neurological system. All twelve of our biological systems must work harmoniously with each other in order to keep us running smoothly; they also have to work in balance with our consciousness, our emotional state. He explains that our minds are the processing center of our bodies, it needs to be in harmony with our body, and that this harmony is the representation of health.[30] This is also essentially what numerous spiritual and motivational leaders and experts have been saying for years. The balance of mind, body, and spirit is not strictly a consequence of how fit we are or how healthy we eat. If it were, then millennials, people with orthorexia, or anyone for that matter, could be healthy and live forever. We're not that simple. Even a perfect balance, which doesn't exist, wouldn't stop the aging process anyway. Health is about a deeper state of awareness of ourselves, our collective consciousness. To quote Eckhart Tolle,

"Awareness is the power that is concealed within the present moment. . . . The ultimate purpose of human existence, which is to say, your purpose, is to bring that power into this world."[31]

Another great quote that touches on this concept of harmony of health was from a recent podcast interview I had with Tamas Kiss, co-founder of Ate, a nonjudgmental and mindful food journaling app. In describing his journey prior to creating the Ate app, he dropped a profound statement. Tamas said, "Health is emotional, mental, and physical."[32] A very simple yet profound statement describing Tamas's journey through fitness only to discover that his mind was not there yet. Although Nathaniel looked healthy, underneath the good looks and tough career-driven demeanor, a lot of emotional challenges were eating him up. There were signs about his eating challenges and food rules that were bound by a deep hidden fear. He wasn't present. Like Tamas, his mind had not caught up.

Nathaniel described a little about himself and the reason for the visit. He explained that he was a vegetarian and was trying to be a vegan, but it wasn't that easy. He couldn't maintain his energy levels, and he wanted to gain more muscle. He described his daily routine:

5:00 a.m.—Coffee black and catching up to his social media feed on his phone

5:30 a.m.—60 minutes strength training and conditioning four mornings a week

6:45 a.m.—Coffee black and checking email and work schedule (sometimes on his way to the airport for a client training trip)

7:15 a.m.—Breakfast—Organic, gluten-free granola bar, 6 ounces of low-sugar coconut-milk yogurt, and ¼ cup of blueberries, all while checking his computer, listening to the TV in the background, and scrolling through social media on his phone

7:45–9:30 a.m.—work

3: Compassion

9:30 a.m.—30–45-minute power yoga about twice a week, sometimes three depending on whether he was traveling or not

12:00–12:30 p.m.—Lunch—Usually a heaping salad plate with some combination of fresh kale, spinach, micro-greens, a combination of various fresh veggies he would have available in his fridge, about half a can of organic/low-sodium/fair-trade chickpeas or lentils, about 1.5 ounces of mixed raw nuts and seeds, ¼ cup of vegan cheese, and about 3 tablespoons of an organic sesame seed oil-based vinaigrette with only five ingredients or less

The is an example of his perfectionism of eating a super high-quality food selection. This idea of a superfood is another extreme term for categorizing food as bad or good, which is any food that is not ultra or overly processed. Simply put, in my experience to date, I have not seen anyone capable of indefinitely sustaining this type of eating. Let's continue.

2:30–3:30 p.m.—Take his dog on a 40–50-minute walk (At this point I was thinking, *Where does this guy find the time?*)

3:45 p.m.—Vegan protein bar, which had to have pea protein only, 12 ounces of herbal tea, and some days he made a power green juice cleanse (wheat grass, broccoli, and/or cauliflower with spirulina and vegan protein powder mix)

At this point, Nathaniel paused to ask what type of vegan protein powder is the best, because he believed his plummeting energy levels at this time of the day were due to the quality of protein and not the lack of food. It was a momentary about-face from our conversation. As he asked, I could see that for the first time he was listening to himself describe the obsession with his perfectionistic eating. His body was telling him to *eat*, yet he focused on the protein powder. This was definitely a small breakthrough, but he needed to continue describing the rest of his routine.

4:00–5:15 p.m. (or till about 5:30 p.m.)—Most days at home he would continue with work, and maybe a couple of days a week he would work till 6:30 or 7:00 p.m., but that was typically only toward the end of the quarter when more reports and deadlines loomed.

5:30 p.m.—He would go on a 5–7 mile run 4–5 days a week. On weekends, he would do anywhere from 15 to 18 miles.

Running was his jam. It was his escape—his drug, his high. He was planning to do an ultra-marathon, which is double to quadruple the number of miles compared to a typical marathon of 26.2 miles. Oh, and that's nonstop, no breaks, just keep running. There was a little problem. During his training for an ultra-marathon, he wasn't recovering from his long weekend runs like he used to. He was running 60–70 miles a week, and he said at this point in his training he needed to be up to 100–125 miles a week. The obsession and intensity with ultramarathons and health reached beyond the food. It's not to say that ultramarathoners are obsessive or have orthorexia, but Nathaniel wasn't doing it for his career or for a major cause or charity. He was trying to impress Raquel. He wanted her to see he was amazing, but all she wanted was for him to love himself. What was interesting was that as he described his training and eating regimen, he seemed nonchalant about it. As if the amount of training and obsession about his eating was no big deal. You would never suspect anything was wrong with Nathaniel and his laid-back demeanor, but, boy, was there a lot of pain and fear! He continued describing his routine . . .

Back from a run or the gym (oh yeah, I forgot to mention the days he didn't run, he went to the gym and did about 45 minutes on the treadmill and 20–30 more minutes on weights) . . .

6:45–7:00 p.m.—Recovery snack/drink—vegan protein bar or a spirulina protein drink

3: Compassion

7:00–7:30 p.m.—Dinner—some type of Buddha bowl with a bed of mixed greens, roasted veggies, organic quinoa, and cauliflower rice mix, vegan parmesan-flavored cheese, and two or three drinks (stiff straight up drinks like vodka, bourbon, or gin, with maybe an ice cube)

At this point, things got difficult for Nathaniel (as if they hadn't been already). He told me that at night he would get these cravings and had a hard time falling asleep unless he ate something. Instead of eating, most nights he had a couple of drinks and took melatonin to help him fall asleep around 11:30 p.m. or midnight, yet he started his fitness routine again at 5:00 a.m. to prepare for his first workout of the day. He began to tell me that it was all the amount of sleep he needed, but then I asked him, "Well, but what about that middle of the day slump you hit?"

And he responded, "Well, that's one of the reasons I came to see you. I feel like I'm just burning out and I don't have as much energy as I used to in my runs and toward the end of my workday. Then at night I'm feeling really hungry." After providing his typical eating routine and talking about his runs, Nathaniel seemed a bit proud about his routine at first, but as he was paying more attention to what he was telling me, he quickly realized how obsessed the routine actually sounded.

He then said to me, "I see that I'm hitting that midday slump, and of course now that I hear what I'm saying, I must sound like I'm always obsessing about every little ingredient in food. I'm also getting really hungry at the end of the day, but now I wonder if it has to do with how little I eat."

I then asked about all the coffee he was drinking. He responded, "I don't really enjoy coffee, but it's been part of my ritual for the last few years. Yeah, I guess it all sounds a little over the top, huh?" He then described his weekend routine, which started with going out with friends on Fridays. Unfortunately, it was hard for him because they would frequent pubs and bars with few vegetarian options, so he would usually enjoy a few pints of beer and maybe some nuts. Yet again, another example of how unsustainable, unrealistic, and socially isolating diets can be.

Saturdays were his "sleep in" days. "I'm usually up around ten-ish, but of course it depends on events from the night before. I typically get in anywhere between 11:00 p.m. and 2:00 a.m., I order a whole pizza, and eat the whole pie along with a few stiff drinks. Then on Saturday I go on my long runs and skip breakfast, mainly because of the hangover or crappy feeling from the pizza and drinks. When I get back, I grab my usual—a protein bar, veggie and protein powder smoothie, and a shot of wheatgrass juice in order to [as he put it] help detox me from the night before." It was a sign of punishment and reward. All week long he would eat vegetarian superfoods (so he called them) as a form of punishment, and then on weekends he would "reward" himself (in quotes to denote the irony) by indulging in forbidden foods like pizza, which technically was vegetarian in his mind. It was a mental fuck: punishing himself by restricting, using coffee instead of food and avoiding carbohydrates, then overeating and drinking alcohol because his body just couldn't handle the restriction; then the emotional and self-deprecation and shame, which he would try to erase or correct by overexercising the next morning. No wonder his energy was crashing midday—his body was screaming for help.

The Awakening— Compassion Starts to Affect Change

One story in particular stood out to me as an example of the role fear was playing in his life. Nathaniel went to a pool party and ran into his ex-girlfriend Rachel, but she was with her new boyfriend, and Nathaniel couldn't handle it to see her with another man. He couldn't build up the nerve to even talk to her. Essentially, he felt he just didn't measure up to her new boyfriend. "He's about eight years older, really good-looking, and he started his own super successful technology firm. I don't know. I'm just not sure," he said. "I'm just not sure what I did wrong in that relationship. I had a cool apartment, a successful career, and she just wasn't into me. I guess I didn't measure up to her

3: Compassion

new boyfriend. I just wasn't enough." And then he started to reveal a few more insecurities.

His family was from South Carolina, where he grew up in a small town. He rarely spoke to his father, who was the very figure of the hyper-masculine patriarch of the family: rarely showed any emotions, worked long hours, loved to hunt and tinker in his shop with cars and anything mechanical. Nathaniel did not show pain and emotions, and he never cultivated strong relationships with other family members. His parents were busy, and Nathaniel was often left to take care of himself. It was difficult for him to socialize and develop intimate relationships in his current hometown, Atlanta. His ex-girlfriend was his college sweetheart, and they had a lot of great memories together, but he said they just started to drift apart. He couldn't understand why, but he suspected she just wasn't into him after college. Nathaniel revealed that he had been afraid of losing her, but he didn't know how to express it. It was the little things that started forcing a wedge between them. He explained how he was always so jealous and didn't want her to hang out with her girlfriends, but he avoided confrontation and emotions as much as possible. He would take her on nice vacations, but at home he wasn't really there for her. Nathaniel would be out with his friends instead of taking time for her. He was distant and not responsive. He wouldn't acknowledge her feelings, and she would often tell him she felt like an armpiece he displayed to his friends. She wanted his attention, she wanted to share his emotions, but she kept getting the cold shoulder. They continued dating after college and lived together in his new apartment, but then she broke it off after a few months. He was devastated.

After the breakup, he escaped by working more, traveling significantly for work. He gained some weight and was just not in a good place in his life. He was heartbroken and lost. This went on for a few months, and then one day he just decided enough was enough. He was going to change his life and win her back. And so for the next year he went on a vegetarian diet, started working out every day, and discovered his passion for running. He signed up for a few races and marathons, and he was laser focused on impressing her with his weight loss and fitness in order to try and win her back.

When he ran into her at the pool party, he was nervous. He wanted to talk to her, but she was with her new boyfriend, and Nathaniel just didn't know how to approach her. He hoped that she would notice how much weight he lost and how much better off he was. Then he started drinking a few more mixed drinks to help with his nerves, and because there weren't any vegetarian food options that stood up to his dietary standards, he simply avoided eating. Nathaniel had about four drinks and a couple of beers. "I didn't hear you mention food except for the protein bar and smoothie earlier in the day," I said. And then he mentioned, "Oh yeah, I forgot. I did end up eating a few veggie tacos after the pool party because it was the best option I had. At the party, I wasn't paying attention to my hunger. The drinks kept me full, and they helped soothe my nerves about talking to my ex." Sadly, he never ended speaking to Rachel after all.

He continued, "The night was just a wash. I got home around 1:00 a.m. and ordered two pizzas again. I just didn't want to eat in front of anyone, but that's my problem, David. On Fridays or Saturdays, when I get back home, I'll order a couple pizzas and just eat them by myself. The next day I won't eat a thing, but make sure to go for a run and then hit the weights at the gym." And then he sat there for a while and didn't say anything. I could tell he was finally listening to his internal narrative.

I transitioned to a different approach. "OK, so you're eating what you think is perfect all week long, and then on the weekends you enjoy pizza and some drinks. I, too, enjoy pizza and beer on weekends, and I tend to eat a little more because I really love pizza. It just feels good, but there is nothing wrong with that." I said next, "After listening to what you typically eat and from the three-day food log you provided me, there seems to be very little consumption of any carbohydrates in your diet to sustain the level of activity. You're not eating meat and have a seemingly healthy diet, but did you notice that you also have a variety of these food rules about ingredients, protein, carbohydrates, and eating out? It seems like these rules really limit the amount of food your body needs to sustain itself. I understand your idea of eating healthy like this has helped you feel better and lose weight, but I wonder if restricting during the week leads to the overeating of pizza, bar food, and alcohol on the weekends. You then only punish yourself again with extreme workouts and then reverting back to your food rules and vegetarian plan. It just sounds very extreme."

I saw him pondering that for a while. "Hmm, I never noticed it that way," he said. He was seeing it now from a completely different angle. Nathaniel realized he was in quite a pickle. I started to explain the importance of carbohydrates and how athletes, and all of us, need them as the main source of fuel for his muscles. How glycogen is a form of glucose that comes from the food we eat that is then stored in our muscles and liver in order to provide fuel during moments of intense energy needs, like when we work out, go on a run, or experience stressful events. More importantly, it's also necessary to fuel the body's natural biological and physiological functions all the time. Maybe his diet restrictions and food rules cut back so much energy that it began affecting his running. He started to see that his obsession for food might have gone a little too far. He wasn't about to stop being a vegetarian, though, and of course that wasn't my intent anyway.

Fear of what Nathaniel thought he was or had been—overweight, and not good enough for Rachel—had really settled in his mind. It was clouding his true self, a deeper sense of himself—someone kind, intelligent, funny, and loving. He started to realize that he was punishing himself during the week and then going buck wild on the weekends. Rewarding himself for the discipline and hard work. It was a vicious cycle of bingeing on pizza over the weekends and then feeling both physically and emotionally horrible that he had to go on long runs and eat "super clean" all over again. Orthorexia can be a gateway condition to more severe forms of disordered eating, or itself can be an intense eating disorder. Nathaniel knew this wasn't sustainable. He understood that something wasn't going right. Nathaniel started to realize that he was seeking more than eating healthy; he was trying to escape the man he was. He was afraid he couldn't win Rachel's heart unless he was this super-human, this persona of a perfect man that had it all. Remember the prison of the ideal of masculinity from above? The perfect apartment, car, job, looks, physique, and diet, just like those images on magazine covers or celebrities. A fictional character we see in the movies. What was really important was that Nathaniel needed to confront his fear.

I got it. I understood. I was listening to him, and I empathized since I had a similar food journey. It was as if I was listening to a mirror image of my life—you remember my story at the beginning of this book. I, too, was in this orthorexia mindset in my late twenties. I was running away from who I really was, and my world came crashing down in front of me as well. I told Nathaniel this, and through my story he started to see his. He started to realize that he needed to face his demons. I told him that FEAR really is only in his mind. It stands for **F**alse **E**xpectations **A**ppearing **R**eal. He needed to head toward his fears to get past them. Eating super healthy, exercising like a madman, and coming off as this perfect image of a guy was only fooling himself. Nathaniel really resonated with this idea. I explained that manhood and masculinity cannot and should not be defined though such a narrow lens.

Forward Momentum

I asked him next, "What's the lowest hanging fruit?" What could he do now going forward?

He thought about everything we discussed, looked at me, and said, "Well, I guess I need to really start with fueling myself better. The most important thing I think would be to start adding back some carbohydrates to my diet." Nice! All this was self-directed—anything he would have said would have been the right answer. He already knew the answer but was afraid of what might happen: gaining the weight back, not getting Rachel back (though she wasn't coming back to him at all—that ship had sailed). He was afraid that if he ate those foods, people would stop thinking of him as that perfect persona, or more importantly *he* would stop thinking the same.

What were his next steps then? One small bite at a time. He decided to start adding more carbohydrates back into his diet. I gave him a few ideas, like starting with breakfast, adding about a serving or two of any grain that he thought was safe. He decided on a quinoa and muesli blend (still an orthorexia-type behavior, but it was a small step in the right direction). He thought he needed a grain for lunch or snack as well, and I told him this was a good idea to help keep him fueled, but what's more important is what his body would tell him. The key was to experiment and take his time because the body may not provide clear cut answers or quick wins. His body was in it for the long haul.

Two weeks later, he came back a totally different person. He was smiling more. He had a lot more energy. He felt a lot better about himself, and he started to tell me that his run times improved. He also decided to cut back on his physical activity, but he said he wanted to stick with the strength and conditioning routine. He made some changes, started feeling better, and was pleased with where he was. He told me he felt so much lighter, like he was finally breaking the shackles of his routine. He never realized until our last meeting how obsessed he was about food and his body. I reminded him he wasn't crazy, that we all go through these challenges in life, and it's hard to see in ourselves the changes that need to occur. We turn a blind eye or simply aren't aware. I'm reminded of the quote from the amazing Maya Angelou: "There is no greater agony than bearing an untold story inside of you." Bearing witness to one's own challenges can be extremely difficult, but not impossible. It is definitely where one must begin. While we needed to work on a few more of his challenges, this was a great first step. He wanted to do more. OK, I challenged him on this.

I asked him what worked best since we started our sessions. He said that having a little carbohydrate at breakfast really did the trick. He didn't feel the need to drink as much coffee, and he realized that he was getting sick of eating the same protein bar all the time. He also slipped in that he started taking a cooking class and met a cute girl.

Then I asked him what he thought he needed to do going forward. "Well, I need to start making healthier meals for the rest of the day."

"Alright, let's just sit with that approach for a bit." He looked at my face, and I could see he realized that that might not be the best idea. I asked him, "Do you think you can handle cooking or preparing healthy meals for breakfast, lunch, and dinner each day on a regular basis?"

Again, he thought about it for a while and couldn't really figure it out at first. I asked him to take a look at being a vegetarian, and how much that required of him. How much time he had to spend each week to plan and prepare meals. He then explained, "OK, maybe what I need to do is just get better at eating those grains in the morning."

"Well, what do you think?" I asked him.

"Yeah, I see where you're going with this. If I start losing focus on that one small bite, I go back to the way I was doing things before."

Yup, that's exactly what I was thinking, but then he said something pretty impactful. "You know, David, I started thinking more about myself, but it was weird, but weird in a good way. This time, I was thinking about the man I am, and not the man I used to be. I didn't want to go back to who I was, but I had to confront that old me in order to change."

Wow! As if I had scripted that line for him to say. No, not at all! This was all him and he was on it. "Yes, one of the things we fear the most is losing our sense of belonging, or fearing we can't possibility become the image of the man society expects from us. Interestingly, at the same time it's easy to stay in that comfort zone even though it can be lonely or isolating." Or as Jen Sincero, author of the *New York Times* bestselling book *You Are a Badass: How to Stop Doubting Your Greatness and Start Living an Awesome Life*, calls it—the Big Snooze (BS for short). I read to Nathaniel my favorite quote from the book:

"Very few people are even aware of what's available, however, because we live in a fear-based society that loves to get all uppity toward people who wake up from the Big Snooze, blast out of their comfort zones, and follow their hearts into the great unknown. Oftentimes, taking great leaps of faith is labeled as irresponsible or selfish or insane (until you succeed of course, then you're brilliant). This is because: Watching someone else totally go for it can be incredibly upsetting to the person who's spent a lifetime building a solid case for why they themselves can't."[33]

Boo-ya! Right!? It's the BS that enhances the fear and perpetuates the same cycle of control, restrict, punish, overeat, and then do it all over again.

F.E.A.R. (which, remember, stands for **F**alse **E**xpectations **A**ppearing **R**eal) is created in our mind based partly on our past experiences. We don't want to get hurt, but it is through those difficulties and challenges in life that we grow. The key here was that Nathaniel started to work on what was important: building only one small change at a time, which was also a form of self-kindness and compassion for himself. I provided him with what he already knew was important. He came to see me because he needed more energy, and all I did was reassure him of what he was afraid to do: eat more carbohydrates, enjoy food again, stop the restricting and bingeing game. Although he was afraid of gaining weight and becoming the old Nathaniel, he somehow knew that his current lifestyle wasn't sustainable. He was ready for the change. He needed the guidance, and more important, he needed permission to eat again. I was just a sounding board to do what he was afraid but knew what to do. I was his Sherpa guiding him up his mountain, and Nathaniel hearing my story seemed to help him see his.

It wasn't easy. Eating carbohydrates isn't what's going to transform a person, but we often don't realize that the transformations we need in life are simpler than we realize, simpler than what we expect. One small bite is about heading toward the fear and rumbling with it. Becoming our mind's observer. Building self-compassion through self-kindness and mindfulness. Nathaniel needed to observe his mind, be expansive, be receptive to the beauty of what is available to him. What is interesting is that what we fear most is the power and potential of positivity within ourselves. What we fear is that we are glorious, amazing, and incredible. We are more intelligent beyond our imagination, yet we choose to stay in our comfort zones because it's easy and familiar, even though it keeps us perpetually locked in our misery. When we overcome this fear through small steps—through one small bite—we find a completely new world open to us.

Isabel

Self-Compassion Came as a Surprise

> "Self-compassion is a way of emotionally recharging our batteries. Rather than becoming drained by helping others, self-compassion allows us to fill up our internal reserves, so that we have more to give to those who need us."
>
> —**Kristin Neff**

I think it was October 2015 when I received a fax referral from Isabel's primary care physician (PCP). When I called Isabel to schedule her first appointment, she was expecting my call, albeit with some reservation. She had seen a registered dietitian nutritionist (RDN) in the past, and her experience was not great. She started to ask me what my approach was, and so I told her that we focus on an anti-diet approach that helps people build a positive relationship with food and make peace with their body. It's an individualized method to meet her needs and wants. What sold her was that she was being heard for the first time! She talked about all her challenges, and all I did was listen to what she needed. Isabel got to choose what she wanted to do. "That was the deal breaker for me because I thought you were going to give me more food rules and have a prescription of exactly what to do. For over three months, I avoided making the appointment and told my PCP that I couldn't make it because of scheduling conflicts."

Isabel was fifty-one years old and raised her daughter and son alone. Her twenty-seven-year-old daughter and boyfriend lived in her basement with their nine-month-old daughter, Isabel's first grandchild.

Isabel's nineteen-year-old son was back from college for a semester to take a break for a few months. Isabel was a CPA and had a stable position with a large accounting firm, but she often had challenges with coworkers. Her commute was about an hour each way, and she would get up most mornings at 4:00 a.m. to avoid traffic. Most days consisted of numerous and endless doctor appointments after work for various health issues such as fibroids, arthritis, diabetes, chronic back pain, high blood pressure, blood clots, and high cholesterol. She also had two total knee replacements and several dental procedures done. Needless to say, she had major life challenges, and again another example of how many people deal with overwhelming challenges—all are superheroes without a doubt!

However, Isabel was an amazing woman. In addition to her family accomplishments, she was able to get her bachelor's and master's degrees. It was all the strength she could muster in order to leave her kids' emotionally and physically abusive drunk of a father. It was nothing shy of incredible. She was also active in her church, attended Sunday service, went to Bible study once a week, and was always willing to volunteer when she could. Isabel was amazing because she wouldn't hesitate to help others. But at what cost to her?

For the first eight months, we worked solely on building her self-kindness voices, being mindful of her food choices, and what factors led to those choices. We discussed various aspects of her life and health that interfered with her ability to pay attention to her body. During some of our sessions together, she would describe difficulties prioritizing herself and wasn't aware of how much she tried to people please. She didn't know when to say yes to herself, to things that mattered in life. And she kept overwhelming herself.

We then created some organization and a better structure around prioritizing herself, to stop and have meals, and paying more attention to her hunger and fullness cues. She started grocery shopping more, packing her own meals from home, and trying to eat based on what gave her the most lasting energy and made her feel better in general. Yet, Isabel

3: Compassion

was still quite resistant to trying new foods. It wasn't obvious at first, but Isabel was so accustomed to her food choices over the last thirty years that she thought she was pretty much stuck in her ways. She rarely changed what she ate and had a lot of food aversions for fresh vegetables and fruit. If the fish wasn't fried, then she wouldn't touch it. She rarely tried any meat other than chicken and ground beef and was terrified of carbohydrates because of the numerous diets saying that they supposedly reinforced weight gain. She had years of self-criticism and negative narratives about herself and trusting new foods.

When she was a child, her father used to force her to eat everything on her plate. He was abusive and extremely aggressive, and because they grew up poor, they rarely had variety on their dinner plates. Isabel was forced to always clean the plate, eat everything on her plate regardless of the taste and appearance of the food. Her family rarely had fresh fruits and veggies and were only familiar with the canned versions. Isabel lived with a deep-seated fear of trying anything new that was not authorized or allowed. She was never given any autonomy to choose her own foods, and because her father was so strict, they all had to eat exactly what he wanted. She never learned to cook and only did what she was told, until she got to college. By that time, she was ready to break free, and she had all this newfound freedom. She ate whatever she wanted, whenever she wanted, without regard to what she needed.

Isabel's ability to trust herself and listen to her body was discombobulated through early childhood years of food control, then a free-for-all in college, and then a deprioritization over time of herself over others. Diets that she began in college with passion would end just as abruptly, and that was the cycle for the next twenty years—lose, gain, lose, and gain all over again, and various attempts at the same approach. Making matters worse were the years of body image issues, childhood emotional neglect, and an abusive romantic relationship. Needless to say, Isabel's self-compassion meter was stuck on zero.

Therefore, she was relieved not to have to start another crazy diet or fitness program. She wanted autonomy but didn't know what that looked like unless it was complete chaos, which she feared as well. She was a self-identified perpetual dieter. Therefore, when she started working with us, she really enjoyed her sessions and felt like she received a lot of compassion and kindness. No judgment about her past, eating patterns, or body. She began to understand her intuitive signals of what she needed and wanted to eat. Even though it was scary to learn to trust herself, Isabel found a way to experiment with new foods. But compassion doesn't occur in a straight line, as we have already discussed, and there remained major complications. She wasn't happy with her body.

One day she came to my office after attending a bariatric surgery information session at a local hospital *(please see Appendix A for details on bariatric surgery)*. We had discussed bariatric surgery once before, about how she had tried a bariatric final phase eating plan in the past to support a friend going through the surgery.[34] It's important to understand that while Isabel enjoyed our sessions, and gained an enormous understanding of herself and built some trust back again, she still significantly struggled with her weight. She had incredibly strong emotional demons swirling in her head about how she looked and how her weight directly affected her health, which was so intricately tied to her self-worth. Not to mention that she was constantly bombarded by fat-phobia messages and weight-stigmatization from all directions—social media, TV, the news, the latest internet browser pop-up ad, from her doctors, from her co-workers, and from her family. Fat-phobia messages that made it seem she was not beautiful, not worthy, and almost not human.

Unfortunately, this is the society we live in—one that views fat as a disease, labeled that way by the American Medical Association and other health professionals. We are not aware of the deep-rooted diet culture mentality that is steeped into our society. Yes, there are numerous studies showing a *relationship* between obesity and excess fat and various types of chronic illnesses, but there isn't a single study that shows *causality*. However, the weight-stigma is arguably equally as damaging to a person's health. The negative stigma of "being fat is being bad" translates to an enormous segment of society thinking they are bad, that they don't belong to a society that believes thinness is beauty, being buff and toned is manliness. These are extreme expectations to put on society, when in actuality a low percent of people fit that false image we see in the movies. The parallels to the financial disparities in our society are striking: you can call that extremely small minority of "perfect" people the one-percenters. By perfect, however, please note there is no such thing. I would bet even those one-percenters feel they're not perfect either—you have to wonder why plastic surgery is a pretty big business. In short, we have a fat-phobia epidemic, not an obesity epidemic.

Forward Momentum

It's never a straight line. Life happens, and it's going to make us fail, fall down, stumble, and struggle, which is so necessary for growth to happen. Isabel was dealing with major emotional and medical challenges. As a result, she believed bariatric surgery was her solution. There was no changing her mind; she was dead set on this decision.

Consequently, she followed all the requirements pre-gastric bypass surgery. And there were considerable requirements she had to meet even before a date for the surgery could be established. Before surgery, Isabel battled with insurance requirements such as providing proof that she had attempted other weight loss programs, or meeting her deductible for her plan, all which created various interruptions and missed work at times. Then there were other life challenges like coordinating her care and medications with various physicians and juggling the care of her granddaughter and life in general. There were numerous forms, medical tests and visits, classes, evaluations, and nutrition requirements prior to surgery, but she stuck with it as best she could. From the time she decided to go forth with bariatric surgery and her actual surgery date took approximately nine months. It was a challenging amount of coordination and planning that disrupted a lot of her life and family. Remember, she was the matriarch and supported a lot at work and at home.

Shortly after surgery, she dealt with some medical complications, and had to go back to the hospital a couple of times due to infections, malnutrition, and severe abdominal pains. Needless to say, she had lost a considerable amount of weight but at the expense of eating challenges such as difficulty swallowing food, keeping it down, and often throwing it up. She had to take an extra week off unpaid leave from work to adequately recover, and her family tried to help but they already were stretched as well. It took Isabel approximately three months before she was able to have a regular meal. The amounts were less than a cup per meal, and in many cases, she would fill up after just a few bites of food. She was eating extremely low amounts of food, and this was concerning since we discussed the Minnesota Starvation Experiment and the effects on these men's mental and physical health.

At her three-month follow-up with her surgeon, among other things, they checked her weight, and she was down a large percentage. Then the surgeon said, "You're doing good, but you could stand to lose some more." It was a devastating comment to say the least, but so many people that have had bariatric surgery tell me similar stories. I'm sure the surgeon meant well and was using a tough-love tactic, but over time those types of approaches can deteriorate a person's soul. This comment put Isabel into a tailspin. She cried for days wondering what more she could do, yet she was also familiar with that tough-love militant approach. One could say that's just what she needed to get her motivated to lose more weight. The problem is that type of approach is judgmental and places blame for a failed medical approach on the person. Look, if weight-loss surgery or diet programs were put to the same standards the FDA uses to approve medications, they just wouldn't be approved. The *surgery* wasn't working, not Isabel. That tough-love approach is latent form of hostility that might seem like a great approach, but the psychological and emotional effects long-term could be devastating. However, over time her blood sugar levels did improve, which of course was because she wasn't eating much. Her back felt a lot better partly because she wasn't working much and was pretty stable for months with significant amounts of rest after her surgery and complications. She also realized she was sleeping better, but this was also because she had a lot of time off work and slept in often. Isabel had established a meal pattern that she thought was good enough to get back to work.

Over the next few months, Isabel continued to lose weight, and after a couple of years the challenges became manageable. She felt better and her medical condition improved for a while, but many challenges still remained. Like so many people that have had bariatric surgery, her weight plateaued, and she struggled to reach an unrealistic goal weight: her high school weight. Simultaneously, her life was still pretty packed, and emotionally things were difficult. She was doing everything as she was instructed to do, eating small "healthier" meals and working out, but what wasn't happening was finding that self-compassion. She only knew to be harder and harder on herself, and this approach after a while just beats a person down. Isabel was no different. She couldn't sustain the self-deprecating narratives about herself.

The surgeon's comments were devastating to her and echoed in her mind for years. She was hard on herself because that tough-love mentality and beating herself up was familiar to her. It was her way of motivating herself to keep things going. But this time that old trick just wasn't working. She wasn't twenty-something or even thirty-something anymore. Her body wasn't going to support yet another weight loss, and this type of motivation is emotionally draining even for the toughest of people. She thought there was something wrong with her. It started to affect her self-worth more profoundly than before, particularly because bariatric surgery was the last straw in weight loss. Isabel knew that she needed a different direction. She was curious about whether our work with intuitive eating, anti-dieting, and compassion-focus approach would be more helpful. There was still a desire to lose more weight, and frustration that she started gaining some of the weight back about two years after surgery.

Isabel started working on paying more attention to what her body actually needed. Two years after surgery, she knew she had to slow down and pay attention to what her body was telling her. At times her surgery forced Isabel to slow down, like when she would eat too fast and didn't chew sufficiently and then felt the food just get stuck. It was a painful reminder, but Isabel learned to pay attention. Learning these subtle cues was instrumental to building her intuitive signals of hunger and fullness again. She had to re-learn all those signals. In fact, I often tell people that when they have surgery, they'll be learning how to eat all over again. They'll be at their infancy of their eating and digestive process all over again, so slowing down to listen is vital. Isabel eventually gained a considerable amount of weight back, despite the surgery and eating less. She went to the gym religiously, but it still wasn't enough. She was yet again so frustrated, but this time she knew things needed to change. The challenge was helping her understand that this anti-diet and self-compassion approach wasn't a backdoor approach to more weight loss. Hearing this was difficult for Isabel, but it was important to help her realize that her health wasn't just about her weight; it was also her mental and emotional state that also affects her overall health.

Over time, Isabel became much more kind, mindful, and aware of the little things in life. She started with just one simple exercise every day. A couple of times throughout the day, she would pause for thirty seconds and just check-in with her thoughts and feelings. This pausing didn't require much. She just stopped and paid attention to what she was thinking or feeling. Again, building mindfulness and awareness to what her body was telling her even if there wasn't anything major going on, but sprinkled throughout the day to help her slow down. It was her one small bite that made a major difference. Over time, the emotional baggage of weight and how she looked started to improve. She became more involved in the moment, and her negative self-narrative started to move further from her normal way of thinking. She was more focused on paying attention to signals and facts, and not old voices, that ultimately started to help changed her life.

Isabel's journey was challenging, to say the least. It is an example of how some people have to go through challenging or traumatic events in their lives before they become more compassionate with themselves and about what truly matters. However, this doesn't have to be the case. We can learn self-compassion at any point in our lives. Our brain is capable of developing new self-compassionate neural connections—new methods of doing old things. But each of our own journeys and experiences are fundamental to learning, to growing, and to being the person we want to be. We all have to suffer or be challenged with difficult situations at some point to discover a different way. Self-compassion recognizes that the messy middle is the part of life where we learn, adapt, and become curious. When we accept where we are in life, then moving forward is part of the equation. It's knowing that we can only get out of difficult issues if we build self-compassion.

Compassion is about all these things. Just like Nathaniel, it's about vulnerability—the courage to move beyond your fears. It is about self-prioritization, self-kindness, and knowing that we're not in this alone. We are all in this together. Remember Meredith and how slowing down helped her significantly towards transforming her life? Well, in the next chapter you will read about how all of us discover our self-compassion through these very elements—prioritizing, kindness, and awareness.

All

Self-Prioritization, Self-Kindness, Self-Awareness

I'm not offering any new Shero's or Hero's perspective or describing their journey here. You've already read how Meredith needed to slow down and pay attention to the things that really mattered in her life. You learned about Angela and her back-and-forth with curiosity until she truly found her direction, her purpose. You learned how I, too, discovered my inner voice through the difficult challenges in my life—losing my mother and father to cancer. Catalina was curious about finding a new way and move away from the old diet approaches.

When I talk to people about self-prioritization, it's not about being selfish, ignoring other people's problems, or only thinking about what's important to you. It's about pausing—taking small incremental moments in life, every day, to pay attention to the body and understand the basic physiological needs, as well as desires. Yes, desires. Because the longer we try to ignore those desires, the more intense they become. Those desires can turn into obsessions, and those obsessions can overwhelm our lives, our emotional state. Self-prioritization means that eating is essential for life. No diet is going to change our physiology and human nature. Provide the body with the fuel it needs, and enjoy food because—well, let's not kid ourselves—food is joy. When we truly pay attention to our bodies, or to our natural hunger and fullness cues, to our needs *and* wants, we will learn to satisfy ourselves with less.

With regards to self-kindness, it is about finding that voice you would use with your best friend or your loving pet. Do you remember the last time you did something wrong or made a simple mistake? What voice did you use with yourself? Did you talk to yourself with a forgiving and understanding voice? A nurturing voice? Or did you choose to demoralize and insult yourself because that's what you've always done? "You idiot, you keep making the same mistake" might have been the comment to yourself. In many instances, the self-deprecating talk seems to come out automatically. Isabel used that tough-love approach because that's how she was raised. So much of our self-narrative comes from our childhood. We learned how to talk this way to ourselves partly because many of us were emotionally neglected as a child. Take me, for example. I was the youngest of nine kids. My parents loved me dearly, but they were so busy raising our entire family and working all the time that although I grew up with lots of siblings, it was as if I was an only child. Ironically, I was spoiled and doted on as a child, but this was my parents' way to show their love and make up for lost time. Childhood Emotional Neglect is a common mental health issue, but it is so under the radar to many people.

Dr. Jonice Webb, author of the book *Running on Empty: Overcome Your Childhood Emotional Neglect*, talks about how well-meaning and loving parents can also be neglectful to their own children, yet be completely unaware of their neglect. Part of this emotionally neglectful parenting is due to their own upbringing. They too were raised neglected or left to deal with their own internal demons.[35] This neglect is therefore a vicious cycle. The emotionally neglected child grows up to be a parent as well and raises their own children in the same way.

It also plays out in the food we eat and the relationship we have with food and our bodies. We neglect to eat because we don't prioritize ourselves, because other things and people are more important that we are. As a result, we neglect to fuel ourselves adequately, to take the time to sit down and enjoy food with family or friends. Now, of course, not everyone is raised by neglecting parents. Many of us live in a capitalistic society that puts enormous pressure on us to excel, to be great, to be the next Steve Jobs or Beyoncé. We live in a Grind and Hustle culture that respects and rewards extreme busyness. These are insurmountable pressures that blind us to the basic need to eat or sleep. Think of it this way:

3: Compassion

If you had to urinate you might be able to hold it for a little while, but not for long. Sooner or later, all you can think about is relieving yourself. You obsess about it. You can't focus on anything else and you just gotta go! Food is no different. When you don't prioritize your relationship with food, when you ignore your basic physiological need to nourish and fuel, you are not prioritizing or being kind to yourself. Interestingly, you probably aren't even aware of what's going on. This becomes a silent lack of compassion and prioritization.

This is why emotional self-awareness is vital! As discussed previously, it takes being intuitive and listening to the body. Self-awareness is a skill. It takes time to home in and get better at it. Being aware of natural physiological signals are important, but you can start with paying attention to how you talk to yourself. Take Catalina, for example. She was curious and began to pay more attention to herself and her needs. Self-awareness allows us to slow down and capture those negative comments and reframe them. It allows time to take in the facts and not the judgmental voices that break us down. By being self-aware, you can hear your hunger and fullness tell you when to eat, what to eat, how much to eat, and when to stop, but it is also not perfect. Eating intuitively and listening interoceptively is not a backdoor to weight-loss and a diet scheme. Self-awareness informs your body and soul to find satisfaction in food and life. Self-awareness is a powerful tool, but it has to be practiced.

That is what I mean by one small bite. It's not a diet plan, a special "superfood," or a supplement. It's not a super intense fitness program like the ones Catalina was doing. It also isn't a way of saying that you have to stop everything in your life and only do one thing—or else! No, it's not that. Small bites are often just a mindset. A way of shifting how we think or perceive of the common things in life. Compassion is at the core of that new perception, and we need to nurture it and truly pay attention to how compassion for ourselves is compassion for life.

In the next section, we're going to discuss how being committed to these small bites are vital to your transformation.

4
Commitment

> "A change is brought about because ordinary people do extraordinary things."
>
> —Barack Obama

In this next section of the book, you'll read how various people took the leap of faith. Commitment isn't just in the mind—"I gotta do this regardless of what my body needs"—it's in the heart, and it's in the soul. You'll read how, despite all the odds and challenges in their lives, these superheroes, common day folk like you and me, learn to trust their bodies again. They were curious about how to make things better, and their curiosity was piqued. They were compassionate. They paused, were present, prioritized themselves before others, and practiced. It wasn't easy, but they did things in line with what they valued, not just what they believed. They listened to their bodies and paid attention to purpose and meaning.

While writing this book, there were various moments I felt like giving up. I had so much going on that I didn't think I could do it. It was so hard, and sometimes weeks would go by where I didn't pick up my laptop to write or edit. I felt like an imposter. And then my coach said something that hit me square in the face—I'm writing this book because I love it. It's a part of my soul that needs to get out. I'm doing this because I know my stuff and I'm not an imposter. I'm doing this to serve others, to reach so many more people that need this information. To help others avoid the same snake-oil supplements, fad diets, extreme fitness programs, and the false propaganda of diet culture that my parents went through. It felt right, and it felt good to know not just in my heart and my head, but also in my soul that this book had to be written.

This is what commitment is all about. Doing something because it's the right thing to do, despite the challenges in life. These stories have examples of how commitment is the key to lifelong meaningful healthy change.

Isabel
Unwavering Commitment

Remember Isabel and her decision to have bariatric surgery? Talk about being committed! Isabel made up her mind that bariatric surgery was the route for her. Despite the work she had done with intuitive eating and building a positive relationship with food and her body, she decided to go the diet culture route. This is what's so interesting—not just with Isabel, but with so many people who want to improve their health. It's another example of how a person's journey isn't a straight line. Whether it is alcohol or tobacco addiction, the key to a person's transformation is commitment. However, when it comes to a person's weight, it's a bit more complicated. I don't want to trivialize or make it sound like tobacco cessation is easy by any stretch of the imagination. It's just that we don't need alcohol or tobacco to live. OK, I know, some may argue to the contrary about the alcohol, but work with me. Kidding aside, unlike many other substances we take, we need food to survive, but food isn't just about living. It's not as simple as cut out the food and exercise more, calories in and calories out. And as you have read from the Heroes and Sheroes so far, it's not that simple.

Now, I'm not talking about blind faith, where someone is asking you to do anti-diet or weight-inclusive approaches on a dare. It's not about trying to use willpower to control your thoughts or life. Those methods are hardly effective and never endure. What I'm talking about is a commitment to value your life. Isabel had realized that she'd tried everything. She had been working with me for over a year and in that time she had lost weight, gained it again, and then given up on diet culture. Suddenly, diet culture sneaks back in when a family member loses weight and swears about the latest diet. Old familiar emotions rush back and drive those false hopes and dreams yet again. After a while, she just had enough. Now, I don't advocate for people to have surgery or try to lose large amounts of weight (you read earlier my arguments and the research about how the single biggest predictor of weight gain is weight loss). At the same time, I don't judge someone if or when they decide to have surgery. I am privileged to be in a thin body and have never known what it's like to be in a heavier body, so telling someone they shouldn't have bariatric surgery is inconsiderate. Isabel was tired of diets and fitness programs that didn't work. She worked with therapists and people like me to make peace with her body, and that just hadn't worked for her. The key here is that this time she was 100 percent committed to the surgery. She was 100 percent determined and devoted to this change, and it was evident shortly after the procedure. Unfortunately, it didn't work out the way she planned.

I was impressed by her level of commitment. One of the things I saw in her was when she found something that worked, like a meal plan or pre-portioned plate, she was completely committed to it. Her determination and commitment were two of her greatest strengths. Isabel chose a great bariatric program with top-notch surgeons, registered dietitian nutritionists, nurses, and the whole healthcare team. After her surgery, she went to all her classes and appointments, followed her diet progression plan, but progressed to solid food too fast. She couldn't hold food down. She was vomiting and had diarrhea quite often. Additionally, she had several complications with her medications, particularly with the amount of insulin and other diabetes medications, which caused a few bouts of very low blood sugar. Consequently, as we mentioned in the previous section, she ended up in the emergency room a couple of times. It was pretty scary!

Isabel went through one of the most challenging experiences anyone can have. However, she was committed to working at it, and over time her condition improved. Eventually, she could hold down food, and she progressed slowly, with protein drinks, pureed foods, and then finding the right combination of food options. She got her medications worked out, and, after a few months, she was no longer taking insulin. After about three months, she started walking and doing some light physical activity. Walking alone was a challenge because she had both knees replaced several years before her gastric bypass and walked with the assistance of a cane. She would often be out of breath just walking a few feet, but once she was walking after surgery, her body started adjusting well.

Isabel never imagined anything was harder than childbirth, but bariatric surgery proved to be a bigger challenge. Subsequently, she made incredible changes in her life. She joined various art groups and she started painting. She traveled more with her kids, hired a personal trainer, and went religiously to the gym four or five days a week. Unfortunately, she continues to have challenges diversifying her diet, but she's eating more fresh fruits and veggies than prior to surgery. Isabel has also started her own accounting firm and has been growing her business ever since. However, you know how this story ends. Being healthy isn't a moment in time; it's a constant adjustment. As Daniel Siegel points out, it's a balancing act between all the independent biological systems, like each individual instrument in an orchestra being in sync in order to play beautiful music.[36]

Now this story is extremely important because it is the complete opposite of the whole approach and premise of One Small Bite. Isabel decided to make an enormous change, not small little changes over time. But there was one common element to this dramatic change, and that was her mindset—she had committed to this new way of thinking. Although the journey was epic, she needed to go through it. The irony was that she still had to learn to eat intuitively after all. She learned to balance her meals, maintain a structured meal pattern throughout the day, prioritize herself and her health, and be active. And she learned it little by little, even after the surgery. Isabel worked on small changes over time, and she became a lot better at it. This was the true transformation Isabel experienced. Along the way she spent more time with her children. Her new firm was taking off, she had more energy, and her mood was ten times better, despite the weight gain. Her employees would often tell her how she radiated, and they were inspired by her. Isabel became a new woman, and she didn't look back. She was committed to being the person she wanted to be, not something else.

Like Isabel, you'll learn from the next Shero Tiffany, who learned to commit to something much more important.

Tiffany
Control Is an Illusion

Just the other day I was having a conversation with Tiffany about why she was trying to avoid carbohydrates. She told me that she just couldn't trust herself to eat carbohydrates because once she starts, she can't stop, and that's how she gains weight. She told me that every time she goes on a diet, things go well at first. She loses weight, she feels better, and she has more energy. But as soon as she starts eating carbohydrates, she immediately balloons up (her words). She said, "So, the best way to control my weight is to avoid carbohydrates all together."

OK, I'll bite. I then asked her, "How do you do it?" How does she avoid carbohydrates throughout the day? And just for clarity, I asked her to tell me what types of carbohydrates she is actually talking about. This was when it started getting interesting. She started going through her daily meal patterns.

For breakfast, she usually starts her day with her twenty-ounce coffee tumbler with about a quarter cup of half-and-half. Then, if she has enough time, which she admitted wasn't often, she'll eat a two or three egg white scramble with dark leafy greens like spinach or kale and adds about an ounce of shredded cheese. But in most instances, her morning coffee and cream would be enough till she can get something for lunch. Or at least that's what she thought. Later in the morning, she might grab a large bag of cashews at the office and just snack on that until lunch. Interestingly, it wasn't very clear what types of carbohydrates she wanted to avoid—essentially, all of them! But she continued.

For lunch she'll often grab a salad with some type of protein, or a Buddha bowl, which is essentially a bowl with a bed of greens like spinach or arugula, and possibly some additional veggies with some type of protein on top, and a sauce for flavor. She used to have it with quinoa but decided to stop eating quinoa as well since it was a grain and she felt it was still too starchy. So now she just gets the protein and the veggies only. She also described that some days she skips lunch altogether (depending how busy she was) and that the cashews or nuts with a little more coffee would hold her past lunch. She actually would ignore her hunger and work through it most days. Tiffany said, "I just don't like feeling hungry. I don't have time, so I tend to keep myself busy and just push through lunch some days." I asked her how she felt on those days. She admitted that when she skips lunch, she often gets headaches later in the afternoon. She may grab a few snacks of whatever is around, which usually consists of candy, chips, or soft drinks, but sometimes she'll just take some ibuprofen and she's good to go. I explained to Tiffany that it's common for a lot of people to start feeling cravings, urges, and temptations for hyper-palatable foods in similar situations, and how excluding carbohydrates can intensify those feelings to eat something with more intense flavor and rapid energy. Her body is talking to her; well, actually, it was screaming at that point.

She went on to say, "During the rest of the day it gets a lot harder to avoid carbohydrates and sugar because everyone in the office has some type of treat laying around. It just seems that everyone is trying to pawn all the sugar and junk on me. I think they feel bad for eating it and so they want me to join in." She went on to say, "When that happens, I try to avoid certain areas in the office, and I make sure to schedule a meeting, work on a project, or maybe go on a couple of walks at that point." The walks and distractions can be helpful, but not if the body is communicating hunger. This is another example of how diets and food rules cause more social isolation and avoidance to deal with challenges. Which, in reality, makes a lot of sense. If the body is communicating "I need energy" and it's dismissed, then the brain is going to look for a way out. The brain functions on the law of conservation of energy. I'll discuss more on that later. Tiffany's body was hungry, and by avoiding carbohydrates she has complicated her life even further.

4: Commitment

I then asked her what happens at night or for dinner, and that's when she broke down. "I just can't stop at that point. For several months, everything about my no-carb diet is just perfect [remember, perfection is enemy of progress]. I'm able to get home, make dinner for the family, and even sit down with them and enjoy their company. I have no problems letting them eat whatever they want. I may eat a little with them, but often I'll have my usual: carrots, celery, or cucumbers with a cheese stick or two, or a small sugar-free yogurt and nuts, and everything is fine. And I'll do this for several weeks, and I am able to keep the weight off. But after a while, I just break! I have a mental and emotional break down, and when the rest of the family is asleep, I go at it. It'll start with a bag of chips. I sit in front of my computer and start snacking on them, and then maybe have some hummus. I then add some veggies again, because I figure I should keep it healthy, but then I'll grab two slices of bread, spread some almond butter, and maybe have some jam or cut up a banana on it. Sometimes I'll have some wine as well. And some nights I'll keep going, until I just can't eat anymore. Then I feel horrible! I have an upset stomach, heartburn, and then I can't sleep. Then my mind goes into guilt and embarrassment of what I just did. I feel like such a failure." Again, listen to all the signs: social isolation, control, perfectionism, avoidance, guilt, shame, fear, feeling like a failure.

The good thing was that up to this point Tiffany and I had been working together for about three months, and she was pretty comfortable telling me things. We had been working pretty hard at building her awareness of her hunger and fullness cues. But more importantly, she was developing her ability to pay attention to her body's signs and observing her feelings around eating behaviors. She was demonstrating a sense of clarity and awareness about her own behaviors and mindset that allowed us to candidly discuss her motivations, habits, and thought processes. She was present with her feelings of failure, guilt, and shame and her perfectionistic tendencies.

I asked her to tell me what she observed about herself after describing her eating experiences. What was she able to see or understand about her lack of fueling in the morning, and how that affected her choices at night, and thus her emotional state? Did the anti-carbohydrate approach really help her?

She grabbed a tissue, composed herself, and started to reflect out loud. She realized that because she was trying to control herself and avoid eating any carbohydrates, she made things worse. Tiffany remembered a discussion we had a few sessions prior when we were reviewing her food journal, and she wrote about skipping breakfast and avoiding carbohydrates one day. It was her daughter's birthday, and when her daughter asked why she wasn't eating any of the cake, she remembered feeling horrible. What was she doing? She couldn't enjoy a little cake with her daughter, who she loved so much, on her special day? Tiffany didn't want to feel that way any longer. The benefits of not eating carbohydrates were starting to deteriorate the fabric of her social life. Additionally, Tiffany couldn't go out with friends because of the fear of eating carbohydrates. She would avoid restaurants and certain events with family just to avoid eating carbohydrates and sugar. It even reached a point where her family had stopped inviting her to anything because they were afraid she wouldn't come, and they had to make different foods all the time. These types of social challenges made Tiffany feel worse, not better. The short-lived gains of more energy and weight loss, which were mainly due to the stress response from a form of starvation, just could not endure. She felt so isolated and guilty, regardless of how hard she tried to avoid carbohydrates.

Awareness of the Illusion

She saw what was happening. It took her some time, but Tiffany developed her awareness and sense of self-observation. At the start of her low-carb approach, she thought she wanted a rigid diet with strict rules to control herself because that's how her parents used to control her when she was young. This was an enormous discovery, she admitted. They would often tell her that she couldn't control herself, that she wasn't

4: Commitment

trusted to eat. Over time her parents' lack of trust in her eroded her own ability to trust and listen to her own body. She couldn't trust her own feelings, and they would get her to stop eating even if she was hungry because it wasn't "lady-like." Or they might have forced her to clean the plate despite her fullness level because there were starving kids in some distant country somewhere. It didn't stop at food and eating either; Tiffany was controlled by her parents at every turn. What to study in high school, what colleges to apply to, and what career path to take. She was required to be on the swim team in the summer and to take piano even though she didn't like it. Almost every night, if Tiffany wanted to play outside with her friends, she first had to finish her homework, do her chores, eat her dinner, and then clean up. By that time, it was already dark, and all her friends were back home themselves. Tiffany never had the opportunity to trust her own abilities. Avoiding carbohydrates was a form of the same rigidity that she was so accustomed to.

When it comes to diets and food rules, it typically boils down to control, which I tell people is really an illusion. We are not in control of anything; we just want to believe we are. Now, before you start sending me hate mail or negative comments about this whole control issue, please let me clarify. True and absolute control is not possible; however, we can manage certain areas, people, or situations in our lives for a short period of time in order to help us get things done. Sometimes those things are helpful, and sometimes those things are not. The point is that Tiffany was trying to exert a level of control on something she didn't need to control to begin with. She was trying to control her eating, to prove to herself that she was the person from the past or to avoid some distorted idea of what might happen in the future. But she didn't really know that, and neither do any of us. Her old thoughts and ideas of what she was, what she believed herself to be, and what she identified as, was a self-fulfilling prophecy. But she had never been given the opportunity to trust that she could develop her own path or find her own way. She was perpetually stuck in what she didn't want to do, but what she had to do. It was such a familiar feeling and very reactionary. She was going to be thin no matter what it took. In reality, we can never fully control our thoughts, images, or ideas. If you tried, you'd waste an enormous amount of time and energy—just like Tiffany did.

I had Tiffany do a simple exercise to help her realize how little control she actually had over her thoughts and images. I simply asked: Don't think of a red apple! (You try it. Don't think of a red apple!)

What happens? What do you think of? You think of a red apple, of course. I know, some of you are probably saying, "I didn't think of a red apple. I thought of a green apple," or maybe something red. The point is, the mind cannot separate the image of a red apple with the word "don't," so the red apple pops in your mind. You can try to train yourself to think a different way, like don't eat carbohydrates, but your mind cannot separate the word *don't* from what your body needs as fuel—at least not for long. The harder you control your thinking, the more you try to stop thinking or try to be controlling, the greater the likelihood the thoughts will return without your permission.

Tiffany started to become her mind's observer, to be aware of her thoughts, and to give them space; just be with them in her mind. Yes, this isn't the typical nutrition counseling where she had heard how she should try to eat a more balanced breakfast. And, yes, we did discuss the importance of starting her day with a more balanced breakfast to kickstart her metabolism, give her energy, and help her pay more attention to her hunger throughout the day. She was pretty successful at keeping with her breakfast goals, but her fear of eating carbohydrates was also pretty powerful. That fear drove a lot of that automatic control mechanism she was so well trained in that she obsessed about carbohydrates even more. That's part of the reason at night she felt out of control and ate anything, even carbohydrates. And, by the way, she couldn't clarify what types of carbohydrates because she developed a fear of any type of carb. Therefore, for this simple apple thought exercise, it was important to just get her to become more aware of herself. We started seeing how her negative narratives got formed, and instead, whether those stories (controlled or not) were useful or helpful in her life. Practicing awareness

4: Commitment

and knowing or "seeing" her thoughts or feelings was half the battle. Being aware of what needs to change is truly enduring! Tiffany started to realize, little by little, that her battle with her weight continued because she didn't "see" what really needed to change.

Moving Forward, Making Space

Eventually, Tiffany realized that a balanced breakfast with enough carbohydrates would often help her feel more satisfied. This was her one small bite she wanted to work on. She was committed to this one small bite, which was helping to cause a mind shift. She realized that avoiding carbs wasn't helping, but we couldn't move too fast just yet. It wasn't a matter of completely liberating all her meals and having carbs all the time. This would have been too intense, and just the opposite of one small bite, right? When we reviewed her food journals, she started to realize that when she ate breakfast with a combination of foods including carbs, she felt better throughout the day. She had more energy, and she wasn't as cranky during the day. She smiled more and she had a much better mood and outlook. She was more productive and even helpful with projects and getting things done. More important, she realized that when she had a little carbohydrate with her breakfast, she didn't feel so hungry at the end of the day. She didn't have the urge to snack as much after dinner, but her appetite for lunch was so much better. She would eat with her family and enjoy the time with them. One of the most surprising benefits that Tiffany noticed was that her daughter was also much happier. It was as if she got her mother back, similar to Shonda Rhimes saying yes to her daughter. It was a magical moment to connect to with her. Tiffany broke down in tears of joy, because she was so glad that she was no longer trapped in her old image of restricting and avoiding carbohydrates. She had created a new image of what really mattered in life and to what she really wanted: a true and deep connection with her family and, more specifically, with her daughter. Tiffany never realized that she was sending her daughter the wrong messages. She never realized that her desire to lose weight and to avoid carbohydrates was affecting her emotional relationships.

I often tell people that their relationship with food is a mirror image of other relationships in life. A common comparison I use is our relationships with our partners. The psychologist John Gottman, who wrote the famous bestselling book *The Seven Principles of Making Marriage Work*, talks about how people in a relationship play the roles of the righteous and the victim. For example, the righteous can never be wrong and can often take on a narcissistic attitude, trying to control through embarrassment or shame, and the victim can be overdefensive.[37] The irony is that with food, people are playing those roles in their head. When Tiffany would binge and overeat at night, she would be extremely critical with herself. She would talk down to herself with comments such as, "You deserve to eat like this!" "You're not worthy." "You might as well be fat and ugly because you can't control yourself." "You're such an idiot." Both the righteous and victim would battle on in her mind at a subconscious level. Ergo, controlling her thoughts, especially around food, had its way of manifesting into this self-deprecating war in her head.

Tiffany wanted so badly to be something she wasn't because she never believed she could just be herself. She might have never even understood what being herself meant either. Breaking the grip of control was so liberating. Ironically, she actually felt more in control when she didn't try. She wasn't eating as many carbohydrates because she knew she could eat it whenever she wanted. She also started having more balanced meals with a serving or two of grains or some starch at each meal, just enough that she felt satisfied. After some time, her self-critical voice started to dampen.

At a later session she made a profound statement. She said, "David, I started to realize that the way I was talking to myself wouldn't be the way I talk to my best friend or my daughter. I wouldn't tell them they were not worthy, or idiots, or deserve to be ugly, so why was I doing that to myself?" It was a huge realization. That one small change in thinking really mattered. It was just one small bite that started with a

4: Commitment

little carbohydrate for breakfast. Imagine that! She didn't have to give up carbohydrates or sugar, she didn't have to try to control herself. She needed to be compassionate and forgiving. By doing so, she learned to trust herself more and more. In one of our last sessions together, Tiffany expressed how she finally discovered more about herself, "It was like finding myself after all these years."

Tiffany learned that by being committed to preserving and maintaining what was most important to her—and because she recognized that she couldn't pursue rigid control over everything in her life—she achieved great changes. And those changes all started with that one simple bite. Yes, it was about trusting that she could eat carbohydrates. She had to head toward her fears, but she was committed to what was truly important. The irony was that by letting go of control, she gained so much more. The years of food rules that carbohydrates would make her fat or ugly just wasn't what her body was telling her, thus she transformed.

Claire

Remember, The Tortoise Won the Race

I often tell many of my clients the famous fable about the Tortoise and the Hare. I'll ask clients, "Who wins the race?" and, of course, everyone knows the story and who wins. Intellectually, everyone knows that being committed to one thing is vital for moving ahead in life. Being committed to something means moving toward change and growth as a person, but emotionally the story is quite different. Just like our Sheroes and Heroes in this book, the tortoise was committed to finishing the race. Yes, it might have also been interested in winning, but emotionally the tortoise probably knew that no matter the outcome, the hare couldn't continue to bully and embarrass the other animals. The tortoise was committed to a valuable lesson; that success comes from committing to do something slow and steady and avoid acting quickly and carelessly. We often don't realize the haste of how we do things. We don't take the time to pay attention to what our bodies are trying to tell us. Claire had to learn this as well in her journey.

In one of our sessions, I mentioned this same Tortoise and the Hare story to Claire, and she stopped me dead in my tracks. She said, "I know, I know, you've told me a dozen times, I get it now. You have been telling me this in various ways, and it has taken me quite a bit to figure out." Claire had major challenges with overeating. She had been diagnosed with bulimia nervosa about five years prior to working with me.[38]

Claire was twenty-six years old, lived with her two cats, and worked as a marketing director for a restaurant conglomerate. She tried having steady partners, but her bulimia would always create significant problems, fights, and major distrust in her relationships. Claire traveled a couple weeks a month for her job, which also made it difficult to find a partner. Traveling so often also complicated her bulimia situation in that the likelihood of binge or purge episodes increased exponentially when she was away from home. As a result, she also felt out of control because she just didn't know where and what to eat. Her career suffered too. She had been with her current employer for about four months, but prior to that, she had bounced around between a few companies over the last five years, which was partly related to her absence and productivity issues that stemmed from her struggles with bulimia. With her previous employer, she ended up developing several medical problems that interfered with her work. During a meeting with a very important client, Claire suffered through severe anxiety, felt her heart beating oddly, and fainted during a presentation. She was rushed to the ER and was extremely close to having complete kidney failure.

Additionally, Claire dealt with major body image issues. She engaged in various extreme exercise routines and believed that exercise was the key to tone her body and look amazing. Disappointingly, exercise would help her feel better, but only momentarily. In fact, when she didn't vomit her food, she would exercise for two hours at a time to help avoid eating or work off her food. She would start with a hot yoga class, then strength training, and then would engage in some type of cardiovascular exercises as well. An eating disorder like bulimia can often take over a person's mind and even debilitate someone. Nonetheless, all of her extreme exercise and purging behaviors were taking a toll on Claire, her health, her career—her life! Unfortunately, Claire had to finally resign from her current position because her bulimia episodes were out of control. After her hospitalization, Claire had decided to enroll in an eating disorder clinic, where she did quite well. But this wasn't her first time. The difference this time was the hospitalization and practically life-threatening condition she faced. Much like Isabel having a major life circumstance shift her way of thinking, Claire had realized how frightening it was to end up in the hospital. She didn't want to continue losing great opportunities in her career. She loved her last job and really thought she could advance her career and position there. Unfortunately, her bulimia wouldn't allow that. She realized she needed help, yet the scarier and more challenging part was asking for help, and what that would entail.

Awakening Didn't Come Easy

Claire had started working with me just as she was ending her intensive out-patient (IOP) treatment program at a local eating disorder clinic (ED).[39] As a condition of her discharge, Claire was required to start working with a therapist and a registered dietitian nutritionist. This time, Claire was committed. At first, things were really hard. She would go through about half a box of tissues during her sessions just dealing with her emotions and challenges around food and her body. There were times she was extremely frustrated with the treatment process, yet because of her commitment to change her life, she would catch a glimmer of hope that things were getting better. She would have major wins and feel great, and at times she would revert and self-sabotage because she was afraid it was too good to be true. Her old belief system of "food makes me fat" and distrust in herself was completely at odds with her values of health and spirituality. She struggled with her antiquated and skewed belief system; the old bulimia behaviors would creep back into her life. However, this time it was different. This time Claire listened to her thoughts and got ahead of them. Her extreme exercise diminished little by little. Her main goal was to just pay attention to joyful movement, and find activities she enjoyed with friends, or finding the right amount of exercise in the week that allowed her to enjoy other things in life.

Her journal became a powerful self-reflection tool. In the past, her journaling was an accountability tool and measurement stick of sorts, and not as a nonjudgmental awareness tool. In the past she would count calories or grams of everything to make sure she wouldn't go past a self-imposed level. Instead, this time around her journaling would help her capture her emotions around her eating patterns. Seeing these patterns and emotional connections to her behaviors was transformative for her. This time she was seeing her journal in a completely new light. Her journal entries were not always easy, they weren't pretty, but she was open minded because of her commitment to change. Journaling became a way to escape the day-to-day grind. A way to capture what was both in her conscious and subconscious mind, thus emptying some of the clutter that blinded her to old eating behaviors. Because of journaling, we were able to help her see that she would often skip meals to finish work, which would cause her appetite to increase later in the day. Skipping meals meant eating alone, and being alone made it easy for her old restricting and purging behaviors to occur. She learned to build a support network and have people to talk to when things at work would be challenging.

It wasn't easy, but Claire was committed to her new life. Don't get me wrong, I'm completely aware that a vast majority of people dislike journaling. Heck, I have a hard time keeping one myself. But when I do, and when I ask my clients to do it, even for just a short period of time, it enables us to slow down and pay more attention. I'm not going to pretend and make you think that journaling is a panacea and will miraculously transform someone's life. No, but it *can*. Don't worry, I get it—journaling isn't for everyone. But the power of writing your thoughts on a piece of paper is incredibly powerful in that it allows you to empty the mind of the convoluted narratives that only amplify those emotions we try so hard to control. I can make the same argument if you do a to-do list, or just doodle, the emotional release could be transformative. And remember, control is an illusion, and emotions or thoughts can't be forced away. Journaling for Claire helped her empty her mind to process her emotions, especially with a little help from yours truly. My job was to help interpret what I see for her (and you), so that we can explore the possibilities and opportunities that are there. Remember, I'm just the sherpa and Claire was the Shero.

Summary
Commitment

If there is anything that the Sheroic journeys of Tiffany, Isabel, and Claire taught us is that being committed to one small thing is vital for who we are as humans. To be committed isn't just saying you're going to do something; it's moving through the doubt and fear and doing it, no matter what. It isn't blind faith, though—it's about understanding our basic human needs: food, movement, sleep, hygiene, and human connection. Commitment is about eating in line with our values. For example, if you value family, eating in line with this value is how food brings you closer to your family. Choosing foods that fuel your body efficiently and keeps you healthy offers you more time and a longer life to spend with the people you love. Being committed to something that is in line with your values would then inform your belief system. As a result, being committed and aware of your values as our Sheroes had learned in their journey, gives you the ability to better listen to your body—to feed and nourish your body and not eating more or less than what we need and want. Being committed also means that we are not giving more to others than to ourselves. These three Cs (Curiosity, Compassion, and Commitment) so far have been at the core of what drives the ability for people to transform their lives, build a positive relationship with their body, and make peace with food.

If you go to my website www.orozconutrition.com/book, you'll be able to learn more about Commitment and the rest of the 4 Cs.

Now we're going to learn about the last of the 4 Cs—Consistency—and how this one last C helps people completely transform. We just learned how committed Claire was with her recovery, but what is important is how Consistency glues it all together. Let's read on!

5

Consistency

*"Each one of us has a fire in our heart for something.
It's our goal in life to find it and keep it lit."*

—Mary Lou Retton

Consistency is about determination. Often that determination requires hard work, but it can be profoundly satisfying in the long term. Satisfying and inspiring work as long as it's in line with your values. Again, your values determine what truly matters in life. If you value time with your family, then cooking a nice meal that everyone will enjoy, that fuels and nourishes your body, can be enduringly satisfying. It starts with that simple mindset shift, like saying no to staying late at work. Obviously, learning to cook and eventually burning the meal can be pretty frustrating, but to get to that mind shift means you have to recognize that you need to put in the time. Developing a new skill or striving to achieve a new habit can seem overwhelming, especially if your expectations are too high. Don't plan to be a Michelin Star chef, just start with the little stuff. Make the time to be at home a couple of nights a week. The key with consistency is that it starts with one small bite. What makes a person great is the little stuff, not the big stuff, but over time the little stuff allows you to make it look easy and that's great.

One example of consistency I often like to quote is a section in the bestselling book *Atomic Habits*. The author, James Clear, describes a conversation with an Olympic coach about consistency and determination. James asked the coach, "What is the difference between the best athletes and everyone else?" And the coach replied with obvious traits like genetics, luck, and talent, but surprised James by also saying that the biggest difference comes down to who consistently shows up and works through the monotony of the same training day after day. They would get up and do it again, and again, and again. They would put in the time and effort, and they had the grit.[40]

I remember telling Anita that story during one of our nutrition counseling sessions. Ironically, immediately after that session, I listened to an interview of an Olympic downhill skier describing her race. She explained how every skier before her, including herself, had fallen in the very same spot, but the difference was that she had practiced for it and was able to get up one-one-hundredth of a second faster than the silver medalist. While winning the gold may seem like an incredibly impossible feet for the average person, we don't often see or hear about the years of hard work that skier had to put in before that one point. It's a skill she had to hone over time, and it probably started when she was six years old. Changing your nutritional habits is similar. Consistency with one small thing that really matters in life allows your mind to be opened to accept the challenges and monotony of the hard work to push through, learn from your mistakes, and persevere. Consistency is therefore the glue that keeps the 4 Cs together. You'll read next how Anita persevered, as well as the other Sheroes and Heroes in this next section.

Anita
The Tortoise Keeps Winning

Anita was an athlete in high school and college. In fact, she had a full athletic scholarship for track and field, and her specialty was the decathlon. Her coaches would praise her for always showing up and giving it 110 percent, and she always pushed and persevered during the most difficult times, which paid off through several world championships, gold medals, and making the US Olympic team until she suffered several joint injuries in her senior year of college. However, Anita was also a stellar student, getting nothing but straight As, and graduated with a 4.7 GPA (crazy how GPAs can go beyond 4.0 now—signs of societal pressures for perfectionism and overachievement at all costs). Yes, she had a type-A personality and was a self-proclaimed perfectionist. Examples of this perfectionism is obvious to this point, but she also graduated from college with honors, summa cum laude, and had several job offers even before the ink was dry on her diploma. Instead of jumping into her career right away, she ended up getting her MPH (Master's in Public Health) and climbed up to a senior level management position with one of the largest nonprofit organizations in the world, helping people combat deadly diseases worldwide. Needless to say, Anita was an amazing person and was only thirty-one years old by the time we started working together.

Anita was referred to me from her OB/GYN for nutrition counseling due to a diagnosis of PCOS (polycystic ovary syndrome). PCOS occurs in about 5 percent of women of reproductive age and is characterized by large cysts that form around a women's ovaries, which can cause complications with fertilization. Symptoms of PCOS include some or all of the following: irregular menstrual cycles, excess production of the male hormone androgen, acne, rising insulin resistance, weight gain, and hair loss on the scalp. One of the most common challenges for women and PCOS is the weight gain, but this is also the most stigmatizing both onto themselves and from others, including doctors and health professional. It is commonly blamed for the development of PCOS, yet there is actually no known direct cause of PCOS.[41] However, like most women, Anita suffered through a sense of frustration, disgust, and failure that she did this to herself. That she let herself get fat and because of that she developed PCOS and is now having difficulties getting pregnant. She tried various diets in the past and like the other Sheroes and Heroes so far met the same consequences; weight cycling (multiple loss/gain); rigid and unsustainable food and diet rules of restricting and avoiding some type of nutrient or time-based restriction; social isolations or confrontations with family and friends; unsustainable fitness programs that led to more joint injuries; loss of time and money over and over again. Anita knew she needed to do something different, but there was a greater problem.

Up to this point, most of Anita's eating challenges started developing in middle school, and throughout high school she became a master at hiding them. By the time she was in college, most of her disorders started to intensify and hiding them became a little harder. She juggled between extreme restrictive behaviors and intense fitness training schedules to no fitness at all and episodes of all-night food and alcohol binges. Her eating behaviors were becoming much harder to break, and they followed her everywhere. However, Anita was always determined and devoted to anything she set her mind to, and she would find ways to conceal her eating behaviors from most people. She believed that if she would just eat "normal" (whatever that meant), that she would stop the crazy weight cycling. Her weight problems, she believed, really started to intensify after her injuries in college. She couldn't fall back on hours of training like she did prior to her injuries, and because she devoted herself to her career, life responsibilities threw a monkey wrench into her to time at the gym. Controlling her eating, therefore, was the fastest way

5: Consistency

she could change her weight, but she realized the harder she tried to lose it, the greater she gained. Anita wanted so badly to control her eating and body shape because it was the low hanging fruit, yet her emotions were really driving the challenges.

We learned earlier how Tiffany wasn't given much guidance on how to trust herself and her body. Anita's youth was not very different. How to deal with her emotional situations especially around food was also not a common parenting approach for Anita's parents. This is such an emotional awareness kryptonite. Many of us, including so many of the Sheroes and Heroes in this book, weren't trained or taught how to deal with emotional challenges very well. Anita was no different—how she felt about her body, constantly judging herself, being extremely self-critical, and looking for perfection—was something that a binge eating disorder would help her do. She could avoid feeling anxious, tired, distracted, scared, lonely, or self-loathing by numbing her pain with food. Like Catalina, there was a constant punishment of restricting and eating perfectly during the week, especially around coworkers and friends, followed by her rewards at night, on the weekends, and even with chocolate candies she hid in her desk at work. But her biggest challenge around food was being alone at night.

Awakening to Awareness

It's hard to make changes when you are so unaware that something is wrong. You could be miserable and not even realize it, or realize you're not happy but be unwilling or unaware you can change your situation. For Anita, it was about the fear of gaining weight that kept her stuck in the cycle of overeating. Give me a second to clarify something about the words overeating and bingeing. I'm going to continue using them for convenience because I know what they mean to most people, but professionally, bingeing and overeating is a very natural human phenomenon. It's the body's direct response to restriction of one type or another. One of the best examples comes from an episode on Christy

Harrison's podcast, *Food Psych*, where she interviews Evelyn Tribole, one of the co-authors of the book *Intuitive Eating*, which I've cited on several occasions throughout this book. Evelyn compares food bingeing to diving into crashing waves at the beach, taking a deep breath of air, and having to hold it until you can come back up. But you realize that there's another wave crashed right behind the first one, and you have to hold your breath a little longer. When you finally come up for air, what do you do? Yes, you take a huge gulp of air. However, you don't say you just binged on air. You don't feel embarrassed or guilty that you did. Of course not! This is a natural human function. Your body's response to gulping air is directly related to the restriction (holding your breath under water) of air. So, we really don't overeat or binge. What we do is respond to our body's physical and emotional cues to get in as much food as possible because there is a common, but extremely serious threat of starvation. I often remind people that the single biggest predictor of overeating is directly linked to restricting or avoiding food.

Anita needed to become aware of what was going on, and when she did. We started working simply on paying attention. Looking for patterns in her day and discussing what they were. For instance, she paid attention to how an email from her boss could just set her off. She would often react by fixing the problem, which would often mean Anita would avoid eating yet snack on her chocolates in her drawer. She started realizing that she would sneak the chocolate, and once she started, she made sure to avoid letting people see her. She would skip lunch, partly because she didn't often feel hungry, which made sense since she was snacking all the time. Slowly, Anita started seeing more examples like this throughout the day. As such, she was determined now to start working on her eating patterns right away. She was ready and committed because she was finally aware and accepted she needed help. This is an important first step in the self-care process. I like the explanation that Dr. Jonice Webb gives. There are four major ways necessary to taking care of yourself:

1. **Nurturing Yourself**—putting yourself first, eating meals that satisfy you, exercising, and resting and relaxing
2. **Improving Self-Discipline**—learning and developing the skills to regulate and manage your behaviors through a nurturing and supportive approach
3. **Self-Soothing**—implementing methods to help you soothe during difficult emotional situations instead of reacting and defaulting to old habits
4. **Self-Compassion**—well, we talked quite a bit about this one, but I like the way Dr. Webb puts it: "It is best developed from the inside out."[42]

Anita consistently showed up to our nutrition sessions; she made the effort to do the hard work and rumble with her vulnerability. Without fail, her fear of weight gain was always there, but now she was more aware of her body's needs. She was aware of how her eating patterns and control issues made things worse. Unfortunately, these fears and control issues were only amplified by the typical treatment approaches for PCOS. She was told she had to restrict her carbohydrates. Much like a person with diabetes, she had to follow a low-carb diet, but this always frustrated her and made her feel worse because she had tried low-carb diets numerous times. In other words, she felt like a failure or like something was wrong with her. It was so othering, and blame seemed to be squarely on her.

There is no known cause for PCOS. This carbohydrate-restrictive approach, while seemingly make sense since PCOS has similarities to diabetes, was only intensifying Anita's need to binge. Thus, she had challenges admitting she had a problem. She hid it well, but at least now she consistently showed up to confront her fears instead of running toward a diet. She was now more aware of what was going on and committed to changing. Just asking for help was a massive challenge for her. It wasn't easy. It was challenging to admit her condition to her family, friends, and people close to her. She had to tell her partner, which she thought was worst of all. Anita was a people pleaser and her partner just thought

Anita was a super-woman. In fact, many of Anita's bingeing episodes actually happened at night and during the evenings. There were various lunch and dinner events throughout the day, several days a week. Her company required that she take her clients out for meals all the time, especially on business trips. She had tried so hard to hide her bingeing.

In fact, Anita realized that she often felt like she had a superpower back then. She received numerous compliments about her work ethic and about her body. How she could eat anything and not gain a single pound. Moreover, the women in her office were often so jealous of her beautiful figure, but secretly Anita was in denial. She believed she needed those compliments to justify her behaviors, and it allowed her to believe it was all worth the effort and danger. Finally, she realized how misguided these beliefs were. At first it was an awareness of her eating patterns and how that affected her mood, and then it was how her eating patterns reflected mood. It was a back-and-forth challenge that back then she wasn't even aware was going on. This time it was different. We discussed that while these compliments may seem positive, the problem was they implied a certain level of expectation of how Anita saw herself. However, she suffered in silence. She experienced extreme bouts of depression and chronically overate to then deal with intense levels of anxiety, and then she engaged in rigid diets all over again.

Her therapist helped a great deal here. Working with both of us, Anita started to realize that the more she engaged in her behaviors, the more she felt like a fake, like an imposter. At times it was difficult for her to go over a food journal because she felt so horrible about herself restricting and avoiding food all day long so she wouldn't be tempted to binge. But then she would feel so hungry and exhausted that she couldn't wait to get in her car to snack or overeat after her partner was asleep, which was so much easier to do because she was finally alone. Anita was going through these cycles of reward and punishment. The tipping point came with a visit to the ER and her near-death experience. She had enough. She enrolled into the treatment program. Even while she was in the residential program, her desires to binge were still loud and present, but she wasn't exposed to her daily triggers. In the program, she didn't have to prove herself to anyone other than proving that she was working on getting better. Regardless of the behavior, immediately after each episode, she finally realized how the intense level of emotion couldn't be sustained. She was determined to turn it around this time despite the difficulties she knew were evident.

Moving Forward

Anita was diagnosed with Binge Eating Disorder, and even after working through all the awareness and counseling with her therapist, she finally accepted she needed a higher level of care. In most instances, Binge Eating Disorder is not viewed as an eating disorder because often people don't present with the distorted perception of an emaciated white young college age woman. Anita presented with very challenging body image issues, and over time her work began to suffer. Her disorder started to impede her daily living, her productivity at work, and her schedule. She was often in therapy, nutrition, and digestive health appointments with her gastroenterologist (GI, for short going forward). Despite all these challenges, Anita wasn't going to give up. She finally realized that her situation was taking over her life, and she signed up for treatment.

Unfortunately, Anita ended up having to take a few weeks off work, but it was by far the best decision she could have made. She really needed the higher level of support and work. She progressed through the six-week residential program very nicely, partly because she was committed to getting better. She then moved down to a partial residential program called PHP, and then later down to an out-patient type program called IOP, where she was back home but attending sessions, groups, and meal events with the program about three days a week. Once she was discharged, we started working again. After that initial start, she had multiple slips and relapses, although major progress and improvements allowed her to work through most of her challenges. In the earlier sessions with me, she came dressed in black or gray, hair always in a ponytail, and never any makeup.

She was often reserved and tired, like she'd been up all night. She often had high anxiety, but it would be worse when she forgot to take her medication. We would work on mindful eating exercises, deconstructing her eating, building the right meal plans, and creating a structured routine to help her body fuel. This helped her maintain her energy levels, focus, and avoid the dips in energy that could lead to more bingeing. We tried to find foods that would make her feel satisfied and help her learn what satisfaction felt like. She challenged herself with certain trigger foods, like chips, cupcakes, cookies, and soda. And she would work hard at making peace with those trigger foods. Some days she just hated the work and would often be upset with me, but she was committed. More importantly, she was consistent. Even when the journey was tough or she stumbled and fell, she was the Tortoise no matter how hard things got. She discovered all over again how her athletic years, her determination and dedication to herself, but this time for all the right reasons, were going to help her. She had that grit and determination, and consistency was her middle name.

Slowly, Anita started to feel better. She wouldn't cry as often in our sessions when discussing her old urges to binge, but instead she would just be with the feeling and recognizing that urge for what it was— nothing more than an old habit and the body's signal that she wasn't fueling efficiently. She discovered how powerful it was to be with the emotion. In the past, she just wouldn't be able to do that. She wanted to escape and restrict or avoid food, and then it would snowball from there. Anita became her mind's observer. It was a vicious cycle that her past narratives would lead her on the path of restricting, avoiding, bingeing, and then having intense feelings of guilt; and then repeating it over and over. She honed her coping and mindfulness skills, and really focused on eating enough. That was her one small bite! She tried hard to not skip meals, have backup plans, take breaks, and make sure she built more self-kindness. The key was to eat, ironically as it might seem.

During one of her sessions, Anita described that now, after treatment, she felt like she was seeing someone that wasn't there but was trying to help her. Much like the character John Nash in the movie

5: Consistency

A Beautiful Mind. It's the scene right before the famous "pen ceremony" scene toward the end of the movie. This is when John Nash was about to be told he was going to win the Nobel Prize in economics. They show a new character walking to Dr. Nash's classroom who stood outside and waited for Dr. Nash as students were exiting the class. *Spoiler alert!* Dr. Nash suffered from schizophrenia, hearing voices, and seeing people that didn't really exist. When the new gentleman calls out to talk to Dr. Nash, he at first ignores him. As the students are exiting the classroom, he manages to pull out two students, and asks them to confirm that indeed there is a real live person standing next to him. The two students look at each other in bewilderment, as though Dr. Nash is crazy. But they confirm that, in fact, there is a gentleman standing there and asking to speak with him. At which point Dr. Nash finally acknowledges the new person and then they walk to the famous pen ceremony scene.[43]

Anita explained how that's what her recovery felt like. Her urges and desires to binge were like a voice or person that she knew was still there, but she found ways to realize that those old narratives do not define her. They are not really her, and she is able to recognize them.

She told me, "Well, that's what it felt like to be my mind's observer. All the work from treatment and our sessions together has helped me become aware of my old narratives. Like I've had this alter ego that would keep me locked in the past: The world of restricting and bingeing and repeat. It was as if my mind was changed, and more importantly you worked with me to keep focusing on the meals. Get the energy!"

This is a great opportunity to drop another *Star Wars* movie reference. "Well, that's just the kind of Jedi mind trick I play on all of my clients." And she laughed because she, too, was a huge *Star Wars* fan, which I found interesting since that can be rare for some millennials. Yes, the Force was finally with her *(wink, wink)*, helping her build the ability to be mindful and be one with the Force. *(Sorry, I just can't help it!)*

While all this was challenging for Anita, one small bite that worked for her was having regular meals. Yes, she had Plan A, but we also worked on Plan B; a meal plan is only as good as how flexible she is. People really don't walk around with a meal plan in their back pocket. She found that while it was difficult to work on just changing her binges, having regular meals really helped to enhance her mood and her energy. Sticking with this one small change wasn't easy, but she noticed that if she didn't keep this routine (if she skipped meals), she was more likely to binge. She realized that having meals throughout the day stimulated and maintained her metabolism; it helped her avoid the restricting; it helped her be more focused; and eating regular meals allowed her to be more aware of her old and—more important—her new self-narratives.

We experimented with various meal options, but the focus was on what would satisfy her. The single biggest goal she maintained was don't sacrifice her hunger because it's not the "right" food. Sometimes she would try eggs with and without bread with a side of fruit for breakfast, and that would really satisfy her. But there were days she just wanted toasted frozen waffles with butter, sliced strawberries, and whipped cream on top. It was quick, easy, and it reminded her of breakfast when she was a little girl. Satisfaction isn't about only getting a balance of all food groups in each meal—yes, that's helpful—but satisfaction is also enjoying foods that made her feel good. Remember, if she tried to avoid any food, it could easily trigger her old restriction habits, which in turn, amplify her bingeing urges for those foods later anyway. Initially she complained about eating so often and resisted it, saying that it was too much food. She was afraid of gaining weight, but she also knew that her weight wasn't a determinant of her self-worth, and not even her health. It was difficult to maintain her meal plan, but over time she appreciated how much better she felt long term.

And then one day Anita came in for her regular session, and it was as if there had been a metamorphosis. She was alive! Her hair was loose and styled, not in her typical ponytail. She was wearing a colorful new dress and had put on makeup, and she was excited. Anita started to tell me that she felt amazing. It was as if a dark cloud had finally lifted from her mind, like the weight of the world was gone. She felt liberated.

5: Consistency

I asked her how she thought it happened, and she simply said, "David, what I finally realized was that I just needed to keep at it. This is my new reality. I wasn't defining myself by my past or future me. I was being the person I wanted to be in the present." It was as if the old Anita never existed. Then she reminded me of that story about John Nash. "Oh, the old Anita is there, but now I see her clearly and keenly, knowing when that altered ego narrative tries to creep in. It is empowering to finally be able to be present with those old feelings and thoughts. Now I know I'm more than that. To be able to discern the difference and be the woman I want to be."

Anita kept at it! She worked on various mindful eating exercises, deconstructing her emotions around eating and her body image. She also worked on her meal plan, sticking with it to avoid waves of hunger that might increase the likelihood of her bingeing and letting her emotions run wild. We often discussed problems at work, and then circled back to her eating and how the stresses at work would trigger her. At home, she was often alone because her partner traveled quite a bit, so nighttime was tough, but she had honed those new skills. She learned various coping strategies to deal with her urges at night. And she even started forcing herself to stay at a friend's apartment every so often. Some days Anita continues to struggle, but now she welcomes the struggle. The main thing was she just kept at it.

Interlude
Consistency

> "It's not what we do once in a while that shapes our lives. It's what we do consistently."
>
> —Anthony Robbins

Change is about doing something new; it's about moving forward and being receptive to the opportunities that life provides us, if we are open and able to accept those opportunities. Better yet, forward momentum means letting go of the fear of doing something new no matter how much it may scare us. F.E.A.R. You remember what it stands for: *False Expectations Appearing Real.*

Fear is an emotion created by our minds about the possible expectations of what might happen, yet fear is important for a variety of reasons. Our reptilian brain uses fear to warn us of potential starvation or a potential threat from a predator. We learned to fear certain types of foods because they might be poisonous. We developed the ability to taste chemicals and textures in our mouths. This is important because any funny- or slimy-tasting food can mean a food is spoiled or poisoned. And, of course, the human brain developed the limbic and neocortex, or the emotional and executive functioning brain. Therefore, we learned to discern food to be sour, bitter, or spicy, which means that it isn't necessarily a bad thing, but could be informing us that the food may not be ripe, or may not be healthy for us, or we learn to adapt and acquire taste.

What is interesting, though, is that fear is based on past experiences, and eating is just that—a collection of eating experiences that help inform our brain what something might taste or feel like. Take for example the first time you eat a new food. You have no idea what it might taste like, so you probably won't salivate and nor display many familiar feelings toward it other than you might be scared because the last time you tried something new it tasted horrible. In actuality, you probably have no understanding of what to expect. Eventually, you will either learn to enjoy it or be stuck disliking it due to a bad experience.

A good explanation of these psychological food phenomena comes from Paul Rozin, professor of psychology at the University of Pennsylvania. He has researched the psychological and emotional connection to food experiences and cultural belief differences around the world for over twenty-five years. In an interview with Shankar Vedantam from the podcast and radio show *Hidden Brain*, he explains how children in Mexico or India learn to eat very spicy food—food that I know my daughter would probably spit out in an instant and then turn to a fire hose to cool her tongue. Dr. Rozin explains that eating is dependent on societal norms and customs. We learn to adapt and acquire taste over time, and that collective adaptation is key to understanding the basic intuition to eating that we are all born with. He states:

> "The brain compensates for all sorts of things. We adapt to things. And this is a case of more than adaptation where you're turning something that's negative into something positive. I mean, to me, that's an amazing thing, that we can start with something that's innately negative and make it really positive. . . . And what I realized is that it's a miracle that takes place in humans all over the world, not just about hot pepper. It's also about liking coffee, which is bitter, and people don't like it originally—and they like it."[44]

Social norms like diets cause people to ignore their body's natural physiological signals to eat when you are hungry or stop when you are full. Obviously, eating is necessary, but what we choose to eat is an experiential act. What we've experienced in the past informs our present, or our mind at least is trying to prepare us for what something used to taste

5: Consistency

like and what we experienced the last time we had it. Our experiences are, therefore, a defensive mechanism of our prehistoric ancestors developed to protect us from danger. The problem today is if we don't try new foods because of a bad experience, our minds then fill in the gap, and then we're left with a poor variety of foods to choose from.

Next, you'll read how our next Hero, Joel, discovered how past experiences were holding him back.

Joel

Heading toward Scary Foods

Joel is thirty-nine years old, divorced, and worked as managing supervisor for a large fulfillment warehouse company for over twelve years. Joel was a picky eater growing up. As a kid and young adult, Joel had bad experiences with food and eating. His mother, when she was home, wasn't a good cook and mostly had frozen or canned meals for them to eat. As early as eight years of age, Joel would often fend for himself, eat alone, eat the same foods most days, and never be exposed to fresh fruit and vegetables, other than maybe tomatoes and lettuce on a burger or fruit in a can from time to time.

Joel also developed unfortunate beliefs about his mother as well. To Joel, his mother just didn't seem to care about him, but that was far from the truth. She had two jobs, was a single parent with no college education, and dealt with her own emotional demons. Joel was often left at home with his grandmother, Nana, whom he loved very much. Nana cared for Joel, helped raise him, and showed him the affection his mother lacked. Joel's mother just wasn't around much. Joel didn't know his father, and he often had to deal with his mother's dysfunctional boyfriends and all their various food rules; many would tell him that he had to eat his mushy veggies and lots of meat if he wanted to get strong. To make matters worse, Nana suffered from lung cancer from years of smoking, and Joel remembers the images of what looked like rotting food next to her bedside. These images were burned into his mind of his dying grandmother, and those food images only exacerbated his fears. Again, *false expectations or images appearing real*. At Joel's young age, he just didn't understand that the food she had to eat had to be soft and easy to digest because his grandmother had a hard time chewing, digesting food, and keeping it down due to the bouts of chemo and radiation therapy. Still, the damage was done.

As an adult, Joel would stick to the same foods most days and, in fact, he was known at work to be *the routine man*. He wouldn't touch spinach or leafy greens because they were too slimy. For a while, he thought he was allergic to fish and said he disliked the fishy smell, but he had no problem with fried fish sandwiches from fast food. He would only eat foods he was familiar with or knew were pretty safe (sandwiches, burgers, pizza, fast food, and, his favorite, fried chicken tenders).

Over several years, he became pickier and pickier about his food choices. His pickiness would often be the catalysts of some of the biggest fights with his ex-wife. It was one of those recurring arguments that killed their relationship. He never realized at the time, but there were multiple emotional layers and meanings behind the arguments (like the inability to trust, his fear of abandonment, his fear of food, and a very introverted personality). As a result, Joel would just immerse himself further into work, putting in longer hours and working weekends, mostly to avoid his fears. He would stonewall his wife, but more importantly, he was stonewalling himself. He wasn't confronting his demons, which drove a wedge in any relationship, including his relationship with food.

Joel was also pretty intense in his behaviors. Let me explain: he woke up every weekday around 4:30 a.m. and started work between 5:45 and 6:00 a.m. Most days he worked eleven to thirteen hours, and even put in five to six hours on weekends for overtime. While the job was difficult, he maintained minimal interaction with people, which helped him get things done since he was such an introvert anyway. At work, he was a star! He worked with the same company for over twelve years; he started as a picker and sorter and worked hard to climb up to his present position as managing supervisor. He was devoted to his job, but it also took a toll on him. He was absent from his family since he would spend most of his days, including weekends, at work and not at home. Ironically, he was just as regimented with his diet, which wasn't

5: Consistency

much of a stretch since he was so picky with food anyway. He followed a regimented approach to eating and rarely deviated from the same foods week after week.

He brought his four-day food journal to his appointment, and we reviewed it together.

> 6:15 a.m.—one 24-ounce coffee tumbler with half-and-half and about 1 tablespoon of sugar

> 9:30 a.m.—one 2.5 cups bowl of Honey Nut Cheerios with 2% milk (at his computer)

> 12:30 p.m.—two ham and cheese sandwiches on honey whole wheat bread with mayo and one 12-ounce can of diet soda

> 3:15 p.m.—another 12-ounce can of diet soda

> 7:30–8:30 p.m.—five or six fried chicken tenders, honey, a side of mashed potatoes, and another 12-ounce diet soda

Joel also mentioned that from time to time he would have pizza for dinner or lunch, but only if it came from his favorite pizzeria. The only fruit he liked were bananas and sometimes the fruit in those plastic cups from the grocery store, but he did say he would be open to trying apples. Joel was definitely a man of routine and traditions. He would eat at the same time almost every day, watch the same shows on TV, and hang out at the same local bar or restaurant one or two Fridays a month. His four-day journal looked like he just copied each day, but with his stoic demeanor during the session and his picky eating, I quickly realized it was his actual routine. Joel didn't have many friends, and his ex-wife and teenage daughter didn't talk to him much. He was pretty much devoted to his work, and he was terrified of change, but you wouldn't know it. Like many of the Sheroes and Heroes in this book, Joel was intense, and there was a lot of hypermasculinity façade. His picky eating seemed to be a method of control. His deep-seated fear of food seemed like years of unresolved trauma. That egg was going to be hard to crack.

Change is difficult for many of us. Unpredictability, the lack of controlling an outcome, perfectionism, or an expected threat can drive our primal instincts—flight, fight, and freeze—to go into overdrive. Our reptilian brain again kicks into overdrive: a systematic release of stress hormones that turn certain bodily functions on or off; our blood pressure rises, our heart rate increases, our digestive system is turned down, and we become hypersensitive and focused on the imminent threat, which is often a perception and not a reality. Often, these primal reactions are created in our heads from past experiences and are then wired into our self-narrative. This self-narration blocks our minds from being open and prevents us from moving forward.

Joel's fear of mushy food, images of his dying grandmother, and separation anxiety were all perceptions that echoed and repeated the same fear-based or negative narrations in his mind. Joel really didn't know anything different; he was so accustomed to his routine that they were self-identifying his personality. They were familiar to him, and to him it was just who he was. But he knew he was miserable—he just didn't realize food was at the core. He didn't have anyone to talk to, partly because he alienated so many people throughout his life due to challenges with managing his emotions. He was also afraid of reaching out to anyone because of the fear of rejection. He had a similar personality type mentioned previously—alexithymic. This type of person is also described well in Dr. Jonice Webb's book: "Alexithymia denotes a person's deficiency in, knowledge about, and awareness of emotion. In its extreme form, the alexithymic is a person from whom feelings are indecipherable, both their own and other people's. The alexithymic lives his life with no willingness or ability to tolerate, or even experience, emotions."[45] Change was extremely challenging for Joel because it required confronting his emotions, and that was so foreign to him. Yet, he knew something had to change.

Awakening the Conscious Eater

The straw that finally broke the camel's back came one day when his company established a new corporate wellness program. They required a yearly employee health and biomedical screening of every employee. Since he was such the company man, he just kept his head down and complied with the health screenings without hesitation. During the screening, the nurse provided his results and told him that his cholesterol and blood pressure were both pretty high, and that his blood sugar was slightly elevated. It hit him pretty hard, but not just because he feared dying; he was quite embarrassed. Ironically, what scared him the most was the fact that so many people were in the room hearing the same thing.

He wanted to get confirmation, so the nurse recommended he see his primary care physician. The last time he went to the doctor was about five years ago when he broke a finger after a crate fell on his hand, and he had actually gone to the ER. Prior to that, he never went to a regular physical in his life. Similarly to Nathaniel, Joel demonstrated classical male hypermasculine traits such as alexithymia, rigid food and diet rules, difficulty with social interactions, and strong anger issues. In my experience, food challenges with men tend to be about extremes. For Joel, that meant not deviating from his routine, and for other men, like Jeff for instance, it means the need for intense flavors and portions. It helps us men feel manly, or at least what society implies is manly.

Surprisingly to hear, Joel gave me the analogy of cracks in the dam: "This whole biomedical and health screening at work is just like that story of the boy sticking his finger in the hole of the dam. It was just one tiny little crack in the dam and people would ignore it. Then one day there were several little cracks everywhere, and water was leaking everywhere. The dam was going to break. My life was like that dam; cracks everywhere and the cumulative effect is ultimate failure. I was trying to hold it deep inside, but it was going to bust through. And worst of all was that I was completely ashamed about it." The years of plugging up holes, not confronting his fears, and being stuck in the same routine was leading to health cracks. On the other hand, Joel was willing to make some of the changes, even though he was hit with this devastating news. But it wasn't because he was afraid of having high blood pressure or developing diabetes; it was deeper than that. Just like Jeff and Nathaniel, the only way Joel finally listened to his body was through a traumatic event. Another example of extreme expectations of what it means to be a man in our society. Still, he was listening now!

While fear can be a motivator that sparks people into action and has the potential to change a person's life, I often find that it is not an enduring motivator. Yes, Joel was listening now, but it's important to be careful that more extreme situations only lead to similar reactions of more pickiness or overeating. This concept is similar to external controlled motivation outlined through the Self-Determination Theory (SDT) below:

> "The most central distinction in SDT is between autonomous motivation and controlled motivation. Autonomous motivation comprises both intrinsic motivation and the types of extrinsic motivation in which people have identified with an activity's value and ideally will have integrated it into their sense of self. When people are autonomously motivated, they experience volition, or a self-endorsement of their actions. Controlled motivation, in contrast, consists of both external regulation, in which one's behavior is a function of external contingencies of reward or punishment, and introjected regulation, in which the regulation of action has been partially internalized and is energized by factors such as an approval motive, avoidance of shame, contingent self-esteem, and ego-involvements. When people are controlled, they experience pressure to think, feel, or behave in particular ways. Both autonomous and controlled motivation energize and direct behavior, and they stand in contrast to amotivation, which refers to a lack of intention and motivation."[46]

5: Consistency

Suffice to say, Joel had to have the extrinsic motivator, the health screening, and tough news that his health was at jeopardy as an initial motivator to prompt change. Although Joel was externally motivated by negative consequences to get healthier, it nonetheless served to get things started for him. He realized that there were deeper emotional issues that needed to be explored and solved. Joel didn't quite understand what his picky eating signified, but his mind started to open. The strong need to control his eating and the connection to his separation anxiety were obstacles now being challenged by extrinsic forces. He knew he had to change something.

Initially, I used to think these health screenings and corporate wellness programs were so helpful: a key method in the prevention of chronic diseases. In fact, early in my career, I contracted with various worksite wellness programs and delivered many myself. Yes, I used to drink from the same punch bowl and provided those very weight-loss programs and pushed diet-culture messaging. Over time I observed that the human resources directors were often pressured from the company brass to deliver better results from these programs. They wanted more fitness competitions, more diet plans, cooking demonstrations, weight-loss ideas, health and wellness newsletters, or any trick or tip that would force employees into shape. This was called engagement, but it was only a form of healthism at best. Healthism, in case you are wondering, is this cultural belief that people must attain this ideal of health—a person that on the exterior looks thin, has perfect biomedical laboratory values, is physically fit or athletic, and is without any health issues; an Adonis; a perfect human being. Yeah, the problem is that just doesn't exist. Healthism is a way of controlling people. It puts the blame solely on the individual for not achieving an impossible ideal image of a health. Companies weren't seeing the health changes in their employees because the expectation of health was so skewed, unrealistic, and unsustainable (yet again, examples from my list of why diets don't work). The problem was that with all the best intentions, these programs only perpetuated the same diet and shame culture messages found in other areas of our society. In my experience, these programs never brought the supposed ROI (return on investments) that many companies wished for, despite all the good intentions or the one-offs like with Joel. Let me add that I'm all for enhanced worksite wellness programs, but they need to be completely voluntary and separate from the company workplace (more on this in a minute).

With that said, I'm not a fan of biomedical screenings or wellness programs at the workplace. I realized that these screenings alone were riddled with shame and embarrassment. Unfortunately, what I saw in these programs were employees subjected to embarrassing medical screening processes that were rarely private. These screenings place employees in such a predicament because they tend to offer large financial incentives tied to the cost of their health benefits. In other words, an employee is essentially financially charged for having high blood pressure, diabetes, or being in a larger body. Furthermore, these screenings would often be held in large rooms with minimal, if at all, private stations. Screeners would check weight, height, waist circumference, and blood pressure and either do a finger blood prick or a venous blood draw, all while dozens of people were in the same room. It's like doing your yearly physical but instead of in the privacy of your physician's practice, it would often be in a company auditorium, conference room, or large open space packed with people. These types of programs are the epitome of shame culture, this sense of healthism that other people into hierarchal systems. Employees are incentivized to attend, and if their results are "poor" or viewed as a higher health risk, they are then incentivized to take part in wellness programs like fitness challenges, weight-loss programs, nutrition education, or diet programs that further others or isolates people. Again, a method of placing blame and the responsibility of health solely on the employee. These screenings are a form of shame that induces more intense levels of stress, not just to the employees subjected to these programs but also to the human resource directors or program coordinators that have to provide them. We know from Brené Brown's research how shaming people into change has a dangerous and negative long-term effect.

In my experience, we cannot continue to put the blame of chronic illnesses solely on the individual. I need to be clear, I strongly believe we should provide programs and systems that help employees maintain their health, but embarrassing someone like Joel, without understanding the history of emotional challenges, is only an external short-term motivation that will not endure. Yes, Joel was motivated to get help, but he faced embarrassing screenings, felt shamed into getting healthier, and was pushed into more emotional challenges. He had to go through various practitioners before working with us, and he refused to engage in any of the programs at work. While he was a company man and followed all the rules, he didn't like having all his private health information displayed in front of coworkers and company executives.

Worksite wellness programs need to be voluntary. Yes, there should be fun fitness programs, but they should be kept simple like walking groups, or simply taking more breaks throughout the day. Companies can offer more mindful and emotion-based programs like meditation or break rooms, onsite counselors and life coaches, or access to and lists of therapists or psychologists to help with mental challenges. I have a small company, so I understand the enormous financial challenges of just offering health insurance, therefore I advocate for stronger government support for small business in healthcare options. I support more flexible work schedules and various options for telecommuting or teleworking. I think it's great if a company can afford to offer membership discounts for gym or fitness centers, particularly to those with a weight-inclusive and body positive or body neutral focus. I think health insurance should include more than just one free medical physical screening a year, there should be no copays or deductibles when possible, and access to discounted medications. I also feel that wellness programs should be extended to offer more family leave options. But I understand how challenging this can be for small business. Without a doubt, health is a social justice endeavor that requires various private and public sectors to coordinate, but suffice to say that shame-based wellness programs are not the end-all-be-all, and certainly not a long-term solution to enhancing the health and well-being of individuals.

Forward Momentum

Nonetheless, Joel was motivated. He started working on changing his health, and thought it was extremely important, but he wanted to do it his own way and not through his company's wellness programs. He worked with a few physicians at first, but he quickly experienced long waitlists for appointments, as well as short ten-minute doctor visits, who would often just spit out recommendations to change his diet and exercise and just prescribed medications that were often not cheap because of the copays. No one asked about his life situations; no one paid attention to his emotional or family challenges. Like so many, he started to distrust the system. That initial fear and shame-based external motivator slowly started to wear off. He started to ignore his health again, didn't change his diet, and blamed the system for pushing pills instead of supporting and guiding him. Empathy and understanding were dead in his mind. It took another two years or so before he decided to find help again. This time, he found a physician that would listen, one who took twenty-five minutes with him and just paid attention. She asked many questions and just let him talk. She recommended a healthcare team that consisted of her as the gatekeeper, a dietitian for his nutrition, a therapist for mental health, a physical therapist to help with joint issues, a sleep specialist to help with sleep concerns, and a social worker on staff to help coordinate and find practitioners that were all covered by his insurance.

Joel was one of the lucky ones because his company health insurance was pretty good. I often think of all the people who struggle with adequate health coverage.

When Joel and I started working, he had difficulties trying new foods, but he explored and worked with me. I listened and asked a lot

5: Consistency

of questions, and he was actually OK trying meatless dinners once or twice a week. It was slow going at first, but his mind opened up. He was driving his own change; I was just his copilot. The meatless nights soon encouraged him try new foods, to think outside the box. He was free to make his own choices, and at first it was simply rice and beans for dinner. After a while, he was preparing meatless tacos, and he even made a few bean-based slow cooker meals. He impressed himself. Although it was a bit challenging at first, he found an internal motivator.

At first Joel was quite resistant to change. It felt quite scary. He often fell back on old habits and reverted to his standard dinners, but he knew he had to work at it. He realized the positive intrinsic momentum building. It was a faint realization at first, but it was there. He was surprised to enjoy other food groups beyond his typical routine, and he observed and was pleased with how they made him feel. For example, he started experimenting with a variety of nuts with his cereal in the morning; he tried nut butters for sandwiches; he even started learning to sauté a few veggies to combine with his meat and potato dinners some nights. One night he even made a Thai curry shrimp bowl with cashews—OK, it was really one of those premade freeze-dried meals that required water, but what a change! At one of his appointments, he was so excited about the Thai curry shrimp bowl that he actually started tearing up. He explained how the big fight with his ex-wife that led to their eventual divorce started because he didn't want to eat shrimp. The shrimp was actually a representation of his emotional isolation and fear of intimate connection. It was like a flood of emotions trapped by the years of control and fear of letting go were finally coming out.

Routine is both a blessing and a curse. Doing the same thing over and over again is helpful in getting things done and being efficient, unless of course that routine is keeping us stuck in the perpetual loop of old habits or the fear of old experiences. Russ Harris explains this in the chapter called "Demons on the Boat."[47] We make a deal with the demons to drift aimlessly out in the ocean and never head to shore, and they promise to stay below the deck. However, if we head toward the shore (in this case, Joel trying different foods), they'll come out and threaten us with their fangs, claws, and creepy demonic figures. But we get bored, tired, lonely, miserable, and more anxious when we depart from our established routines if we don't confront those demons and deal with them directly. In Joel's case, he had reverted to his habits; instead of confronting the demons, he avoided talking to his wife and daughter. This caused deep wedges and further separation with them. The decision to stick with his way of eating was only one manifestation of his fears that were ingrained in him from an early age. Change was, therefore, one of the single biggest challenges for him, yet he needed to finally head toward that shore to realized there were no real demons. Drifting aimlessly out in the ocean, doing the same things repeatedly was not getting him closer to improving his health. Joel was not able to experience the spiciness of peppers, the mushiness of purees, and the sliminess of okra to live because his deep-seated fears were never challenged.

Doing something new or different requires learning something new. It requires slowing down, being curious, having self-compassion, and learning how to navigate obstacles and barriers to what we don't know. It takes courage to do this. There is no order or hierarchy in how we let go of our past, move forward, and find that one small change. Change comes through different channels for each of us, including Joel. However, once we start moving forward, we build momentum. We start with small changes that add up. Those small changes start to become familiar, and our brains learn to adapt and build muscle memory. There is a cumulative effect; it gets easier, and that's exactly what happened with Joel. He started with small bites, small changes, that then started to add up.

Joel felt lighter, his clothes fit better, he was thinking clearer and more aware, and his focus was on his mood and his energy level. It was as if a cloud had lifted from his head, and he could finally notice old habits that were keeping him stuck. For instance, he noticed that his typical midday coffee break was his body's method of letting him know his energy level and mood were low. Joel saw how important it was to

5: Consistency

talk to people, communicate more, and open up about his feelings, and he worked a lot with his therapist to enhance his awareness. Although it wasn't easy, he started to find people he could talk to. He called his daughter more often and even spent a few weekends a month with her. Joel also decided to get a new follow-up physical and saw his blood sugar and cholesterol improved. More importantly, Joel was a new man. He felt more confident, started to open up more, and even had a better relationship with his ex-wife and daughter. He wanted to be around and enjoy his daughter a little longer.

The changes Joel made came in waves. It wasn't easy. He simply started with one small bite, to have a meatless meal every Monday, yet every so often would revert back to old habits. We worked at avoiding diets or food rules that that limited his mind. Over time, Joel became more confident and more open to change. He was starting to enjoy his life a little more and enjoy new foods, and he was listening to his body. Some days he would enjoy steak and potatoes, and other days he explored tofu. OK, that really took a lot more time, but he really found a routine that worked for him. He was more pleasant at work with his fellow coworkers, and he started to cut back on the long workdays, yet he was still more productive. Interestingly, he never joined any of the worksite programs offered at work. He didn't like the lack of privacy, and since he was a bit more to himself, he would much rather work with his therapist and me.

As far as his picky eating, it took quite some time, but that started to improve considerably. He discovered more plant-based meals but never gave up meat all together. This was important because he wanted autonomy to choose his own way of eating. He was eating more in line with what he valued this way. Here's an example of his new typical eating style:

> Breakfast—A bowl of Cheerios with 2% milk, but now he started adding some mixed berries and mixed nuts; he still enjoyed his 12-ounce coffee with half-and-half (no sugar).

Lunch—He'd often bring his typical ham and cheese sandwich and chips, but now he has an apple or pear, and he started giving up his diet sodas for the 24-ounce water bottle he keeps with him and fills up a couple of times a day.

Snack—He was already snacking, but he'd experiment with a fruit and peanut butter or cheese to help mix it up. He also started having a can of carbonated flavored water or every once in a while his diet soda, but it was much less frequent.

Dinner—Meatless Meal—stir-fry: broccoli, red and green peppers, green beans, shredded carrots, and mushrooms, edamame (soybeans), and a good serving of rice, with a delicious Asian peanut sauce

The one small bite was challenging himself to have a meatless dinner at least once a week. He kept a simple grid in a small notebook and put a checkmark each time he had a meatless meal. He would even check off when he had a new fruit or veggie. Surprisingly, his curiosity opened his mind to exploring other changes. For instance, he experimented with other beverages, or just water instead of soda a few days a week. In fact, he found that relatively easier to stick with than he thought. He started adding a few more nuts, especially at breakfast and for snacks instead of chips. He was eating out less, which helped him save money. From the money he saved, he bought his daughter a new computer. Joel even decided to take a few cooking classes. And best of all, he made just a few small changes to his diet, not because he was afraid of getting diabetes or having a heart problem but because he had a mind shift. The motivation was no longer about avoiding diabetes or high blood pressure, it was reconnecting with his daughter. Little by little, he noticed how closer they became. She enjoyed learning to cook with him, and it gave him precious time with her again. The motivation was internal now.

You might be thinking: "You see, David, those biomedical screenings and corporate wellness programs do work. Joel was able to change

5: Consistency

his life around." I don't disagree. Shaming Joel into a health screening might have initially motivated him to change, but what truly affected him—what truly scared him—was the fear of dying alone. Of being lonely. Of losing the connection with his daughter and living his life fully. And those connections were deeply personal, intrinsic motivators.

He didn't want the same fate for his daughter either—he didn't want his daughter left with no connection to a father. For so many years, Joel was disconnected from his emotions. No one ever taught him how to recognize his feelings and what they meant. Joel still enjoys pizza and chicken wings. He still enjoys an occasional beer with friends at a pub. But now he also enjoys a new world of hiking, camping, and grilling out with his daughter. Joel still deals with some of his old picky eating challenges—he has difficulties eating enough veggies—but his transformation was epic. Yet it came slowly. This transformation took about four and a half years, and it wasn't a straight line either. There were months where he didn't attend sessions with his therapist or me, and just went back to his old ways. There were medication changes and challenges with his schedule at work. There were financial challenges that kept him from going grocery shopping, and sometimes he just wanted to give up. The key was that he kept at it. He now had a light that shined toward true connection, and interestingly, food was the way he connected most with his daughter. Joel's journey continues today, and he's discovering how to enjoy activities and new foods all the time, but he recognizes that it's a long game with various destinations.

In most cases, fear is the trap that keeps us looped in the perpetual negative world in our heads. Stop and slow down. Listen to your body, and the old habits that need to change. Another great quote that I hear often on Pat Flynn's podcast *Smart Passive Income* is "What got you *here* isn't what's going to get you *there*." Choose one small change that will make an impact on your day. Be open and aware that there are opportunities to learn about yourself. Things you've done in the past might have been helpful to get you where you are today, but there are new opportunities that might be missed if you keep to the same way of doing things.

To help you get started on that one small change, I have a completely FREE downloadable version of the same journal Joel used at my website: www.orozconutrition.com/mindfuljournal. That one small bite, coupled with some commitment and consistency, will prove immensely valuable over time.

Know that the fear of losing control, of being imperfect, or facing the unknown is often what holds us back, but we're not taking a giant leap, just a small step, but a *ton* of them. It's simple, but not easy; it's a leap into faith; it's a cumulative effect. There are no demons in any bow of any fake boat that will harm us—quite the contrary. Actually, it's the drifting aimlessly out in the ocean that will eventually kill us, so let's choose to head to shore.

Marcie

Our Fine-Tuned Biological Machine

Have you ever wondered why, after we go on a diet, we start gaining the weight back? Well, by this point you have read my seven reasons why diets don't work, so I would imagine you have a pretty good idea why. But let me tell you about this very same conversation I had with Marcie not so long ago. Please meet Marcie. She was so frustrated by the years of losing weight and gaining it back. Sometimes gaining it back right away and at other times slowly over a couple of years. Marcie got excited by the hype of a new diet that promised the secret to magically burning the fat off for good. This new diet promised to be easy and convenient; all you have to do is drink this or eat that, or cleanse with this product and detox with that. It may offer tons of meal plans and recipes so you can "easily" follow it, but once Marcie started the diet, it was as complicated as assembling a new piece of Ikea furniture. Some diets have rigid rules, overwhelming steps, and are nothing more than snake-oil and charlatan tactics. Marcie was frustrated because she just didn't understand what was going on with her body. She would commit to a new diet and fitness plan, albeit contrary to her lifestyle and body's needs, and then she wouldn't lose any weight. She wanted expert advice but not a new diet. She was done with dieting and thought there had to be a different way.

Marcie was interested in a more holistic and intuitive approach to enhancing her health (which was code for "help me lose weight"). She liked that I was about building a positive relationship with food and eating, and she was intrigued by the fact that I didn't have any gimmicks or quick-win solutions to a complex and long-term issue. However,

Marcie still had this "will this work?" mentality. During our initial conversation, it was clear she had years of strong fears of foods that she thought would make her gain weight. She followed quite a few diet rules, restrictions, habits, and beliefs, such as no white food for breakfast or dinner; you shouldn't eat anything after 7:00 p.m.; you can't have fruit with your meal; carrots are high in sugar; bread and carbohydrates will turn into fat; and so many more. Copious amounts of food fears and beliefs had confused and overwhelmed her. To get a better idea of what would help Marcie the most, we first started by looking what she had to eat the day prior.

She started with the following: "Well, for breakfast I had my usual cup of coffee with cream at around 4:45 a.m., just after waking up. I love my morning routine [very similar to some of the other Sheroes' and Heroes' routines, isn't it?] because it's one of the only times I have some peace and quiet and time for myself."

At this point, I quickly noted the possibility that she has little time for herself. OK, check that!

She continued, "Then I got ready, filled the rest of my tumbler, fed and let the dogs out in backyard, woke my wife and the kids up, got everyone's lunch ready"—not hers though—"and then I was out the door by 5:50 a.m. I like getting to the store early because there's less traffic and I can get a lot of work done before everyone gets in. I had a protein bar at my desk at around 8:30 a.m. I like to have something to eat and finish my coffee while I check my inbox, organize my day, start my daily to-do list, and try to catch up loose ends for the day prior or get ahead a bit if I can."

A common habit I often see is when people start having these protein bars. On one hand, they are hungry, and on the other, they just don't have time. There's a common belief that protein won't make you gain weight. Or, more insidiously, there's the social belief that carbohydrate will make you gain weight. I often tell clients that try as we might, we can't outwit the body. This is another indication of the fear of carbs, or a food rule to avoid for the fear of gaining weight. Again,

5: Consistency

it's important to point out how little Marcie had to eat up to this point in her day, yet how much work she'd already done. She relied on the coffee to get her started and keep her going instead of food. This repetitive habit may seem convenient and probably saves her (and all of us) time, but in the long run, she taught herself how to suppress her appetite temporarily. Just to be clear, not everyone has to have a large breakfast to start their day, but her morning routine was just another habit on top of all the other habits and rules that can contribute to the body having difficulties regulating energy levels.

Marcie mentioned that she starts her weekly 10:00 a.m. team meetings with an order of breakfast pastries and an assortment of fruit, but she doesn't touch them because she believes those foods are "unhealthy." Another example of how her fear and misconceptions about food could stifle her energy levels and overwrite her hunger cues. Technically, I'll go out on a limb here and say that this belief system, that pastries and fruit are unhealthy, has been a brain washing that diet culture has insidiously infiltrated within our shared social consciousness. It also exemplifies a few of my seven fad diet ingredients such as socially isolating, unrealistic, and unscientific. Diet culture and weight stigma has put the fear of God into her mind about pastries and fruit. I don't know about you, but how fun is life without enjoying a few of those?

> Lunch—"I had a late lunch around 2:15 p.m. because the meeting went over, and then I had to catch up with emails and put together some items for a client right away. I grabbed a butternut squash soup, and now that I think of it I only had half of it, and a couple of bites of the baguette that came with it."—She had mentioned that she tries to avoid anything white because her doctor thinks it will drive her blood sugar, and she could develop type 2 diabetes. Again, fear of carbohydrates and old beliefs that carbohydrates make her fat. Just a side note, what's worse: the years of stress response that a piece of bread has the potential to kill you of a chronic illness, that would probably take decades to develop, or the actual effects of the bread? Let's

get to this answer in just a little bit; for now, let's continue with her typical eating pattern.

Dinner—"I just kept pumping out work. I was super busy that day because the meeting in the morning put me back quite a bit, so I was playing catch-up the rest of the day, but that's how it is most days. Then I picked up the kids from their after-school programs, drove to the supermarket, and grabbed some food from the hot buffet for dinner because I knew my wife wouldn't be home and I didn't have time to cook. I served the kids their dinner, which they had each in their rooms, and I had to help my oldest do her homework. I took only a few bites of some curry chicken thighs with sautéed veggies, and a couple of bites of rice. I couldn't eat right when I got home, because my wife wasn't back from work yet and I needed to let the dogs out. I also got a message from my employee at work about a file she needed for a client's project. I was nibbling on some of the food, but yeah, it was about 9:15 p.m. before my wife got home last night, so I had the rest of dinner with her with a couple of glasses of wine. I had a little more work to finish that night, so I had some chips and a little more wine. I try to get a little work done most nights so I'm not so far behind the next morning. I think I went to bed around midnight." Late-night snacking and alcohol, that's what she said was one of her biggest challenges; the snacking at night, and the other was her sweet tooth. She said that at night it was like a radar for sugar and desserts. OK, you do see the irony of her giving up the pastries in the morning. The other challenge, if you haven't already guessed it, was how much she worked: rarely stopping to enjoy a meal, not able to slow down and notice her hunger and fullness cues. She had little time for herself, but she desperately needed to take it.

Trusting Her Body

Actually, Marcie had quite a few challenges. First, she didn't make enough time for herself. The problem was that she is a Shero. The typical characteristic of the selfless mom/boss/partner punctuated by doing so much for others—her family, her employees, her dogs—that the only time she had for herself was her morning coffee ritual. Echoes of the very same challenges of so many other Sheroes and Heroes in this book. Marcie also deals with packed schedules each day, generally subsisting on coffee and sheer adrenaline to get her started and keep her going, but her hunger intensifies in interesting ways as the day progressed. This was further amplified by a lot of old food rules that continued to dictate how, what, and when she ate, which simply overwhelmed her. Some days she just didn't know what to eat. Think the radar sweet-tooth—that's also known as a starved brain screaming to be fed. Sadly, she was also scared, frustrated, and confused about her health and her weight cycling. Who wouldn't be? There were so many different rules and times of what and when to eat that her body was responding adequately by gaining the weight back, increasing cravings for sweets, and wanting to snack at night. Her metabolism couldn't be maintained relative to all her physical and mental requirements throughout her day. Simply put, she was starving herself and her body reacted by slowing her metabolism, increasing the stress responses, releasing cortisol, epinephrine, norepinephrine, and glucagon in order to liberate glucose and triglycerides into her blood stream to keep her going—at the body's expense. You have to check out my story frame called The Oil Rig Comparison (Appendix B). It will make a lot more sense.

Remember, the glucose and fat broken down in her chronic stress response day after day is the very stored fuel that is required for her body's natural functions while she sleeps, or when she's sick, or when she needs the energy for a true emergency. But when it's used as the regular form of fuel instead of receiving a steady supply from food, her body is going to react by increasing her appetite; in her case specifically at night: gaining the weight back, amplifying that radar sweet-tooth, snacking—and there were other challenges as well. She started to lose focus, was easily distracted, and snapped more at her employees and family.

Anytime Marcie started another diet, her day was easily disrupted and emotions escalated over the smallest of problems. Diets became such a burden and impossible to sustain. On top of it all were the years of extremely strong beliefs that carbohydrates would make her gain weight, which caused so many fights with her wife and family about what to eat.

Come on, let's look at the facts. Low-carbohydrate diets have been around now for over fifty years. The same for low fat, high fat, low protein, or high protein. It just ain't working! If diets did work, we would only need one. Still, the fear of carbs has been imprinted in our collective consciousness so strongly that the belief is greater than the reality. Marcie had overwhelmed herself with so many diet rules and requirements that her metabolism and physiology were simply overwhelmed and confused.

To reiterate, I refer to these situations as starvation mode, which is really the body's response to less food, restricting calories, avoiding carbohydrates, or any form of dieting or pseudo-dieting. Our body works similarly to the way we extract petroleum from the earth. I know, cheesy analogy, but it drives the point home—at least, I think it does.

The years of weight cycling had played havoc with Marcie's body, although the signals were difficult to find, we slowly unpacked the key to transforming her relationship with food and her body. Little by little, she discovered how much it was about learning to trust her body again. The more she trusted herself and listened to her body and mind, the more she sprung forward to her transformation. Alternatively, a major benefit to trusting her body was that it no longer responded to dieting and weight loss because her metabolism just couldn't keep up. It was time for a redo! That, too, was her body's way of communicating.

Again, what she needed was to refocus her efforts on learning to trust her body's intuitive signs, but she had to start slowly. She had to slow down and re-learn how to pay attention to subtle hunger cues, such as how easily irritable she became without a satisfying meal. While

5: Consistency

breakfast was important for her, she also discovered that she easily over-ate if she didn't slow down and pay attention to how she was talking to herself. We focused on paying attention to her self-narrative at first. It proved difficult to understand her deep-seated feelings due to the years of diet behaviors and food rules that easily snuck into her head whenever she was busy or stressed.

Oddly, she found that instead of focusing on food she concentrated on how much she loved to sing. Singing was her escape and release. It was a great way for her be active because she would also dance, which helped her relax. As a young girl she used to love singing with her church choir, but more importantly she remembered how much it would soothe her. Finding something other than food to cope with her stress and emotional challenges was vital for her transformation. As a result, she started her day with a little song, which in turn would inspire her to grab a little meal. She would occasionally sing positive and uplifting tunes that helped her get through the day as well. In fact, on weekends she took up piano again and started playing music with her wife and daughters. Slowly she discovered that singing was her one small bite. She enjoyed it and it was always right there; whenever she wanted, she had it available to help her manage stress. This was one easy thing she could easily commit to it, and it was so simple for her to be consistent with it. What was truly important was how singing made her feel complete and filled her soul.

Singing had an unforeseen domino effect. Eventually it led her taking breaks to just sing, which made her feel better and get home in time for dinner with her family. This then allowed her to go to bed earlier and then get up earlier. But it wasn't because she told herself she had to sing, she just arbitrarily picked a time to take a break that it became a method to pause—to pay attention to herself. She felt amazing. Over time, she started trusting herself more. She wouldn't bother buying more food than necessary, and that helped her be less tempted by excess food laying around the house. Marcie and her wife were pleasantly surprised in a few other areas, like how much money they saved not buying so much food or going out to eat less often. Marcie noticed that she started to eat foods she long excluded out of her diet such as pasta and bread. She was enjoying her meals more with her family. They looked forward to a little family sing-along after dinner. But more importantly, Marcie trusted her body again.

The process of building a positive relationship with food and making peace with her body was about discovering what truly filled her in life. Like Isabel, she needed to slow down and enjoy life a little more. Eventually, music and singing would fill her more than any sweets or bag of potato chips would ever fill. She didn't feel the need to overeat anything because she gave herself the gift of reconnecting with her wife and family. Singing and music was Marcie's one small bite. For Marcie, singing was transformational.

Interlude

Consistency

> "Getting an audience is hard. Sustaining an audience is hard. It demands a consistency of thought, of purpose and of action over a long period of time."
>
> —Bruce Springsteen

When you're good at what you do, you can do it with your eyes closed. There's an efficiency and effectiveness to being repetitive and doing things without thinking. Whatever the skill or profession everyone learns to be fast and efficient. You develop the ability to get things done without thinking. At home we're the same way. We do the same things over and over again, and each day has a certain pattern and a certain rhythm to it that helps us save time and energy. This is what I call the autopilot mode.

While extremely helpful in making us efficient at what we do, if we don't pay attention to how those automatic tendencies (you know, the small stuff), then this type of consistency can negatively impact our long-term well-being. This is what I mean when I say getting stuck on *autopilot*. We can actually get lost in the ego self, the self that remains in what Jen Sincero calls the Big Snooze (or BS for short).[48] Autopilot, while extremely important in our lives for sure, can blind you to your own reality. You may never be aware of how your actions are affecting your body.

Here's a simple analogy. Think of strength training or lifting weights, exercises that help us grow and tone our muscles. If we lift or pull the same weight over again, without increasing the weight, changing the technique, or any other variables in the slightest, our muscles won't grow. In fact, when we change our workouts to include more weight or increased repetitions, the body wakes up connections called neuromuscular junctions because new muscles are required to lift or push. Similar to life, when we stop, slow down, and learn new habits, we help enhance our health. It's a form of cognitive exercising or strengthening. However, if we only look at magazines or stream shows of athletes while sitting on our couches, we don't see the fruits of our labor. We can't grow, develop, or prosper emotionally as well. Autopilot is the easy zone, the BS. It's the place we're so familiar with because we've done it repeatedly in our lives. Why change?

Steve

Stuck on Autopilot

Take Steve for example. A fifty-eight-year-old senior logistics officer for a major airline, married with two daughters, one in college and the other a senior in high school. His years in the Army really helped him solidify routine and discipline to his day. He'd wake up every morning between 4:45 and 5:00 a.m. and grab two cups of coffee and half-and-half while catching up with news and emails on his smartphone. He would then go to work, where it was one meeting after the other. Typically, he had lunch every day at 12:15 p.m. and then home for dinner between 6:00 and 7:00 p.m. Then he would get back on the computer and work until about 11:00 p.m. most nights. And this routine would go on for months.

Like Steve, these habits happen without even thinking. It's like an assembly line. Things just move together like they always do. Autopilot is extremely familiar, and the brain loves the familiar because it's easy and means it can conserve energy. Remember, the brain functions primarily on the law of conservation of energy. We don't have to think about it, which frees us up to do something else. Then we start learning to multitask. We think we're able to do multiple things at the exact same time, but in actuality we're not doing any one thing well. This was Steve's challenge. He was stuck in a routine of skipping breakfast, living on coffee in the morning, and then grabbing whatever food he could to avoid interruptions. He learned to save time and be more efficient in his profession and with his wood working hobbies. He converted his garage into a woodshop, and tools and equipment were immaculately clean and organized. It was like walking into a woodshop museum. This efficiency and precision, and subsequently his autopilot mode, were the main reasons why his career took off. The challenge was that he couldn't see how his autopilot mode was affecting his health. A lack of physiological awareness, what Evelyn Tribole and Elyse Resch call a lack of interoceptive awareness, was missing in his life.[49] He paid little attention to his body's needs and just lived in his comfort zone, his autopilot mode. It made sense; it was easy; and the brain likes to conserve energy.

One weekend, Steve planned a hiking trip with his buddies. These hiking trips happened twice a year, so he was excited about it because he really needed a break from work. He spent a week planning this hiking trip, packing all his dehydrated food, clothes, and gear. On the day of his trip, he packed everything in the car and drove off for a three-hour drive to meet his buddies at the trailhead. About two hours into his drive, his wife called to tell him he had left all his food on top of the counter. Ironically, this scenario was familiar for Steve. He would usually grab a snack in the morning before leaving to work each morning, but would put the snack right on the kitchen counter right before he left. He'd usually grab his coffee and forget his snack. He'd packed for his trip in the same way. All the food was on the counter just like his snack in the morning. He seemed to do it naturally. He didn't realize that he wasn't going to work, yet he went through all the familiar motions of packing all the right stuff, picking out his gear and clothes, and even checking things off his list, but he was so in his zone (quick and efficient) that he forgot his food. Eventually, he stopped at a local retailer to buy more food, which cost more money and time. Nonetheless, Steve and his buddies had a good laugh on that trip!

Now Steve didn't start working with me because he needed to figure out how to better pack his hiking gear or avoid forgetting his food. Although we did have a few great conversations about hiking and all the cool gear we each had. Anyway, I digress. He came to see me because he was concerned about his rising cholesterol levels, and that he couldn't get back to his twenty-something body. All the things he'd done in the past to tone up and get fit just weren't working. He couldn't

5: Consistency

be consistent with a lifestyle from twenty years ago. Life was much different for Steve now. He had a demanding career, a nice big home, two beautiful daughters, and an amazing wife. However, like many of us, Steve had been brainwashed to believe we can just spring back into that young body through some miraculous diet or fitness program. (Again, it's just unrealistic!) But in Steve's mind, all he thought he had to do was get back to his military training and button up his diet and workouts because he is so efficient at getting things done. Forgetting the food on his hiking trip became the example in our sessions of how his autopilot mode was killing him.

This is partly why vacations and hiking trips are so important. It slows us down and allows us to prioritize ourselves. To recharge our batteries, reconnect with nature, and to get back to what really matters in life. We are forced to acutely pay attention to the small stuff because it's so unfamiliar, yet so important. When you go on vacation, you don't know the local food scene, what, or where to eat. You get to slow down and enjoy the small, beautiful things—the architecture, the cobblestone streets, the winery, the white sandy beaches, the hues of orange-red and gold of the fall foliage, the snow-covered mountains, the beautiful colors of fresh fruits and vegetables on our plates. When you go on a hiking trip, you have to think about where to shelter and what to eat. Therefore, vacations and getaways give back these intense yet tiny and subtle pleasures in life.

The autopilot mode can be a wonderful way to build meaningful and helpful consistencies into our lives. On one hand, the ease and convenience of doing things without thinking can serve us extremely well because it conserves our energy. Our brains process hundreds of data points within a few seconds all day long, and if we are dealing with multiple responsibilities like work deadlines, irate bosses, multiple emails, client demands, financial problems, your next car payment, family responsibilities, your emotions, your loved one's emotions, your health—oh, and by the way, your hunger—it's just overwhelming. On the other hand, being quick and efficient can also blind us to some of our basic needs, like eating or sleeping. What Steve discovered was, like many of the previous Heroes and Sheroes in this book, the transformation happens when he stopped and listened.

Steve wanted a way to get back to his youth, but he was looking in the wrong direction, no matter how many times he'd try to lose weight and improve his cholesterol. He wanted to stop the weight cycling he had been experiencing over the last twenty years: losing large amounts of weight on crazy diets or fitness programs to then only gain it back, sometimes really fast; other times the weight would just creep up slowly over the course of one to two years. Steve described how diets just don't have the same effect as when he was younger. He was on autopilot, and it seemed to work great for his career, but not so much for paying attention to his body's needs. And like Joel, he found out about his high cholesterol only after a bio-screening health event at his company. Therefore, he wanted to start another "lifestyle modification" as he called it, or technically another diet.

He's done these plans before; therefore, it begged the question, "Why didn't he stick with it then?" On paper it looked great, right? He followed the plan and it worked magnificently. But what happened?

Before I answer, let me give a little more background. Steve regurgitated every last detail about the diet, what to eat, how to prepare everything, but after a couple of months, he'd lose his motivation to continue. He would reminisce how life was so much easier twenty-two years ago: "I wasn't married; I'd just landed my new dream job and lived with a roommate. We ate anything we wanted, and I'd go to the gym six or seven days a week. I would hang out with friends at the local pub after work, did quite a bit of activities most weekends like hiking and mountain biking buddies. I was in so much better health back then, and life was so uncomplicated. Going on a diet and fitness plan helped me feel young again, at least for a little while. It's just that after a while my current life gets in the way. So, I just didn't feel the need to continue my diet, and more importantly, it didn't make me feel happy for long. I felt so shallow and pretty lonely even though I was around a lot of people." Like Joel, Steve was quite the introvert, so

5: Consistency

he cultivated close relationships with people that were important in his life. He met his wife while volunteering for a local charity, and they were a perfect match. Arlene was someone Steve could easily talk to for hours at a time, and even twenty-one years into their relationship, they have great conversations. What Steve didn't realize was that he wasn't really happy back in his twenties, either; however, he believed that if he'd lose the weight, he'd be happier, but there's that counterfactual thinking—the memory of how he actually felt and who he was back then wasn't part of the weight-loss equation. He wanted a career, and becoming successful executive was what he dreamed about. Being at a lower weight has nothing to do with that.

To Steve, happiness was another ten or fifteen pounds away, yet he wasn't twenty-something anymore, and twenty-two was not such a great age after all. Oh, and there's the Oil Rig Comparison going on here as well. Like Marcie, his body would respond to weight loss attempts by slowing his metabolism and converting any energy into fat to preserve his life even though he wasn't really in danger. Although Steve's metabolism could go longer because he was a man, tall, and had more muscle mass, after a while, even those advantages wouldn't help for very long. Additionally, Steve was so much better off in his life now, so much fuller with a beautiful family and a great career, great close friends, and a fantastic woodworking skill and a great tinkerer. Still, he wasn't satisfied. His self-compassion meter was way off, and he immersed himself deeper into his work, which caused his autopilot system to get worse. His expectations were through the roof, and he felt there was never enough time. He frequently compared himself to Steve Jobs, Bill Gates, or Elon Musk. That bar was just too high to sustain.

Finally Aware the Autopilot Button Was Stuck

Steve regularly felt overwhelmed with all his responsibilities, so he made an appointment thinking he would get a custom-designed meal plan that would finally fix things for him. Easy, right? See a registered dietitian nutritionist and then—poof! They're the experts and they'll figure it all out for you. Surely things would be better. Customized plan means it's foolproof—his cholesterol would improve, and his waistline would shrink.

Well, you could imagine his surprise as we explored that thought process. We chatted about the Oil Rig Comparison, and how he's not twenty-something anymore, and that seemed to resonate a little with him. Being overweight is not just about someone's external weight but more about the burden they carry inside—an internal weight. Now don't get me wrong, in the past Steve would feel great when he'd drop the pounds. He was quite active and had a lot of energy, yet at the same time he still felt heavy. He felt like something was wrong and things just wouldn't change. How could they? He was stuck in the same routine day after day, which only kept that autopilot button stuck. However, he was ready for change, no matter how scary it would be to leave what was so familiar to him: a twenty-year-old belief system.

And there lies one of the main problems in our modern society. We just don't stop to think about ourselves in the present. We reminisce of the past, or dream about the future (nothing wrong with that unless you're stuck in autopilot). The challenge is that we live in this autopilot life and do the same things every day. We don't stop to pay attention or listen to our bodies. We don't give ourselves the opportunity to get out of our minds and do something different. This is one of the most common problems I see in so many people. Steve wanted to change, but the change was not what he realized. It was a more profound reason. He needed to change his perception of himself, change his purpose. Yes, getting or staying active helps us feel better, and even feel young, but weight loss wasn't going to last. He needed and wanted to enjoy life and grow, but he needed to see it came from within, not from losing weight. Ironically, we all need these life challenges from time to time to help us learn what not to do, to help us appreciate the small but beautiful things in life even more. Again, I'm not against

5: Consistency

having a healthy autopilot mode like when riding a bike or building a house. It's a muscle memory that helps us conserve energy and makes us experts in our fields. Yet if we aren't aware of how it creates other challenges like forgetting to eat, then the benefit it provides is lost in the long run. Just like when Steve had to take time to stop and buy more food for his trip. As the saying goes, "Measure twice, cut once!" We need to slow down and pay attention throughout the day to what our body needs. Take breaks throughout the day and enjoy what we love to do. What truly gives us joy.

Knowing When to Turn Off the Autopilot Button

For Steve, the way to pay attention was to put a pair of sneakers right in front of his coffee machine. You might be wondering what this has to do with turning off the autopilot button. It is an exercise I call *Captain Interrupter*. Steve realized that each morning he would make his coffee, sit with his smartphone, and scroll through all his emails and social media notifications. He'd spend thirty to forty-five minutes just sitting there doing just that. It was one of his autopilot mode strategies. Therefore, I saw it as an opportunity to discuss what small changes he can make that can become his new autopilot. And right there he mentioned how much he enjoyed running, and how it's a great mind escape for him. He reminisced about how much he enjoyed cross-country and running back in high school and college. He explained that when he runs, he gets into a different zone, this realization and awareness zone. Therefore, I suggested that he put his sneakers next to his coffee machine. Doing so could help interrupt his morning flow, but he didn't *have* to go on a run. He just needed to move the sneakers out of the way to pour his coffee. This one small thing was enough. He was intrigued, and ready for the challenge. Soon, he was getting up, moving his sneakers on to his feet, and he'd just go out for about ten to fifteen minutes. Then he discovered he can listen to his podcasts. Soon he thought, why not just put his workout clothes on top of his sneakers? And after a few weeks, he was running a couple of times a week. Nothing strenuous, just one to three miles three or four days a week.

There was a domino effect from the Captain Interrupter technique. He had more energy in the morning. He didn't drink as much coffee, and he started making breakfast. He even packed his lunch a couple of times a week. Just a little aside—eating in even saved him over $45 a week. He didn't need the money, but it was a pleasant surprise. He realized that by just doing one small thing like putting his sneakers next to his coffee machine, so many new changes occurred. He started feeling better, and his family started noticing. There were no diet plans, no food rules, no special fitness programs, just his clothes and sneakers next to his coffee machine. Ironically, a few months later, on his next hiking trip with his buddies, Steve made sure to put his food and gear next to his coffee machine. It was a running joke, but one that served as a great reminder of the importance of small changes.

Allow me to digress just a bit, but I promise I'll make the connection. Here's a simple exercise I have people try when they come to my office. Grab a piece of paper and sign your name with your dominant hand. Really pay attention to how the pen feels in your hand. How it flows on the paper and how you sign your name so easily. Now take the pen, put it in your nondominant hand and sign your name. What does the pen feel like in your nondominant hand? Is it hard or easy to sign your name? Does it feel awkward? Yes, of course it does. Now, some of you may be ambidextrous and can do it, but you still feel the difference. It feels a little awkward or funny. Why? Because we are so used to signing our names with that one hand. Doing it with the other requires us to stop, slow down, and think through it. Oh, and that's where the magic happens.

Yes, change comes one small bite at a time, but what we have to go through the discomfort of that change. It doesn't take much. Like Steve, it became his new autopilot, and a form of muscle memory, because he was consistent. He was willing to lean in to the awkwardness of putting his sneakers next to the coffee machine, but more importantly, he was consistent. He didn't always go on the run, or the walk. He didn't always remember to put his clothes on top of his sneakers. And some weeks work got in the way. But like his woodworking skills, he knew greatness comes from determination and keeping at it! That was his true purpose, and it was really in line with his health and body's needs. And more importantly, he was consistent at it.

I often tell people—in fact, I've mentioned it previously in this book—that most of us are born with two legs, but no one just pops out of their mother's womb instantly walking. Walking is something we have to learn, one baby step at a time. It takes anywhere from eight to sixteen months to start, about two to five years to get it straight, and even then, as adults we still stumble and fall. The point is, we don't remember the challenges, fumbles, falls, and face-plants in the process of learning to walk, but that's because it's not important anymore. What was important was to get from point A to point B. We build muscle memory, and our legs learn to balance, hold, stabilize, and move one foot in front of the other.

I started this chapter talking about how not paying attention to that autopilot mode can cause problems in our health and wellness, but if we slow down and pay attention to what we need, we can actually learn new helpful habits that can transform us. I'm reminded of my mother, who use to say, "In life the only problem that has no solution is death, and at that point it doesn't matter anymore." This isn't about sheer willpower or blind faith. Consistency is about first pausing and being curious about what changes you can make, then building self-kindness for yourself, committing to it, and then keeping at it.

6

Conclusion

Congratulations! At this point, we start *your* journey to *your* transformation One Small Bite at a time!

Up to now you experienced various journeys and experiences from people in this book. More than likely, you have spotted at least one new behavior or one new habit that has resonated with you. A new idea might have even popped in your head as to what direction, what one small bite, you will start now to transform your life. This new habit will finally break the cycle of crazy diets, build a positive relationship with food and your body, and help you finally start *being that person you've always wanted to be*. By the way, that last statement, *being that person you've always wanted to be*, is so important. It is one of the most common statements I make to almost every client I work with. It is the single most important element to anyone's transformation. Be the person you want to be, and don't wait around for the next best thing! Don't think that some new diet is going to come around and change you. Gandhi put it best: "Be the change you wish to see in the world." I would add that you *are* your world.

One small bite is a way of grabbing hold of your life *now*! In the present! At this moment! Why? Because it is only one small change that offers you momentum. One small change that often makes us feel better, yet it's not overwhelming. This change is attainable, realistic, and most important, doable! So often the people I work with are living in the past, thinking about how or who they are based on their past experiences. Or they believe they are destined to become a certain way because of their genes, family history, or past mistakes. Their past experiences, their understanding of who they were, is like a self-fulfilling prophecy; so, they are doomed to repeat it and become it. Or others are so caught up in the future, concerned with what will happen to them if they don't lose weight, or if they don't look a certain way. All the while, they are missing out on the most precious element of their lives—today! *Now*! Themselves—the present!

One of my favorite quotes comes from the movie *Kung Fu Panda*. This scene in the movie paints the picture of so many of us when life feels so heavy, and we feel like we are up against impossible odds. The scene is when Po, the panda, is drowning in his misery and despair. He feels like such a failure and unworthy. He can't possibly be the Dragon Warrior, and he thinks Shifu and the Fearless Five believe he's a joke. Po has just found the Peach Tree of Heavenly Wisdom and has stuffed a mouthful of peaches to numb his misery (just love the emotional eating analogy here). Master Oogway then appears behind Po.

> Master Oogway: "I see you've found the Peach Tree of Heavenly Wisdom."
>
> Po (with a mouthful of peaches): "Is that what this is? I'm so terribly sorry! I thought this was just a regular peach tree." (A peach falls out of his mouth as he speaks.)
>
> Master Oogway: "I understand. You eat when you are upset."
>
> Po: "Upset, I'm not upset, why, why, why . . . what makes you think that?"
>
> Master Oogway: "So why are you upset?"
>
> Po (sighing): "I probably sucked more today than anyone in the history of Kung Fu. In the history of China! In the history of sucking!"

6: Conclusion

Master Oogway: "Probably."

Po: "And the Five [referring to the Fearless Five], they totally hate me."

Master Oogway: "Totally."

Po: "How's Master Shifu going to turn me [lifting up his big belly] into the Dragon Warrior? I'm mean, I'm not like the Five. I have no claws. No wings. No venom! Even Mantis has those . . . thingies." [He takes another big sigh.] "Maybe I should quit and just go back to making noodles."

Master Oogway: "Quit. Don't quit. Noodles. Don't noodles. You are too concerned with what was and what will be. There's a saying. 'Yesterday is history, tomorrow is a mystery, but today is a *gift*. That's why they call it the *present*.'"[50]

As Oogway turns back and starts to walk away, he taps the tree with his staff and a peach falls out of the tree right into Po's hand. I just love the connection between my love for food, martial arts, and the wise and so soft-spoken master tortoise. I tell this story because I too have been through what many of my clients in this book have gone through in one way or another. All too often we go through days of uncertainty, of despair, or of doubt about our abilities—a type of "impostor syndrome." We worry about things that haven't happened yet, or live in the past, thinking we should go back into our shells and caves, back into a lower version of ourselves because we are not worthy or we are incapable. We consistently worry instead of living in the present. The present *is* a gift! And so many of us take that for granted. I love that scene and tell it to many clients I work with on almost a weekly basis. Why? Because it represents the whole premise of One Small Bite. We have only today to make our lives what we want it to be.

When I was writing this book, I felt overwhelmed. I had major staff changes in my office. My partner decided to split, and I was left with the entire rent, twice as much in expenses with no new clinicians to help fill the space and financial void. We had a major flood from a busted waterline in our office and we were forced to close for four days. This was right after the holidays, when the office was closed for a week, and people were on vacation. It hit my business so hard both financially and emotionally. All this was happening right when I was about to turn in my manuscript to my writing coach. I was in the middle of doing the first self-edit and review of the book. And as if all that wasn't enough to derail me, then COVID-19 and quarantine happened. Now, thankfully I was (still am) meticulous when it came to saving money, and I had a decent cushion to fall back on, but it quickly got depleted. I was emotionally a wreck. I was about to throw in the towel and tell Coach Azul that I couldn't do it. And then out of nowhere, during our weekly coaching session, he hits me with my own medicine. "David, just focus on One Small Bite." I felt like Po, with a mouthful of peaches. I was just handed the exact same speech by Master Azul (OK, no peach tree and not the exact same speech, but you get my drift), and then I thought, "Huh, the irony here."

Think about what will happen if you don't take one small step at a time.

- Waiting around for another magical diet (new diet lifespan is five to seven years)
- Starting another diet and lose some weight, or nothing at all
- Letting your metabolism slow down further
- Gaining another ten pounds
- Restricting and avoiding foods again
- Controlling everything around you
- Exercising to extremes and injuring yourself again
- Living in doubt and self-pity, imposter syndrome, and depression
- Believing you are not worthy of more, of better
- Being overwhelmed and out of control

You might be thinking "But, David, where do I start? There were tons of examples from each client. How do I choose?" Start with what feels right, and if it doesn't, try something else. Maybe for you, it's

6: Conclusion

Captain Interrupter, or it's writing a food emotion journal; maybe it's just letting yourself finish the diet you're currently on and starting when you are ready. Maybe you can start by reading *Intuitive Eating*, or maybe it's just pausing for thirty seconds once a day to observe yourself.

The key is to let yourself be curious to what you observe and wonder. Experiment and learn, then build that self-compassion to know it's not about getting it right, it's about getting it wrong. Remember the famous quote from Yoda: "The greatest teacher, failure is!" Then dust yourself off and continue. Commit to the new habit because it feels right, even though it's awkward and difficult, and then be consistent. Build that determination and focus on that change because it feels right.

Lastly, I know it's not easy to do it alone. Feel free to contact me or one of my ON Team members for a free fifteen-minute chat to get you started and set up regular visits. Visit our website at https://www.orozconutrition.com/contact—we look forward to hearing from you!

Complementary Section

Yoda's Greatest Quotes, They Are

As you might have seen, sprinkled throughout the book are some *Star Wars* quotes or references. It is definitely on purpose as I believe that the stories of the Heroes and Sheroes that you have read about are on the Hero's and Shero's journey. Just like Rey Skywalker, Luke Skywalker, his father Anakin Skywalker (Darth Vader), and so many of the other characters of *Star Wars*, they all had to take One Small Bite toward Curiosity, Compassion, Commitment, and Consistency in order to be their own Hero or Shero!

Here are some great quotes from Yoda that helped them along.

1. **Do. Or do not. There is no try!**—*Empire Strikes Back*—This quote is a simple lesson in commitment and the power in giving something our all, not just giving it a try.
2. **You must unlearn what you have learned**—*Empire Strikes Back*—As creatures of habit, we tend to love our routines and our go-to methods. But sometimes, we must shake up our process, and even unlearn our process, to succeed.
3. **Named must be your fear before banish it you can**—*Empire Strikes Back*—When we call out our fears directly, they become less of an ominous force and a challenge we can tackle head on.
4. **Luminous beings we are ... not this crude matter**—*Clone Wars*—Referring to our soul, our beings and not our flesh. We are greater than our thoughts and feelings.

5. **Fear is the path to the dark side. Fear leads to anger. Anger leads to hate. Hate leads to suffering**—*The Phantom Menace*—Like Nathaniel and Isabel, fear is where they needed to head to in order to get to the light at the end of the tunnel; otherwise, they would just stay in suffering.
6. **The greatest teacher, failure is**—*The Last Jedi*—We learn from our mistakes—plain and simple.
7. **Pass on what you have learned**—*Return of the Jedi*—The wisdom we gain in life is a gift to pass along, not to keep to ourselves. Make like Yoda and share your insights with others.

The Tortoise Effect

The Hare just wouldn't stop bragging about how fast he was. All the other animals in the forest didn't want to hear it anymore. They didn't want to hear the Hare boast about how he could beat anyone in a race, yet no one had the courage to challenge him. The squirrel knew he was fast, but said he was too busy to take him on. The hedgehog was busy burrowing his tunnels and shied away from the challenge. The wild turkey just didn't have the time, but not the Tortoise. He challenged the Hare to the race, and of course the Hare laughed at the challenge but figured it was gonna be an easy win. Right up to the start, the Hare continued to brag, make fun of the Tortoise, and even offer to give him a head start. At the starting line, the Hare was still bragging about how easy this was going to be, and how he would be signing autographs at the finish line in no time.

The gun fired and they were off. The Hare sped down the path, while the Tortoise put one foot in front of the other, determined to finish the race no matter what. The Hare was so far in front of the Tortoise that he decided to take it easy because there was no way Tortoise would ever possibly pass him. He found a nice, shaded area just off the race path, closed his eyes for a little, and got some rest. The Tortoise, on the other hand, was slow but steady as he could be. He was tired but, again, extremely determined, hyperfocused on winning the race. Well, we've all heard the ending of this story. The Hare overslept, and the Tortoise just kept moving forward no matter what.

This is the beauty of this story. Just because you think you are slow doesn't mean you can't win the race. We are not predetermined to continue being who we were. The current way of thinking is what shapes the person you want to be. It doesn't take rigid diets or crazy fitness programs to feel better, live longer, and enjoy life more. The Tortoise just knew things had to change. He was curious and built the courage to accept the Hare's challenge. If anything, he was determined and consistent to finish the race, regardless of what happened. But more important, he was compassionate. The Tortoise didn't rub it in, he didn't do anything fancy, he didn't cheat, and he didn't have multiple things going on at the same time. He simply took one small step at a time. Steady as he could, and not forcing anything, he just focused on what he needed to do to finish the race.

Each one of us must make our own transformation, and for each of us it is different. For me it was the news that my mother was diagnosed with diabetes and colon cancer, and my father with high blood pressure and prostate cancer. While it was emotionally difficult for me, I couldn't help thinking that I didn't want to head down that same path. I couldn't stand by any longer and be bullied by my old critical narrative that kept me stuck in that unhealthy autopilot mode. Like many of the Sheroes' and Heroes' journeys here, my path led me down a much darker hole. At the time, I had no clue what I was doing. I didn't realize I was restricting myself so much, obsessed about eating only the cleanest food. I started becoming more socially isolated. My best friends just stopped inviting me to go out with them because of my new obscure "healthy" habits. We couldn't just sit down at a bar, have a few beers and food, and enjoy ourselves.

Yet, I needed to experience all of that. "The greatest teacher, failure is!" What I didn't realize was the true transformation came from within me. To become the man I was inside. Again, the fear we have is only created by our own minds; how we think today is what will shape our lives in the future. That's why one small bite is a mindset shift. It is the beauty of the possibilities that lie ahead for who and what we can be, our own selves. That was the case for Nathaniel, for Meredith, and for Angela, even with three girls at her side. They all embarked on a transformational journey, but one small change at a time. Just like the Tortoise, they each started with one small bite.

It's slow and steady, one foot in front of the other. Committed, compassioned, and consistent—this is not how you win the race but how you grow and transform!

Appendix A
Bariatric Surgery

Bariatric surgery is a form of weight-loss surgery that requires alterations and changes to the digestive system with the intent to help people lose weight. There are two main types of surgeries performed in the United States: the Sleeve Gastrectomy (Gastric Sleeve) and the Roux-en-Y Gastric Bypass (Gastric Bypass or RNY for short).[51] Technically, there are a couple others, but for simplicity's sake I'll stick to these two since they're the most common. The most commonly performed procedure done today is the Gastric Sleeve, which is done on about 61 percent of people who qualify for surgery, and about 17 percent get the Gastric Bypass procedure. Interestingly, just fifteen years ago, my very first job out of grad school was at a major bariatric center in Atlanta, GA. The "hot" surgery back then was the lap-band surgery, which is a procedure that is hardly done on anyone now. Fast-forward sixteen years, I see a significant number of lap bands removed and people either choosing for another surgery like the gastric sleeve or bypass.

The Gastric Bypass is one of the oldest bariatric procedures still performed today and offers the greatest amount of excess weight loss, as well as the highest likelihood of almost "eliminating" type 2 diabetes. I put eliminate in quotes because there is no known cure of diabetes. What I often see is that while initially blood sugar and insulin levels improve, people often have blood sugar complications again whether they gain weight or not. In fact, most people I've worked with gain some weight back after surgery. The Gastric Bypass is both the most restrictive and malabsorptive of the two types of bariatric procedures. People who have the Gastric Bypass are required to take chewable iron, calcium, and multivitamin supplements for the rest of their lives, and they are required to take either a sublingual B12 or a monthly B12 injection. The Gastric Bypass also causes the most side effects, such as regurgitation, heartburn, vomiting, diarrhea, and digestive problems, some of which occur because of dumping syndrome. This is when a higher than normal amount of sugar and/or fat empty into the ilium, which is now the receiving end of food for the small intestine. This in turn causes complications.

In the Gastric Bypass, the stomach is cut into about the size of a small ping-pong ball size pouch and the lower part of the small intestine is then cut and reattached to that new small ping-pong pouch. The remaining old large stomach and intact intestinal track is left behind but is no longer directly involved in the digestion of food. Below is an image of the Gastric Bypass.

Gastric bypass surgery

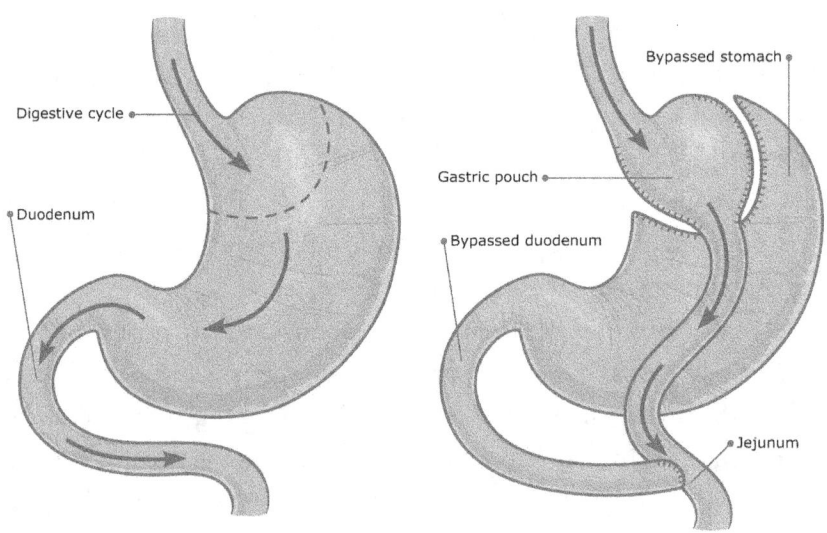

This type of bariatric surgery offers the greatest weight loss compared to other types of stomach surgeries, but it also has greater risks. The risks from surgery[52] include bleeding, infection, leaking, and infection from the site of cut and stapling of the stomach and intestines, diarrhea, blood clots, and in some rare occasions, death. In the long term, the gastric bypass procedure reduces the body's ability to absorb certain nutrients such as calcium, iron, and vitamins B12, A, and E. The biggest challenge is the difficulty with protein absorption by volume, particularly early after surgery. Since the surgery restricts the total amount of food, the body doesn't get enough protein at one meal, and there's less absorption area for protein. This can lead to malnutrition complications like brittle nails, hair loss, and dry skin (which are the mild complications). The malnutrition can also diminish the body's ability to produce red blood cells or immune fighting cells, which can increase the risk of developing anemia, osteoporosis (bones becoming weaker, porous, and brittle), and the development of gallstones due to the rapid weight loss. Many people can also develop swallowing difficulties and acid reflux issues like GERD (gastroesophageal reflux disease). Another overlooked long-term complication that arises from any form of gastric surgery or weight loss is the long-term psychological effects such as disordered eating or eating disordered behaviors. The gastric bypass is both the most restrictive in amount of food you can eat, and it has the highest risk of medical complications short and long term.

As for the Sleeve Gastrectomy procedure, it is much less complicated and avoids much of the malabsorptive complications. The stomach is cut into a banana like shape and the intestinal track is left intact. It doesn't offer as much weight loss as the Gastric Bypass, but it is the most popular bariatric surgery currently performed.

VERTICAL SLEEVE GASTRECTOMY

Appendix A

According to the American Society of Metabolic and Bariatric Surgery (ASMBS), the key organization of surgeons and integrated health professionals that provides surgical and safety guidelines, procedures, training, and research for bariatric surgery, found that in 2011 the number of people having bariatric surgery was 158,000. In 2018 those numbers nearly doubled in seven years to 252,000.[53] In my experience, I see a fair amount of people two to ten years after surgery wanting to lose weight again, a clear indication of how this extremely complicated procedure may only help people lose weight for the first two years, then it's just like any other diet. The weight loss is a significant indicator of future weight gain.

Let's do some quick math: the running average cost for surgery is approximately $20,000 if you're paying cash.

$$\$20,000/\text{surgery} \times 252,000 \text{ people} =$$

$5 Billion

And that's just for the surgery alone. This doesn't include all the tests, copays, medications, medical visits, nutrition and psychological evaluations, classes, and requirements needed. Plus, there are indirect expenses as well, like parking fees for medical and healthcare visits, time off work for appointments, time off for recovery from surgery, travel time, gas, all the food, drinks, supplements, plates, and tools required before and after surgery. It is unclear what insurance plans cover because plans vary so widely, but you can bet it's a lot less than you and I would pay. The other problem is that many insurance plans may not cover the surgery, so there is a significant amount of people that end up having the procedure outside of the United States—I've had clients that had the procedure in Mexico, Colombia, Brazil, India, and even in Poland. What's most alarming about the American Society of Metabolic and Bariatric Surgery statistics is the number of revision surgeries, which amount to about 15 percent per year. That is practically the same amount of Gastric Bypass surgeries alone performed in the same year. Possibly just as alarming is that ASMBS published a peered review paper in their professional journal, *Surgery for Obesity and Related Diseases*, in which the study described the low number of people that qualify for the surgery.

In my experience, bariatric surgery is the most extreme weight-loss treatment out there with little long-term benefits and many false expectations. On one hand, it promises to help people lose incredibly large amounts of weight, improve their health, balance blood pressure, eliminate diabetes, and other promises. Yet, these promises don't work for everyone. What's worse is the profound and deep-rooted psychological messages such as the plethora of weight stigmatization from society. People, media, and culture telling them they are less than human or not normal. It's a form of discrimination and racism. On the other hand, bariatric surgery is also viewed as a copout by people in thin bodies. It creates a lopsided hierarchal standard that other people make them feel like exhibits at a museum. Thin people perceive bariatric surgery as an easy way out of losing weight. Both these forces only further dehumanized people in large/fat bodies, pushing them into further hiding their problems. This is nothing more than enormous amounts of stress, which adds more complications to the body.

Our society is so hyperfocused on an image of thinness and beauty that we often conflate with success, or worse, perfectionism. What's interesting is that I see just as many people that are thin and supposedly the image of perfection with just as many problems. Perfection, like control, is nothing more than an illusion. Bariatric surgery doesn't cure culture norms.

Appendix B
Fat Burning = Oil Rig Comparison

Here's what's happening. The body burns fat similarly to the way we extract oil from the ground through these elaborate and complex oil rigs. Our body is no different. Burning fat is a laborious biological function. It is not easy, so the body tries hard to hold on to it because fat has so many different uses. Please allow me to elaborate on this analogy a little further.

In an oil rig, the drill is turning and pumping the oil out of the ground. But the drill just doesn't spin and pump on its own. It needs an energy source. An engine and motor attached to that provides the energy and movement. And to turn the engine on and keep the motor running, we need to provide it with an energy source, which is gasoline. The irony here is that we get gasoline from the very oil we are drilling from. In our bodies, the engine, motor, and drill are our metabolism. Similar to the motor, our metabolism needs fuel, which is food. If we eat a balance of the three main macronutrients—carbohydrates, proteins, and fats—from various food groups, we will then have an efficient and effective metabolism, or motor, that will turn the drill. Remember, the drill also acts like a pump, and it then sucks up oil that will then be converted back into gasoline. In other words, our body fat is burned if we eat enough food and have balanced meals with various food groups combined in meals and snacks throughout the day. Below are the major six food groups:

1. *Grains*—bread, cereal, oats, pasta, and potatoes
2. *Fruit*—apples, grapes, oranges, and berries

3. *Veggies*—broccoli, spinach, kale, peppers, and carrots
4. *Dairy*—milk, cheese, and yogurt
5. *Protein*—beef, chicken, turkey, and fish
6. *Fat*—olive oil, butter, cream, and nuts and seeds

Often when we have balanced meals, our body will be able to sustain our level of activity, emotional state, and our basic physiology. This way our metabolism runs like a well-oiled machine (pun intended). This often means we need a minimum of two, preferably three, meals a day, and maybe a smart snack or two to make up the calories or food groups missing in meals (for more specific information, download my FREE TDW Meal Planning Guide at www.orozconutrition.com/mealplanningguide). Like a well-functioning oil rig (and keep in mind I am oversimplifying the analogy), I know there are thousands of moving parts and multiple complex systems that regulate and manage just one oil rig, but the body is no different.

Our bodies need a regular fuel source to just maintain; otherwise, the ability to utilize fat from our bodies is not efficient, or heck, it may not work well at all. Therefore, whenever we go on a diet, or cut out calories, eliminate any food group, fast, or skip meals on a regular basis, we hinder the delicate balance of our metabolism. Now the body, like oil rigs, have backup systems—backup generators, safety systems that reroute power to different machines, alternative drills and pipes that siphon the oil when the main system is down. When our metabolism starts to drop, much like a thermostat, it triggers the backup system, which breaks down lean tissue or muscle to give us the fuel we need to sustain our health. However, the backup systems are not designed to run indefinitely. We cannot continue to breakdown our lean tissue to run our systems forever. We just can't store that amount of fuel.

I compare this to tapping into our savings and our retirement accounts. You might need to withdraw money in case of emergency, but you don't pay yourself a regular salary from them; otherwise, you wouldn't have anything for a rainy day or when you retire.

Therefore, when we are not fueling ourselves efficiently (in other words, when we diet), we are breaking stored energy in our liver and muscles. This is stored as glycogen, which is a relatively easy energy source to break down compared to fat. Another key point is that part of the very energy coming from the liver or the muscle is being directed back to the liver and muscle itself to break itself down to provide that energy. What this means for us is that in the long run the body cannot sustain this backup system. It's a backup system, not a main system.

This is another example of the unsustainability of diets, and the risk of weight regained. Therefore, we have to remember that we can't trick the body—it needs food as the main fuel source. The problem is that when we go back to food, the damage is done. Our metabolism has already slowed down due to the use of the backup system, this starvation mode as we referred to earlier. Therefore, the body now becomes more efficient at storing that food as fat. Why fat and not muscle? Well, for one thing, we're not athletes, and we aren't burning through energy like a maniac. We're also not young anymore, so our body doesn't need it to grow muscle, lean tissue, or bones. And why would we use it while sitting behind a desk all day, staring at a computer? I tell people that for every one thing they do to lose weight, the body has multiple overrides to keep you from losing it.

Much like the intricate engineering designs of oil rigs, with its complex machines, pipes, platforms, all the way down to the refining facilities, where the crude oil is converted to gasoline and many other byproducts, the body comprises a complex system of engineering and processes designed to manage energy. The body doesn't use fat as the main source of energy. It isn't a closed-loop system. We need to eat. It has to get a daily supply in evenly distributed meals throughout the day to keep the metabolism, the motor of the body, running optimally, efficiently, and effectively. If it were a closed-loop system, we wouldn't have to eat, and then we wouldn't gain a single pound.

Remember, fat is used for more than just energy. Like petroleum, fat in our body is used to produce hormones, and it insulates our neural connection. For example, our nerves are wrapped in a myelin sheath, which is made of fat. The myelin sheath is similar to the rubber that covers electrical cords or the plastic that covers power lines; it helps insulate nerve connections and allows electrical and chemical signals pass through the nerves. When myelin sheaths don't function properly, we experience significant health consequences. Multiple Sclerosis is a major physical impairment and happens when the body attacks itself and breaks down the protective myelin sheath. Fat is also used in maintaining our immune system and provides various components that make up every cell membrane in our body. As you can see, just like an oil rig, our body has a complex web of systems that are independent but interdependent. Each independent system works harmoniously with others to create homeostasis (more on homeostasis in just a minute).

Therefore, if we start dieting, we reduce the energy source to our metabolism. We cut back the fuel necessary to optimally, effectively, and efficiently turn the drill that pulls fat out of our body to help supplement the fuel, and that helps with all the various body systems. So, it must go to our backup system—lean tissue or muscle. This is where things get interesting. As I mentioned earlier, your body hates tapping into its savings account or retirement fund to run your metabolism—your drill. It will do it to survive, but it's not sustainable. This is the *main* reason diets *seem* to work so well, because muscle can retain a considerable amount of water. For every pound of muscle, there is a potential to hold up to almost three pounds of water, partly because our muscle is made up of about 60 percent water. So, when we go on a diet or cut out food groups (think giving up meat, eliminating nutrients like carbohydrates—going Paleo, Keto, Atkins, etc.), we essentially break down muscle, which in turn releases a significant amount of water weight quite rapidly. Therefore, all these crazy diets seem to work well for many people, some more than others, but they all do the exact same thing. They break down lean tissue stores of glucose, which then releases a lot of stored water, and then in about a week, when you jump on the scale, you think you've succeeded.

Appendix B

Well, you kind of did.

Now don't get me wrong. You obviously lost weight, that's true. Just like an oil rig using its backup system will extract oil for some time. In fact, many people say they feel better, at least initially, which makes sense because your body is not carrying as much weight any longer, and there is some fat burned off, but only at the expense of burning off the lean tissue. This is just unsustainable. Dieting forces our body to use our backup systems to circumvent our primary system. We rely heavily on our muscular system, lean tissue, as a fuel source to take up the slack of our digestive system and food as fuel, and that's just not sustainable long term. Remember, the energy stored in our liver and muscle we need for rainy days, and not to be our daily salary of energy. Your body needs to rely on all your systems equally to be healthy, which is exactly what homeostasis means.

One of the best explanations of homeostasis comes from Dr. Daniel Siegel, author of *Mindsight: The New Science of Personal Transformation*.

He explains the eleven independent systems,

1. Muscular system
2. Endocrine system
3. Skeletal system
4. Integumentary system
5. Digestive system
6. Circulatory system
7. Respiratory system
8. Lymphatic system
9. Excretory system
10. Reproductive system

and the main processing center of the body,

11. The nervous system

while all independent, must work harmoniously together to communicate and share responsibility in keeping the body healthy. He eloquently describes how we need to enhance our body's ability to find health through his concept of Interpersonal Integration or PART:

P—Presence

A—Attunement

R—Resonance

T—Trust[54]

Being healthy is learning and understanding our biological Oil Rig bodies. It has to do with being present and attuned to the body's needs. Food maintains our energy to be productive and remain sharp. We need protein to help build our immune cells and blood cells that keep us healthy. Fat sustains us and makes us feel satiated. It maintains the nervous system, and therefore keeps our brains healthy. Or we can just enjoy all foods, like candy, cakes, bread, or pasta, and that helps us feel better because it's enjoyable. When we are not in tune with ourselves like Marcie, we run the risk of stealing from Peter to pay Paul, as the saying goes. Our body is a finely tuned architecture of human biology; it's messy and at the same time beautiful. It's complex yet extremely simple. Our body has basic needs, but we have learned how to override these basic needs because we get lost in autopilot mode like Steve. We get lost in the past, where we might have suffered from a traumatic experience, or a belief that life was better in the past. We get lost in the future thinking that only the best is ahead, that we need more to get ahead and succeed. We think more money and more material possessions will fill our lives. But it's never enough, so we find a way to use food to fill that void. We find a way to use food as a coping mechanism or manipulate it and try to restrict or control what we eat. Therefore, we breakdown the very intricate fiber of the oil rig; we damage the way our body utilizes energy and slow down our metabolism.

Now when the dieting stops (again it's unsustainable), we go back to eating what we gave up, or eat those new foods in greater quantities, and we start gaining the weight back. This happens for a variety of reasons:

Appendix B

- Slower metabolism—we don't burn fat off as well.
- Less muscle—our backup system is broken, less fuel for true future emergencies.
- Fat storing efficiency—our body will store more fat because muscle is being burned up.
- Irregular hormonal fluctuations—our systems are not working well, more cortisol to store more fat for the long-term.

Notes

1. George Sylvester Viereck, "What Life Means to Einstein," *The Saturday Evening Post*, October 26, 1929, 117, http://www.saturdayeveningpost.com/wp-content/uploads/satevepost/what_life_means_to_einstein.pdf; accessed Dec. 19, 2020.

2. Russ Harris, *The Happiness Trap: How to Stop Struggling and Start Living* (Boston: Trumpter Books, 2008), 141, Apple Books.

3. Kristen Neff, *Self-Compassion: The Proven Power of Being Kind to Yourself* (New York: HarperCollins, 2011).

4. Kristen Neff, *Self-Compassion: The Proven Power of Being Kind to Yourself* (New York: HarperCollins, 2011).

5. Eckharte Tolle, *The Power of Now: A Guide to Spiritual Enlightenment* (Novato, CA: New World Library, 1999).

6. Celeste Kidd and Benjamin Y. Hayden, "The Psychology and Neuroscience of Curiosity," *Neuron* 88, no. 3 (November 4, 2015): 449–60.

7. Harry F. Harlow, Nancy C. Blazek, and G. E. McClearn, "Manipulatory Motivation in the Infant Rhesus Monkey," *Journal of Comparative and Physiological Psychology* 49, no. 5: 444–48, https://doi.org/10.1037/h0047817.

8. "John F. Kennedy; Moon Speech—Rice Stadium," Software, Robotics, and Simulation Division, Space Movies Cinema NASA, accessed Oct. 17, 2020, https://er.jsc.nasa.gov/seh/ricetalk.htm.

9. Martin Luther King, Jr., Dec 24, 1967, Massey Lecture #5, "Christmas Sermon on Peace"; Beacon Broadside, A Project of Beacon Press, Published on Dec 24, 2017, Accessed on Dec 19, 2020: https://www.beaconbroadside.com/broadside/2017/12/martin-luther-king-jrs-christmas-sermon-peace-still-prophetic-50-years-later.html.

10. Kristen Neff, *Self-Compassion: The Proven Power of Being Kind to Yourself* (New York: HarperCollins Publishers, 2011).

11. Brené Brown, *Dare to Lead—Brave Work. Touch Conversations. Whole Hearts* (New York: Random House, 2018), 171.

12. Michael R. Lowe, Sapna D. Doshi, Shawn N. Katterman, and Emily H. Feig "Dieting and Restrained Eating as Prospective Predictors of Weight Gain," *Front Psychol* 4, no. 577 (2013): https://www.ncbi.nlm.nih.gov/pmc/articles/PMC3759019/.

13. Elke D. Eckert, Irving I. Gottesman, Susan E. Swigart, and Regina C. Casper, "A 57-Year Follow-Up Investigation and Review of the Minnesota Study on Human

Starvation and Its Relevance to Eating Disorders," *Archives of Psychology* 2, no. 3 (March 2018).

14. Evelyn Tribole and Elyse Resch, *Intuitive Eating: A Revolutionary Anti-Diet Approach* (New York: St. Martin's Publishing Group, 2020).

15. Brené Brown, *Daring Greatly: How the Courage to Be Vulnerable Transforms the Way We Live, Love, Parent, and Lead* (New York: Penguin Random House, 2012), Apple Books, 87.

16. Brené Brown, *Dare to Lead—Brave Work. Touch Conversations. Whole Hearts* (New York: Random House, 2018), 233.

17. "Probiotics May Help Boost Mood and Cognitive Function," Healthbeat, Harvard Health Publishing, accessed October 2020, https://www.health.harvard.edu/mind-and-mood/probiotics-may-help-boost-mood-and-cognitive-function.

18. Brené Brown, *Dare to Lead—Brave Work. Touch Conversations. Whole Hearts* (New York: Random House, 2018), 33.

19. Zachariah M. Reahg and Michael A. Yasa, "Repetition Strengthens Target Recognition But Impairs Similar Lure Discrimination: Evidence for Trace Competition," *Learning & Memory* 21, no. 6 (July 2014):342–46.

20. Shonda Rhimes; My Year of Saying Yes to Everything, TED Talk, TED February 2016, Accessed on Dec 19, 2020: https://www.ted.com/talks/shonda_rhimes_my_year_of_saying_yes_to_everything.

21. Anna Gatmon, *Living a Spiritual Life in a Material World* (Berkeley, CA: She Writes Press, 2017).

22. Ancel Keys, Josef Brozek, Austin Henshel, Olaf Mickelson, and Henry L. Taylor, *The Biology of Human Starvation*, 2 vols., (Minneapolis, MN: University of Minnesota Press, 1950).

23. Elke D. Eckert, Irving I. Gottesman, Susan E. Swigart, and Regina C. Casper, "A 57-Year Follow-Up Investigation and Review of the Minnesota Study on Human Starvation and Its Relevance to Eating Disorders," *Archives of Psychology* 2, no. 3 (March 2018).

24. Ingrid Fetell Lee, *Joyful: The Surprising Power of Ordinary Things to Create Extraordinary Happiness* (New York: Little, Brown Spark, 2018), 277.

25. Anna Gatmon, *Living a Spiritual Life in a Material World* (Berkeley, CA: She Writes Press, 2017).

26. Kristin Neff, *Self-Compassion: The Proven Power of Being Kind to Yourself* (New York: Harper Collins Publishers, 2011).

27. E. B. Blanchard, J. G. Arena, and T. P. Pallmeyer, "Psychosomatic Properties of a Scale to Measure Alexithymia," *Psychotherapy and Psychosomatics* 35, no. 1 (1981), 64–71, https://doi.org/10.1159/000287479.

28. Ronald F. Levant and Shana Pryor, *The Tough Standard: The Hard Truths About Masculinity and Violence* (Oxford University Press, 2020).

Notes

29. Brené Brown, *Daring Greatly: How the Courage to Be Vulnerable Transforms the Way We Live, Love, Parent, and Lead* (New York: Penguin Random House, 2012), Apple Books pg. 65.

30. Daniel J. Siegel, *Mindsight: The New Science of Personal Transformation* (New York: Random House Publishing, 2010).

31. Eckhart Tolle, *A New Earth: Awakening to Your Life's Purpose* (New York: Penguin Random House Publishing, 2015), Apple Books, 129.

32. David Orozco, "Episode 5: Nonjudgmental Accountability with Tomas Kiss," January 8, 2020, One Small Bite, podcast, MP3 audio, 48:28, https://www.onesmallbite.net/episode-005-a-nonjudgmental-food-tracking-app-with-tamas-kiss/.

33. Jen Sincero, *You Are a Badass: How to Stop Doubting Your Greatness and Start Living an Awesome Life* (Philadelphia, PA: Running Press, 2013).

34. Dietary progression plans vary slightly from surgical program to program. They typically include 4–5 stages of gradual food progressing from clear liquids, to full liquids, to pureed foods, to soft foods, and then to whole foods, which is the last stage. People progress at different rates, but it typically occurs at about the eighth to twelfth week post-surgery. Essentially, phase four or five of the diet progression is when people can eat whole food again but in very small quantities. Meals can consist of between three-fourths of a cup of food to a little more than a cup for the rest of their lives. Individuals are required to avoid drinking liquids with meals, and avoid drinking carbonated beverages ever again.

35. Jonice Webb and Christine Musello, *Running on Empty: Overcome Your Childhood Emotional Neglect* (New York: Morgan James Publishing, 2013).

36. Daniel J. Siegel, *Mindsight: The New Science of Personal Transformation* (New York: Random House Publishing, 2010).

37. John M. Gottman and Nan Silver, *The Seven Principles of Making Marriage Work: A Practical Guide from the Country's Foremost Relationship Expert* (New York: Harmony Books, 1999).

38. Based on the DSM-5 (*Diagnostic and Statistical Manual of Mental Disorder*, 5th Edition), bulimia is a condition where a person engages in eating extremely large portions of food followed by a purging episode, which typically consists of vomiting. In some instances, people with bulimia purge without eating much at all, or some people restrict their consumption of almost any food, or strictly fast, and then binge on food. The behavior is extremely difficult to manage and is one of the most dangerous eating disorders. Many people with bulimia create major complications to their digestive system, throats, and mouths and can experience very dangerous and life-threatening medical complications.

39. An IOP (Intensive Outpatient Program) is a type of therapy treatment within a counseling or eating disorder (ED) facility where people are able to live at home, maintain their job and work life, yet are required to attend group classes, support, and therapy. These group classes might offer the opportunity for the individual to have a meal with the group to help discuss their emotions and challenges with food. Additionally, the program provides and teaches people necessary skills like cognitive behavioral therapy

Notes

(CBT) techniques, mindful exercises, awareness processing, and more that helps them manage ED challenges or behaviors once they complete the program.

40. James Clear, *Atomic Habits: An Easy and Proven Way to Build Good Habits and Break Bad Ones* (New York: Penguin Random House Publishing, 2018).

41. OSHA, HHS, Office of Women's Health, "Polycystic Ovary Syndrome (PCOS)," https://www.womenshealth.gov/a-z-topics/polycystic-ovary-syndrome, updated April 1, 2019.

42. Jonice Webb and Christine Musello, *Running on Empty: Overcome Your Childhood Emotional Neglect* (New York: Morgan James Publishing, 2013).

43. *A Beautiful Mind*, directed by R. Howard, (2001; Beverly Hills, CA: Imagine Entertainment & Universal Pictures).

44. S. Vendantam, "Hungry, Hungry Hippocampus: The Psychology of How We Eat," Nov 11, 2019, in *Hidden Brain* podcast, MP3 audio, 27:00, https://www.npr.org/2019/11/11/778266536/hungry-hungry-hippocampus-the-psychology-of-how-we-eat.

45. Jonice Webb and Christine Musello, *Running on Empty: Overcome Your Childhood Emotional Neglect* (New York: Morgan James Publishing, 2013).

46. E. L. Deci, and R. M. Ryan, "Self-Determination Theory: A Macrotheory of Human Motivation, Development, and Health," *Canadian Psychology* 49, no. 3 (August 2008): 182–85.

47. Russ Harris, *The Happiness Trap: How to Stop Struggling and Start Living* (Boston: Trumpter Books, 2008).

48. Jen Sincero, *You Are a Badass: How to Stop Doubting Your Greatness and Start Living an Awesome Life* (Philadelphia, PA: Running Press, 2013).

49. Evelyn Tribole and Elyse Resch, *Intuitive Eating: A Revolutionary Anti-Diet Approach* (New York: St. Martin's Publishing Group, 2020).

50. *Kung Fu Panda*, directed by M. Osborne, and J. Stevenson, (2008; Glendale, CA: Dreamworks Animation).

51. "Bariatric Surgery Procedures," American Society of Metabolic and Bariatric Surgery, accessed on Oct. 2020, https://asmbs.org/patients/bariatric-surgery-procedures.

52. "Bariatric Side Effects," National Institutes of Health, National Institute of Diabetes and Digestive and Kidney Diseases, accessed on Oct. 2020, https://www.niddk.nih.gov/health-information/weight-management/bariatric-surgery/side-effects.

53. "Estimate of Bariatric Surgery Numbers, 2011-2018," American Society of Metabolic and Bariatric Surgery, accessed on Oct 2020, https://asmbs.org/resources/estimate-of-bariatric-surgery-numbers.

54. Daniel J. Siegel, *Mindsight: The New Science of Personal Transformation* (New York: Random House Publishing, 2010).

About the Author
David R. Orozco

David owns TD Wellness, LLC, a nutrition and wellness practice in Atlanta GA, and he also hosts One Small Bite—a podcast that seeks to optimize men's health through nutrition and vulnerable conversations. David has been in practice for over fourteen years as a Registered Dietitian Nutritionist, and he is a Certified Intuitive Eating counselor. He also holds certifications as an Exercise Physiologist from the American College of Sport Medicine, and he is a Quit Smart® Smoking Cessation counselor. He specializes in weight concerns, diabetes, emotional eating challenges, and eating disorders, and he also provides worksite wellness solutions for various companies and organizations. David was born in Bogota, Colombia, came to the US at the age of three, and is fortunate to be fluent in Spanish. He continues to work with the Latino community and see Spanish-speaking clients as well.

About the Author

David also enjoys cooking. He auditioned for Seasons 9 and 10 of the *MasterChef* TV show with celebrity chef Gordon Ramsey. David also enjoys teaching fitness classes, hiking, and biking and holds the rank of degree black belt in the Japanese martial art of Aikido.

More importantly, David loves fun time with his family, his wife Trisha, daughter Helena, and his dog Fuego. They love to just play at home, travel, explore, cook, binge watch Netflix, Amazon, and streaming TV, and just spend weekends relaxing together.

Contact Info
David R. Orozco, MS, RDN, LD
1201 Clairmont Rd, Suite 100
Decatur GA 30030
E: info@tdwellness.com
W: www.tdwellness.com
P: 678.568.4717
F: 678.951.0508

www.ingramcontent.com/pod-product-compliance
Lightning Source LLC
Chambersburg PA
CBHW072149100526
44589CB00015B/2154